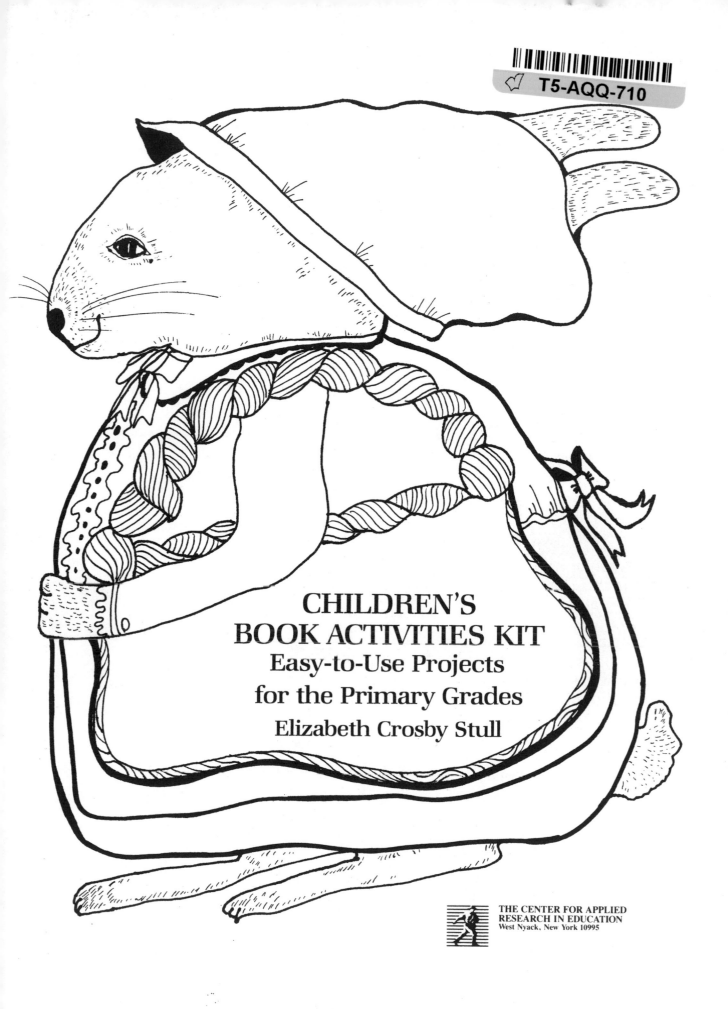

CHILDREN'S
BOOK ACTIVITIES KIT
Easy-to-Use Projects
for the Primary Grades
Elizabeth Crosby Stull

THE CENTER FOR APPLIED
RESEARCH IN EDUCATION
West Nyack, New York 10995

Library of Congress Cataloging-in-Publication Data

Stull, Elizabeth Crosby.
    Children's book activities kit : easy-to-use projects for the
primary grades / Elizabeth Crosby Stull.
        p.   cm.
    Bibliography: p.
    ISBN 0-87628-014-9
    1. Children—Books and reading. 2. Children's literature—Study
and teaching (Primary) 3. Activity programs in education.
I. Title.
Z1037.A1S83 1988
372.6′4—dc19   88-18992
                                                                      CIP

ISBN 0-87628-014-9

**THE CENTER FOR APPLIED
RESEARCH IN EDUCATION**
BUSINESS & PROFESSIONAL DIVISION
A division of Simon & Schuster
West Nyack, New York 10995

About the Author

Elizabeth Crosby Stull, Ph.D. (The Ohio State University) has over twenty years of experience in education as a primary teacher and teacher-educator. She began her career as a teacher of grades 1, 2, and 4 in the public schools of Greece Central, Camillus, and Pittsford in upstate New York, and is currently an adjunct professor at Ohio State where she has taught children's literature.

Dr. Stull has published many articles in publications such as *Instructor* and *Early Years* and is coauthor, with Carol Lewis Price, of *Science and Math Enrichment Activities for the Primary Grades* (The Center, 1987) and *Kindergarten Teacher's Month-by-Month Activities Program* (The Center, 1987). She is a member of the National Association for the Education of Young Children and the International Reading Association.

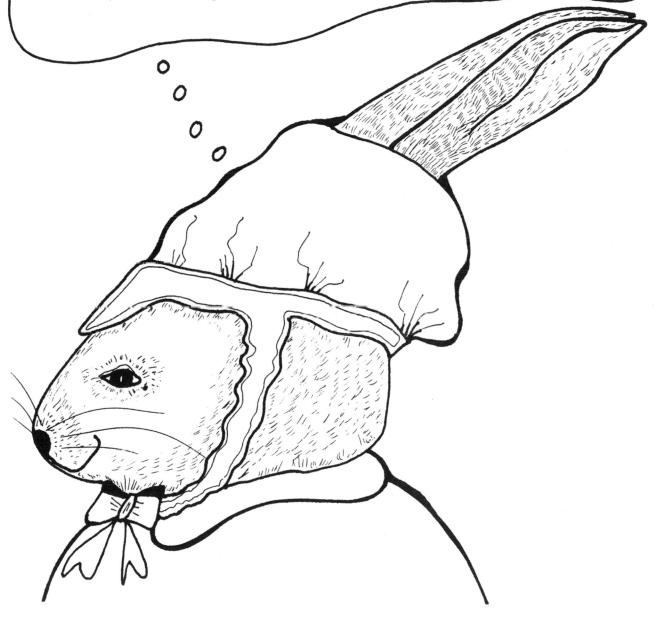

The Bookshop has a thousand books,
All colors, hues, and tinges,
And every cover is a door
That turns on magic hinges.

Nancy Byrd Turner

This book is for Lorren, the hearty
reader! My thanks to Evelyn M. Fazio,
editor, who believed in this project. And a wealth of thanks to *my*
students at Ohio Wesleyan, The Ohio State University, and
Otterbein College, who brought joy to *their* students through
children's literature via "Book-in-a-Box."

About This Kit

Reading stories is a part of our heritage. When children are read to, their vocabulary is increased and their ability to listen is developed. When teachers of grades K–3 read aloud to students, they enable children to form visual images in their own minds rather than relying upon visuals provided, as in television or filmstrips.

Children's Book Activities Kit will help stimulate your students in their creative play and creative art program. Given the opportunity, children will naturally re-create stories in their play. Given the opportunity plus some materials, children can re-create and expand upon a story during creative play. You can capitalize upon this natural tendency by providing the students with new art experiences. Throughout the school year, as suggested by a variety of stories, students can brush paint, sponge paint, splatter paint, or work with crayon, crayon resist, construction paper, papier-mâché, construction materials, cloth, scissors, paste, glue, string, clay, and so on.

In addition, the language development of the children will be enriched as they engage in a variety of activities such as writing; listening; alphabetizing; categorizing; graphing; creative writing; rewriting; recording stories on tape; speaking from print or extemporaneously as author or character; and, finally, interacting with other students in conversation. Language development is enriched by the new words and phrases that are used in the stories along with the help of fine illustrations. The possibilities are rich, varied, and abundant.

The *Children's Book Activities Kit* is designed to help you guide children

- to be exposed to good books or literature
- to develop and expand listening skills
- to facilitate oral and written language development
- to strengthen the ability to imagine (visualize)
- to have a "hands-on" approach to learning with real items in a theme box
- to expand the story through visual art and play
- to know the elements of a good story and become producers (authors and illustrators) of stories
- to develop their individual creative abilities

These goals are met in the *Kit's* ten sections that cover a variety of children's book topics. The *Kit* suggests several books dealing with each topic. The activities that are then listed for each book are designed to extend and enhance the contents of a book, to let the student relive parts of the story in a supportive environment, and to be encouraged to imaginatively engage in activities that are suggested by the book itself.

At the end of each section are ready-to-use, reproducible activity pages that reinforce the skills the students have learned.

As educators, we are always on the alert for ways to make reading meaningful, enjoyable, and interesting for children. We should approach reading in a positive way that appeals to a variety of interests and learning styles. *Children's Book Activities Kit* will help you do just that!

Elizabeth Crosby Stull

Theme Boxes for Children's Books

To create a visually appealing area or center for children's books in the classroom, the following theme boxes are suggested. They can be used to store a variety of good books; to house art supplies, writing material, and construction paper for extension activities; to hold envelopes or cards that suggest interesting activities; and to display real items. The children's book area can be a special place in the classroom where there is a flurry of both teacher-directed and child-directed activity. The ideas contained in this *Kit* can help get you started; then other ideas for extending good books can "flow" from this central area.

THEME BOX FOR ABC BOOKS

Cover a sturdy box with bright self-sticking vinyl. Make giant alphabet letters from patterned paper and glue them onto the box. Paint the inside of the box. With a permanent marker, draw lines on each corner so that the box resembles a giant alphabet block. The inside of the box can be made into sections to store books, alphabet letters, alphabet blocks, and suggested activities. Periodically change the contents inside to keep the area alive and interesting.

THEME BOX FOR NUMBER BOOKS

The "Number Robot" is made by placing a small box on top of a larger box. Spray paint the boxes with silver or cover them with shiny foil. Cover one side of the larger box with felt so that felt cutouts can be used here for counting, working with sets, re-creating the story, and so on.

The smaller box can be used to store math manipulatives. The bottom box also serves as a storage area for math manipulatives and math activities.

THEME BOX FOR PICTURE BOOKS

This box can become an exciting focal point for reading in any classroom. Use a refrigerator box. Spray paint the outside of the box, cut a window for puppet shows, and cut a door out of one side. Place curtains over the openings with spring-type extension rods. The roof can be made by folding a piece of cardboard in half and decorating it with red construction paper shingles.

This center creates an environment for reading and listening to stories, for writing stories, recording stories and reenacting stories.

THEME BOX FOR ANIMAL BOOKS

Use a washer or dryer appliance box. Cover the box with spray paint or paper. Cut a window in one side for puppet shows, and a door or opening so that students can get inside the box. Make large, colorful cutouts of animals and glue these onto the box. Have a container inside for books, activities, and supplies for making puppets.

THEME BOX FOR FANTASY BOOKS

Tape two boxes together with one on top of the other. Cover with self-sticking vinyl that resembles stone. The cylinders on the top can be made from containers with removable lids, and can store activity cards. The bottom box can be divided into sections for storing art supplies, writing supplies, books, and other activity materials.

THEME BOX FOR HUMOROUS BOOKS

Spray paint or cover the inside and outside of a box. Cut the lid into a peak for a roof. Make a big happy face on one side, with a large button nose. One side of the box can be a felt board so that the children can reenact stories.

THEME BOX FOR MONSTERS, OGRES, AND SCARY THINGS

Obtain a medium-sized box with four flaps. Cut one flap off, and tape the other three together so that they are upright. Paint or cover both the inside and the outside of the box.

From sturdy construction paper or posterboard, make a giant creature (polka dots, stripes, or such) to encircle the box. It can look a bit scary and at the same time fanciful.

This creature can eventually be named by the students and can take the students through many exciting books. The creature can also be made from cloth and stuffed.

THEME BOX FOR HEROES AND HEROINES

Decorate a deep, sturdy box in a smashing, glittery red/white/blue design. Use cutouts of stars, and strips of crepe paper for stripes. Make the box look festive.

THEME BOX FOR PROBLEM SOLVING

Place one sturdy box on top of another and tape them together. Cover the boxes with brown kraft paper, and use a felt-tip pen to make wavy lines resembling tree bark. The box on the bottom can be divided into four sections and used for materials and supplies. The "arms" and the "head" of the tree can be easily changed to resemble a person.

To keep the tree theme, cut out rounded shapes from green paper to resemble foliage. (This tree box can be used throughout the seasons by changing the foliage.)

THEME BOX FOR POETRY

Use a medium-sized sturdy box and cover it with paint or colorful construction paper or self-sticking vinyl. Make a slit in two ends; place the head of a big bird in one end and the tail in the other end. The bird can be made from posterboard or cardboard, and covered with polka dot, striped, or flowered material. Or the bird could be covered with bright fake feathers (available from craft shops), or made from material and stuffed. You might want to place the box on a mound of straw.

GENERAL THEME BOXES

Here are a variety of other ideas for theme boxes. Now that you have the general idea, you can create some fanciful ones of your own! Share ideas with other teachers and exchange boxes. Eventually, the children can help create big boxes for the room or smaller ones for individual use.

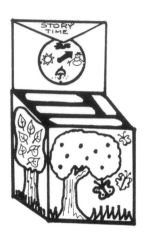

The larger box in the following design can be used for puppet presentations. Children can also climb into it to read, listen to stories, record stories, and so on. The "caboose" contains the materials. This theme box can be changed to look like an actual streamlined train, a delivery van, a truck, or a bus. A clock can be used in conjunction with this idea to denote when the express is taking off. (Tickets could be distributed to passengers and punched.)

Contents

Section 1
ABC BOOKS • 1

Section 2
NUMBER BOOKS • 26

Section 3
PICTURE BOOKS • 52

Section 4
ANIMAL BOOKS • 80

Section 5
FANTASY BOOKS • 110

Section 6
HUMOROUS BOOKS • 135

Section 7
MONSTERS, OGRES, AND SCARY THINGS • 161

Section 8
HEROES AND HEROINES • 190

SECTION **1**

ABC Books

BOOK:

A Farmer's Alphabet
by Mary Azarian. Boston: David R. Godine, 1981.

PAGE BY PAGE

1. Go through the book page by page with the class to determine which of the alphabet woodcuts depict the OUTSIDE rural setting and which ones depict the INSIDE rural setting. Introduce the terms "rural" (country), "urban" (city), and "suburban" (in between). Make a big classroom map of the area. Print each child's name on a colorful house shape, and have the children pin them on the map in the approximate spot where they live.

2. When you have decided which scenes take place outdoors, try to identify the season of the year. The letters B, I, and W are easy. What about A and V? Could they both be autumn? Help children to determine that some letters, such as E and L, could be "year 'round" letters for this book.

3. "Rr Rocker." Ask children if they have ever sat and rocked in an old-fashioned wooden rocking chair. Ask parents to help locate an old wooden rocker that could be loaned to the class for one week. Children can then sit and rock as they take turns looking through books. Place the rocker on a braided rug for a smoother and quieter motion. Perhaps the children could think up a name for the rocker that begins with the "r-r-r" sound. Select five children to play "The Rocker Game," as follows: One child sits in the chair and rocks while the other four sit cross-legged with arms folded in front of the chair making a very quiet "r-r-r" sound. The child in the rocker must say a word that begins with that sound. If the word is correct, the child exchanges places with a group member on the floor. Then, the process is repeated until everyone has had a turn in the rocker.

4. This book has a nostalgic spirit. Invite an antique collector to class; have this person bring five to seven utility items that were used in Early America. Items made from tin or wood could be passed around in a basket for the children to examine after they have been demonstrated and contrasted with comparable items of today. (Examples: egg beater, popcorn popper, toaster, candle maker, rug beater, and such.)

5. Secure a copy of Eric Sloane's *ABC Book of Early Americana* (New York: Doubleday & Co., Inc., 1963), for a rich and varied collection of sketches and explanations of vanishing antiques.

HAND CRAFTS

1. Q is for Quilt. How many different ways can pre-cut triangle shapes be arranged on the nine square to form a repeat design? Let children practice with nine triangle shapes on a piece of paper that has nine squares. They can paste their favorite design into place on the square. All of the paper squares can be put together to make a large paper quilt for the class to enjoy.

2. Arrange for an antique dealer or collector to bring some old-fashioned quilts to class. Allow children to see the stitches and to learn about the names of the different designs (Log Cabin, Schoolhouse, Wedding Ring, Crazy Quilt, and so on). Explain that ladies had "quilting bees" where they got together to sew and exchange news. What news can students exchange?

3. Cut large pieces of calico and gingham. Let children use them at snack time as cloth placemats. Cut small squares and have children sort them by whether they are calico or gingham.

4. This book is entirely illustrated with woodcuts. To simulate this process, use the following method. Collect an assortment of trays that meat, fruits, or vegetables come wrapped in. This styrofoam is thin and can be easily cut into uniform pieces. Make sure that each child has a square. By gently pressing into the surface with a pencil point, children can make a picture or design. Next, paint over the design using either red or blue tempera paint, and press onto a sheet of newsprint. Make two—one for the room and one to take home. (This same process can be used to create greeting cards, invitations, or special announcements.)

5. Right/Left. When designing or preparing a woodcut, everything is reversed. Demonstrate that a "tree" or a "house" on the RIGHT side of a woodcut (styrofoam cut) will be printed on the LEFT side of the paper. Some children understand this during the preparation, and some learn this during the printing process. To work with the left/right concept, have each child hold up his right hand, then his left hand. Locate objects in the room that are "to your right" or "on your left."

OLD-FASHIONED RECIPES

Here are old-fashioned recipes with some help from modern technology!

1. Butter
   1/2 pint heavy cream
   clean jar with tight lid
   mesh strainer

Pour the cream into the jar. Put on the lid and make sure it is tight. Each child can shake the container ten, twenty, or thirty times. (You can finish early by using an electric mixer at the end.) The pale yellow lumps that form are butter. Strain. Serve on crackers.

2. Maple Toast
   Bread
   Toaster
   Maple Syrup

Toast bread as usual. Cut in half. Pour a capful of maple syrup on one half. Soak it up with the other half, then eat both pieces.

3. Apple Butter
   Applesauce
   Cinnamon, Allspice
   Butter

Prepare applesauce by boiling sliced, peeled apples until they are soft. Put applesauce in a slow cooker on "high" setting. Add spices to taste. When the mix becomes dark and thick, add 1 tablespoon of butter for each cup of mixture. Spread on bread or toast.

4. Country Melon Delight
   Watermelon
   Colander/wooden spoon
   Cups
   Large pan

Cut watermelon into chunks and place it in a colander, over a large pan. Mash the chunks so that juice flows into the pan. Separate the seeds from the mash. Serve the mash in cups with the juice poured over the top. This makes a very refreshing drink.

BOOK:

Hosie's Alphabet
by Leonard Baskin. Words by Tobias, Hosea, and Lisa Baskin. Pictures by Leonard Baskin.
New York: Viking Press, 1972.

RICH VOCABULARY

1. This descriptive vocabulary is especially good for the young child who has already had exposure to a variety of ABC Books. For example: "bumptious baboon," (assertive, pushy); "imperious eagle," (domineering); "omnivorous locust," (eats animals and vegetables); "quintessential quail," (purity). Explain that the descriptions fit the characteristics of the animal. What words describe people? What word describes you?

2. Select one of the descriptive words or phrases and integrate it into the classroom experience so that children become familiar with the expression. (Example: T—Scholastic Toad. This label could apply to eager learners. R—The Rhinoceros Express. This could be acted out on the playground. S—A gangling,

entangling spider. This could be used for creative movement. U—The invisible unicorn. This could be used for quiet times. N—The sweet-throated nightingale. This could be used during singing.

3. G—Gargoyle. A gargoyle is a roof spout designed to carry rain water away from a building. It is usually in the shape of an animal or a grotesque (distorted) human figure. Are there any places in your area where children can stand on the street and look UP at old buildings and see the figures? A gargoyle walk would be a different type of outing.

4. Make up your own rich vocabulary ABCs. Explain that these descriptive words, or "frilly words," are called adjectives. Children need experiences "playing" with the language.

5. Alliteration. Work with four letters at a time. Choose the animal/bird/fish that begins with that letter. Then, think of three descriptive words that all begin with that same sound to describe the animal. Begin simply; for example, S —Squirrel: silly, scampering, silent squirrel; W—Whale: wonderful, wet, wide whale. Be accepting of the choices given as long as they begin with the same letter.

MORE ABOUT THIS ALPHABET BOOK

1. Be sure to call attention to the title inside the cover—where the curved S is a snake and the T is crossed with a tree branch, and a monkey is hanging from the middle bar of the E. (This may help some children to remember the configuration of the letter.)

Going along with this idea, help students make an A using three alligators (two to make the angled sides and one for the crossbar), or a P using a parrot with a very curved beak, or a C from a curled up cat. Older children should be able to come up with some good ideas. Explain to the children that before the alphabet (ours is based on one invented by the Greeks) people used picture writing and had to memorize thousands of pictures. Look how easy it is for us—only twenty-six to memorize!

2. Most of the pictures represent creatures from nature. How do they move about—do they fly, jump, hop, swim? List the movements; classify the animals. Imitate them.

3. Have children note the variety in print. For example, call attention to the size of "F" and "R". Also, note "T" (Old English), and "O" (double print). Children are bombarded with neon signs and TV graphics using distinct lettering, and may enjoy this approach. For some, it will increase their awareness of a variety of lines and shapes that represent the same thing.

Make a letter board. On the left, have the alphabet listed as we are accustomed to seeing the letters. Then, children can look through magazines and newspapers to cut out other letters that look different, but really mean the same thing. Paste them in appropriate squares.

EXPLORING NATURE

1. Let's find out about the creatures in the book. Select one or two a day to introduce to the group. Tell something interesting and memorable about them, or read a story book about them.

2. How many of these animals can be found in the zoo? Let's count.

3. How many of these animals can be found in the circus? Let's count.

4. How many of these animals have we actually seen? Where?

5. A—Armadillos are found in Texas. Where are the other animals found? Check library resource books.

6. Pet Creatures. If you could have one of the creatures for a pet, which one would you choose? Why? Which one would you like to take home to dinner to meet the family? Why? Which one do you think your parents would like to meet? Why? Which creature would require the most/least care? Which one would the neighbors or the landlord of your building be most apt to complain about? Which would be most difficult/easiest to catch? What kind of a house would you need to build for your pet creature? Make an illustration of your pet in your home (at dinner, watching TV, playing a game).

BOOK:

The Guinea Pig ABC
by Kate Duke. New York: E. P. Dutton, 1983.

PAGE BY PAGE

1. Go through the book page by page to name the alphabet letters. The letters are nice and big and colorful and the guinea pigs interact with the letters. There is a straight black border around each page, with one word at the bottom that explains the actions of the guinea pig(s) on the page. (Example: A—awake to Z—zzzzz or asleep.)

2. Have students look for all of the bright red letters, all of the purple letters, and yellow, orange, blue, green or violet letters. Notice that R and S are both blue but different shades of blue.

3. Have students go through the book looking for all of the big letters that have straight lines only. How many? Which ones? Make a list.

4. Have students look for all of the letters that have curved lines only. How many? Which ones? Make a list.

5. Some students may go through the book looking for all of the letters that use both curved and straight lines. How many? Which ones? Make a list.

CLASS DISCUSSIONS:
THE GUINEA PIGS TEACH CONCEPTS

1. A—Awake. How is the guinea pig awakened? Discuss with students how people are awakened in the morning (for example, by alarm clock, radio alarm, parent, pet, baby crying, smell of food, and so on). How are they awakened on a weekend? What is each student's favorite method of being awakened in the morning? Are they responsible for awakening someone? Are there do's and don'ts for waking up family members?

2. C—Clean. Class discussion for language development: Does the guinea pig look happy to be bathing? Do children like bathing? Would a bubble bath in a teapot be fun? How many take showers? How many use a brush like the guinea pig, rather than a washcloth?

3. D—Dirty. Class discussion for language development: How do you think this guinea pig is feeling right now? Does it look like fun? Have students tell about a funny experience that they had when they got dirty.

4. F—Ferocious. This is a good word for vocabulary development, and may be new for some. What does ferocious mean? (Fierce, savage, violently cruel.) Encourage students to name wild animals that can be ferocious (lion, wolf, bear, and the like). What does it mean when we speak of the wind or the weather as being "ferocious?" (Examples: hurricane, tornado, blizzard, storm.) Do people ever act in a ferocious way? How can we avoid that?

5. J—Juicy. The guinea pig is enjoying juicy watermelon. Encourage students to name juicy foods. Have them draw a picture of one, and color it with splashy lines so that the juice shows. Label it "juicy."

6. T—Timid. Explain the word timid or shy. When is it all right to act in a timid manner? Discuss potentially dangerous situations when we would be better off to act in a timid manner. For example, "Act timid around a strange dog or cat until you get to know each other."

7. Go through all of the ABCs in this manner, and try to learn some of the new words from the guinea pigs.

ALL ABOUT GUINEA PIGS

1. A guinea pig is about seven inches long. Have students use the ruler to find seven things in the room that also measure seven inches in length. List them in ABC order.

2. A guinea pig is a short, fat mammal, and is a relative of the rat. Make a Rat ABC Book or a Guinea Pig/Rat ABC Book where they are both interacting with the letters.

3. Make a barnyard area in the room for the guinea pigs. Make cardboard farm props and clay guinea pigs. Encourage the use of this area for role playing the ABC book.

4. Enjoy the company of a real guinea pig. Invite someone to bring a guinea pig to class (in a cage) and tell about its habits, favorite foods, pet care, and so on. A local pet store would be a good resource.

5. Another good resource concept book for young children is Kate Duke's *Guinea Pigs Far and Near* (New York: E. P. Dutton, 1984).

BOOK:

Ed Emberly's ABC
by Ed Emberly. Boston: Little, Brown & Co.,
1978.

CONSTRUCTION GOING ON HERE

1. One focus of this ABC Book is the construction of the letter, or how it is formed. Be sure to note this as the book is being read and discussed. After you have read the book, have the children act out each page.

2. Keep the children on the alert for various items on the page that begin with that particular letter. (Example: A—ant, alligator, airplane.) Have the children point out each example. The items are all listed at the back of the book, so give many hints.

3. "N." Notice that the lion is helping with the ending sound. Turn to the N page and see how the letter is being formed. Using a flannel board and felt strips, have three children help make the letter N, just as it is done in the book (| | | N). Discuss ending sounds. Pronounce a word and see if children can determine the ending sound and the letter. Repeat, using words that have obvious ending sounds such as b, p, m, t.

4. Square and round shapes. First, give each child a square cracker. Each child must slowly nibble tiny, tiny bites until the cracker is a round shape. Next, give each child a round cracker. Again, they must slowly nibble tiny bites until they have made a square shape. (Some children may have more success with soft bread.)

5. L. What is the lizard thinking as the L shape turns the corner? How can we tell? Where else have we seen bubble shapes for words or pictures? (Other books, and mainly the cartoon section of the newspaper. Have samples handy.)

6. Give each student a small plastic bag with ten straight pretzels, and round and square-shaped tiny crackers and/or cereal. Children can construct the ABCs and the letters of their names.

BUILDERS AT WORK

1. Check the C page. A crow is eating corn to form the letter C. Bring in a container of popcorn kernels and have children practice making the letter C with

a small handful of corn. To make it easier, they can place the corn on top of a C that has been drawn with a felt-tip pen on a piece of construction paper.

Next, have each child scoop up the corn and place it in a popcorn popper. Watch the corn. What is happening? It's making a sound like "pop" or "p-p-p-p." Give each child a piece of construction paper on which the letter P has been drawn with a felt-tip pen. Explain that everyone is going to get a container of popcorn and can construct the letter P by placing the popcorn on top of the line starting in the upper left corner. When they complete this activity, they can eat the popcorn.

Children can take home the construction paper C and P and tell the story about these letters. This activity might be written up in a parent newsletter so that it could be repeated at home.

2. Cut various lengths of different colored yarns and place them in a little box. Children can practice making (or tracing) upper and lower case letters.

3. Have several sets of ABC blocks in cloth bags. Children can build with them.

4. Use Tinkertoys. The tiger used Tinkertoys to make a T. Let's try it. How many other letters can be made using the Tinkertoys?

5. In a school tote bag, have a small slate, eraser, chalk, and alphabet sheet. Children can practice making letters, shapes, and practice writing their names.

CLAY AREA

1. Explain to students that before there was such a thing as paper, people who could write used clay tablets. Why clay? Because it was readily available by mixing earth and water to form a tablet. Some clay tablets were small and some were 1 ft. × 1 ft. The tablets had to be molded carefully so that fingerprints were not visible. Then, using a stick, letters (not as we know them today) were carefully carved into the clay, and they were baked. Clay tablets were not easy to store, but information was recorded and preserved.

Students can make clay tablets by patting clay, or plasticene, to form a smooth clay tablet. Use the stick of a cattail or some weed such as teasel or a milkweed pod to form letters on the tablet. Use a flat object to depress, or erase, the message. If real clay is used, fire it in a kiln.

2. Have the students do the following activities:

• Roll out coils of plasticene, Play Doh® or clay to a width about the size of a worm, and make letters. (Using this kinesthetic approach is still another way of learning the configuration of letters.)

• Roll out the letters that form your first name; last name.

• Roll out letters and numerals that form your address.

3. Using the clay, mold some of the book characters and shapes. Examples:

B b   bear, basket, berries
H h   hen, hay, hat
E e   elephant, egg

The entire alphabet can be made this way and lined up on 3 × 5 pieces of construction paper along a counter top. Children can play games with them, such as: "I'm thinking of hen, hay, and hat; what is the beginning letter?"

4. Have children construct a sturdy clay bridge. Then, go through this alphabet book page by page and tell how each animal would cross the bridge (concepts: on, over, or under).

BOOK:

A, B, See!
by Tana Hoban. New York: Greenwillow Books, 1982.

BLACK-AND-WHITE PHOTOGRAMS

1. As you go through this ABC book, the entire alphabet is printed in a gray line at the bottom of every page. The one letter that the page highlights is enlarged in black. This gives the child a visual picture of where that specific letter is along the alphabet continuum. (Example: ABCDEFGHIJ**K**LMNOPQR STUVWXYZ.)

2. Reading this ABC book is like reading an X-ray. Each page has bold white shapes of familiar objects on a black background. The white shapes are solid, but the details are not filled in. The photographic process is called photogramming. Obtain real X-rays so that children can examine them carefully. (Resources: veterinarian, dentist, or X-ray technician.)

3. To replicate this book process, get some photosensitive paper from a photography shop. Put an item on the paper, hold it steady or tape it underneath, and place it in the sun for a few minutes. The background will lighten and, when the object is removed, it will leave a dark space because it has not been exposed to direct sunlight. Immerse it in a solution obtained from the photo shop. (This is the reverse of the book: light background, dark objects, where the book has a dark background and white objects.) You can make an entire ABC book this way.

4. Bring in negatives of black and white and color film, and also 35mm slides. Let the children examine them carefully by holding them up to the light. With the ABC book we do not obtain additional clues this way, but in photo negatives we do. They both strengthen our visual awareness.

5. Examine each page very carefully, going over one object at a time. See if the children can identify the actual object from two clues—the outline, and the positive/negative (dark/light) areas within each of the shapes. (For example; on the B page, a button shape is shown. The holes are the negative space and the solid area is the positive space.)

THE ALPHABET SHAPES

1. Count the number of items on each page. Are there any pages with just one item? What letter does it represent? Let the children discover this. (Z has one item—zipper.)

2. What has the largest number of items? Can we identify all of them? Let the children count the number of items. (D has fourteen items because there are so many dots; but B has ten items.)

3. Use the overhead projector to project shapes of objects onto the wall. Have the children try to figure out what they are, then place the alphabet letter shape on the projector to give the answer. (Example: place a pair of scissors on the projector, and have the letter S available for the answer.)

4. Silhouettes. A silhouette (French word) is a solid outline drawing (usually black or dark blue) on a light background. More often than not, a silhouette is a profile of a person. Make silhouettes of the children. Tape white paper to the wall and have them stand or sit between the wall and a high intensity lamp so that the light projects their silhouette onto the paper. Trace carefully, mainly in the face area, and fill in head and hair with broader lines. (Some children have difficulty holding steady for this.) You can cut this out and paste it on dark paper for a treasure to take home.

Using this same process, have the children make silhouettes of simple items in the room that can be placed on a chair in front of the lamp and projected onto the paper attached to the chalkboard or wall. Practice using newsprint or newspaper sheets. What letter of the alphabet does the object begin with? Print this on the page.

5. Shapes of letters can be reinforced by making an ABC set from sandpaper and having children trace around them with their fingers.

THE PAGES OF THE BOOK

1. Try to have many of the book items available in another form—either in picture form or by having the actual object available. This may make it easier for some children who have difficulty with a flat object on the page. Once they realize that the item is actually three-dimensional, some children are able to identify more shapes.

2. Discuss the real colors of the items on the page. Make them come to life by having students draw and label them on a class chart (B—banana, yellow; F—frog, green; I—ice cream, what flavor? and so on).

3. Classify the items. Go through *A, B, See!* looking for food items only. Then go through looking for things that fly, or animals, or toys, or things that move, and so forth.

4. Sit in a circle. After the children have become familiar with the book, have each child take a turn opening the book to any page, then show the page and "act out" the item. Guess what it is?

5. Make up a "silly sentence" using all of the items shown on the letter page. (Example: M—"The MASK told the MOUSE not to eat the MUSHROOMS and the MOON agreed.")

6. Bring in copies of other books for young children by Tana Hoban, such as *Look Again!, Shapes and Things,* and *Circles, Triangles and Squares* (Macmillan).

BOOK:

On Market Street
by Anita Lobel and Arnold Lobel. New York:
Scholastic Books Services, 1981.

MARKET STREET

1. Each alphabet letter symbolizes a type of store on Market Street. (For example, D would be a doughnut shop, or a bakery shop that sells doughnuts.) Go through all of the ABCs and name the type of shop that each one represents. Classify the shops by food (fruits, vegetables, or sweets), articles of clothing, and things that we can use.

2. How many "holiday" letters are there? Have the students list them.

3. If students could buy three items, which ones would they choose? Divide a paper into thirds; have students draw the items and the appropriate letters.

4. Budget. Make out a budget and shop on Market Street for a family of four. You might be shopping from your food budget or clothing budget. What will you select? (Newspaper ads might help.) The word "budget" comes from the French word "bougette," which was a little bag of cash that storekeepers carried with them.

5. Examine the last picture page (with the white cat in the middle). Start at the bottom of the page (A—apple, B—book, ...) and see how many letters of the alphabet you can remember. Keep looking back through the book until you can name at least five items and letters. Then, try to name ten items and letters. Can you name all of them?

6. "Going Shopping on Market Street" Game. Cut out a set of alphabet letters and put them into a grocery bag. Sit in a big circle and have each child reach in and "go shopping" (pick out an alphabet letter). The person who reaches in can try to remember what type of store the letter person stands for in the book. Call on a helper if needed. Then check through the book for verification. Next, the student can name something that he or she would like to purchase from the

store. Put the letter back into the bag, give it a shake, and let the next student have a turn.

7. Charge Account. If we could open up a charge account in two of the stores, which ones would we select? A charge account "loads" the buyer with the responsibility for payment. This term is derived from the word "carrus," a four-wheeled baggage wagon that Julius Caesar, Emperor of Rome, used in his campaigns. It later came to mean "carricare" which was translated as "load up the wagon." When we have a lot of bundles to carry, we say that we are "loaded down." (So, "charge" it to Julius Caesar!)

A CLOSER LOOK AT THE ALPHABET PEOPLE

1. Make a large alphabet person using an item different from the one used in the book. Students can paint it at the easel, use felt-tip pens, or crayons.

2. Look at the letter "I." How many different flavors of ice cream can be identified? Count them and give them fancy names.

3. There is one letter wearing a mask on its face. Look through the book page by page to locate it. (Letter E.)

4. Look at the letter C person. Can we tell what time it is by checking any of the clocks?

5. Look carefully at the letter M person. How many different musical instruments can be identified?

6. Shop for the title. Using the letters O and n for the word "On," what items can we buy? Now try "M-a-r-k-e-t" and "S-t-r-e-e-t." If students were going to shop using the letters of their first names, what would they buy? What can we buy if we use our initials?

7. Suppose these alphabet people could come to life as salespeople. What would they say to people who walked by the shop? Remember, they're trying to get you to come into the shop to buy something. (Stress sales, fresh items, specials, and so forth.) Make an advertisement to carry.

8. Note that each letter person has a head and hands. Draw attention to the feet. How are they made for each letter?

GOING SHOPPING

1. Make a large class graph showing where family shopping is done (shopping mall, grocery store, small store).

2. Check the book to determine how many items are bought by the pound, by the dozen, in pairs, individually, or in some other way. Graph them.

3. Predict the cost of the items. What will be the least and most expensive? Use newspapers and magazines to find the items, how they are advertised to make them look appealing, and what they cost. How close were the predictions?

4. Use the yellow pages of the phone book to find the stores in your area that would sell these items. Do they have special identifying signs, or logos? Students can make a logo book.

5. Be on the lookout for store signs or logos. What do you see outside of fast food restaurants that specialize in hamburgers? Are there any special signs in your town for ice cream stores, car showrooms, toy shops?

6. Have a book available on international symbols that are recognizable even if we can't read or speak the same language. (A good resource book is: Leonard Shortall's *One Way: A Trip with Traffic Signs*. Englewood Cliffs, NJ: Prentice-Hall, Inc., 1975.) How many can the children identify?

REPRODUCIBLE ACTIVITY PAGES
FOR
ABC BOOKS

This little piggy did not go to market. He stayed home and made ABC Books. He has some suggestions for helping you with ideas for your ABC Book.

ABCs of _____ SOUNDS
A – Ahhhh!
B – Boo!
C – Cock-a-doodle-doo!
D –
E –
F –
G –
H –

      Keep going all the way to
Z – z-z-z-z-!

ABCs of _____ THINGS THAT MOVE
A – antique automobile
B – baby's buggy
C – colorful cart
D – darting dragonfly
E – eager elephant
F –
G –
H –

      Put a descriptive word (adjective) in front of each selection. Make sure it begins with the same letter. Draw illustrations.

ABCs of _____
Think up three more ideas for ABC Books. Perhaps you could use something that you are studying about in science or social studies.

    1. ABCs of _____

    2. ABCs of _____

    3. ABCs of _____

Always put a fancy, colorful cover on your ABC Books!

Name _____   Date _____

MAKE A PICTURE ALPHABET

Before the alphabet was invented, way back in the days of cave men, drawings were used to help people write (or draw) stories. These are some familiar symbols:

sun

water

tree

hill

Make your own pictures for these words. Then, draw a story using these symbols.		
rain	wind	cloud
boy	girl	man
woman	love	peace
deer	hunt	eat

To make a story game, these can be cut up into little cards. Place them face down. Select three cards; then, make up a sentence or story using these three picture symbols.

CATEGORIZING THE ABCS

Some letters have only curved lines, such as O and S,

Some letters have only straight lines, such as E and F,

Some letters have both curved and straight lines, such as P and R.

PLACE ALL OF THE CAPITAL LETTERS IN THE CORRECT SPACES BELOW.

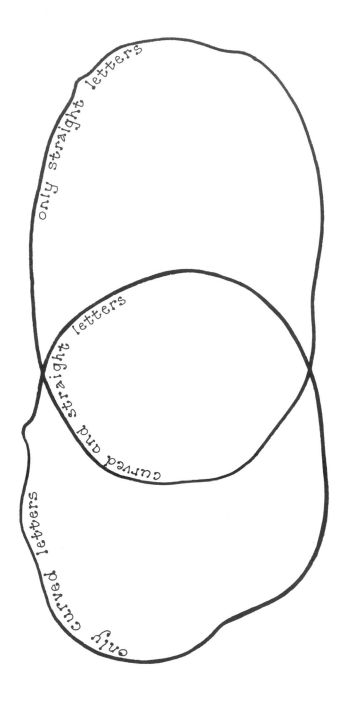

How many curved letters? straight letters? both? Which section has the most? Which one has the least? How many letters are there all together? (Do this exercise on a table top using string for the circles, and cutouts of the ABCs. Then, do this exercise with lower case letters.)

THE ABC TEDDY BERRY BEAR

This bear won a basket of berries for printing all of the capital letters of the alphabet. Now he can help you. Print all of the capital (upper case) ABCs on the berries. The bear has done some for you.

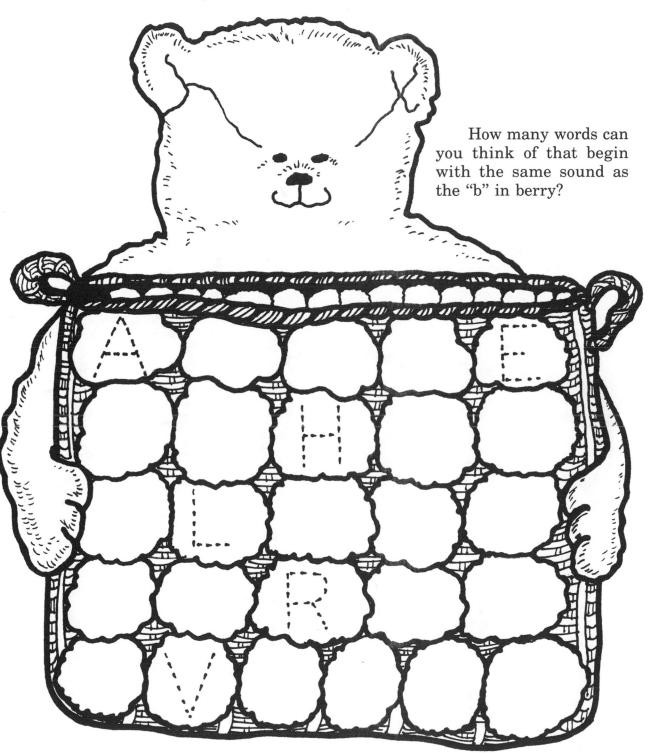

How many words can you think of that begin with the same sound as the "b" in berry?

Name _____   Date _____

The ABCs can help you to become a story writer or a storyteller as you move from A through Z.

1. Print the ABCs on the storyboard.

2. Think up a subject for your story (what the story will be about).

3. Put your finger on the letter "A" and begin the story with an "a" word.

4. Move your finger to the letter "B". The next sentence must begin with a "b" word. Then "C".

5. The letters "X" "Y" and "Z" have a special job because they have to help end the story.

Another way to use the storyboard is with a coin. Drop the coin on the board. What letter did it land on? Use that letter for the beginning word of the sentence. Keep going.

Name _____   Date _____

THE ALPHABET HOUSE

This is where the ABCs live. Today, there are six letters at home. There are three listed, and you can choose the other three. Then, make a list of all the words that you can think of that begin with that letter sound, and write them in the letter house.

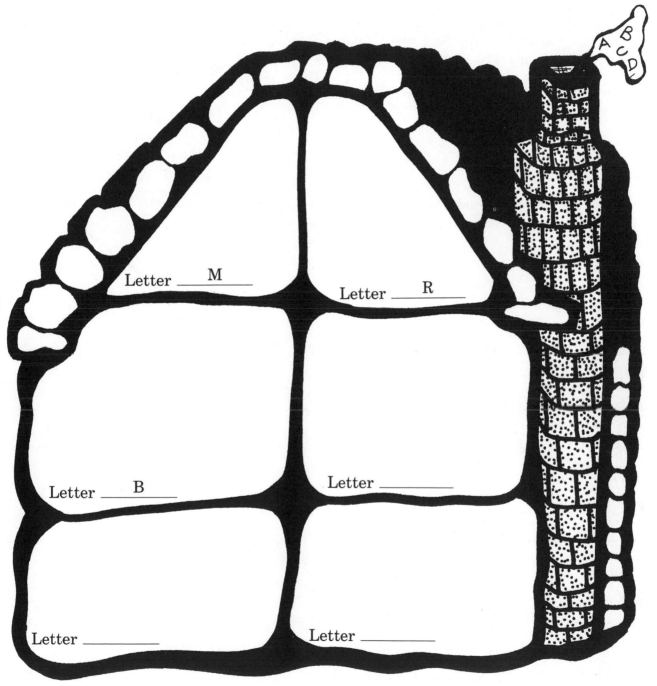

Letter ____M____

Letter ____R____

Letter ____B____

Letter _____

Letter _____

Letter _____

On the back, write a mystery story about the day that two of the letters were missing; or write a story about how twenty-six letters have to cook and clean and do the washing.

Name _____   Date _____

THE ABCs OF HANDS

Spread your fingers, make a fist, move your hands. Close your eyes and think of the things that your hands help you to do!

Then, go through the ABCs. Think of something you do with your hands that begins with each letter of the alphabet. (Examples: A — Ask questions; B — Brush the hair from my eyes; C — Carry my coat.)

The following ABC letters will help you to make your list. Then, make an ABC Book that shows you doing all of these things.

STOP!
TAKE A
GOOD LOOK
AT YOUR
HANDS!

A_____   N_____

B_____   O_____

C_____   P_____

D_____   Q_____

E_____   R_____

F_____   S_____

G_____   T_____

H_____   U_____

I_____   V_____

J_____   W_____

K_____   X_____

L_____   Y_____

M_____   Z_____

Name _____   Date _____

These two birds have built a nest; Now they're taking time to rest. You can help them, if you please; Just fill in the A B Cs.

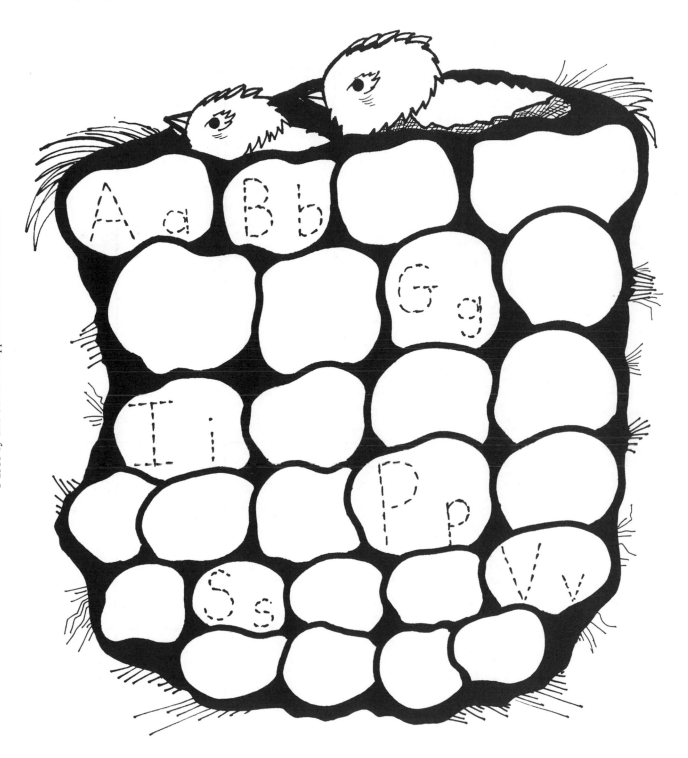

Name —————————————

Date ——————

Name of Illustrator —————————

PLANS FOR AN ORIGINAL ALPHABET BOOK

Use this to help you plan an ABC book. Look at many ABC books before you begin. Decide where you will place the letters on each page. Will you use both capital and lower case letters? Will you have any words on the page? What theme will you choose—animals, birds, food, sports, famous people, cities, and so on.

Endpaper Design	Book Cover	Title Page Dedication		

Author _____

Illustrator _____

ABC Books can also be done as class projects. Each person can be responsible for one page after the planning is done. Enjoy it as a class book, and donate it to the school library.

You can also make an ABC Book with a partner. One person can be the author and one can be the illustrator. When people plan and rewrite, they cross things out and start over. Use as many squares as you need. There are extra squares.

SECTION 2

Number Books

BOOK:

Anno's Counting Book
by Mitsumasu Anno.
New York: Thomas Y. Crowell, 1975.

FROM 1–12

1. Since this counting book is tied in with the twelve months of the year and the changing seasons, it offers many opportunities for counting. As it is read aloud, have the children count the items on the pages. Make it available for them during their spare time.

2. On a large felt board, students can re-create the scenes from the book using the cutout shapes of buildings, trees, and so on.

3. Make up individual envelopes that contain twelve cutouts of circles, triangles, squares, rectangles in three sizes. Students can match them up with identical shapes on a poster board. (They will also be working with small, medium, and large.)

4. Number Mobiles. Materials: Colorful plastic coat hangers, string, tape, scissors, assorted construction paper. Procedure: Students trace, cut, and tie twelve items onto the hanger. They can have twelve of the same items in the book (twelve trees, twelve people, and so on) or twelve different items inspired by the scene in the counting book. (Very young children can add one item each day.)

5. Place miniature items from one to twelve in a box or can with a lid. (For example, eight paper clips, six pencils, four crayons, three miniature cars.) Have the children spill them out, count them, and place them in order by groups from one to twelve.

6. Place a small chalkboard, chalk, and an eraser in a transparent plastic bag. Encourage students to practice forming numerals from one to twelve.

MORE MANIPULATIVES

1. Have colored plasticene enclosed in several jars with lids. Students make coil worms from the plasticene and roll out the numerals one to twelve on a long, narrow strip of laminated oaktag. Have six pieces of yarn or string available in six-inch lengths and have students make a yarn circle around every other numeral, beginning with two. Then, read aloud every numeral that is circled. (Children are beginning to count by twos).

2. Make a set of numeral cards from one to twelve, and laminate them or cover them with clear adhesive paper. Children can trace over these figures using

water-base felt-tip pens; then they can sponge them off. (Very young children can practice making numerals with felt-tip pens at the easel.)

3. Dots and Dice. Have students roll a pair of dice and make little balls from plasticene to correspond with the dots on each die; then count them. Dots (gumdrops) and dice can be placed in little plastic bags and tied with a ribbon. Children untie the ribbon and roll the die. On clean paper toweling, place the number of gumdrops corresponding to the number on the rolled die. Count and verify the one-to-one correspondence of dots on the die and gumdrops. Have the children eat the gumdrops. Have them practice tying a bow with the ribbon.

4. The clock shows the numerals one to twelve. Have students make clocks from paper plates. Put the numerals on with a felt-tip pen (dots could be placed on the rims of the plates in the appropriate spot to insure success). Using a paper fastener, fasten two strips to the clock at the center. Practice telling time by the hour; the long hand never moves from the twelve.

5. Make spinners from paper plates using the same method as that in Number 4 above, but this time just fasten one strip to the center. Spin the spinner. If it lands at "5," for example, have the children find the page in the book that corresponds with that number. Count each of the items on the page. Spin again!

6. Keeping a tally. In this book, a tally of each number is made at the left margin with colored blocks. Have the children make a tally using real blocks, as they turn the pages of the book. Each time the page is turned, another block is added. What happens when we get to #11? (Concept: Tens and Ones.)

Using the blocks, have the children keep a tally for other activities. (Examples: items Number 3 and Number 4 in this section, and activities that are carried out in the room.) After a time, students can move from blocks to sticks, to toothpicks, and to chalkmarks and pencil marks to keep a tally.

THE SEASONS

1. Since this book takes us through the months of the year, have the children say the months aloud as they turn the pages of the book. Note the changes that have taken place during each month, aside from the fact that additional items are added (leaves change color, grass changes color, and so forth).

2. Mini mural. Have four children work together on a large sheet of butcher paper to create a woodland scene. Then, divide the mural vertically into four sections (autumn, winter, spring, summer). Cut the mural into four pieces. Each student can work independently on his season, using media agreed upon previously (paint, chalk, crayons, and the like). When the students have finished, tape the mural sections back together. (It's fun when an animal, for example a rabbit, is caught between winter and spring, and half of it is white and half is brown).

Variation. Working with groups of four, have students draw a giant maple tree on the butcher paper. Divide the tree into four sections. This can be done vertically, horizontally, or diagonally. (Reinforce those terms with students.) Cut it up. Color it independently. When it is finished, tape it together on the back. This makes a very dramatic seasonal tree. (This is a good way to use number books with older kids.)

3. Counting with the months. Take twelve envelopes, and place from one to twelve items in each envelope. (Example: One square in one envelope, two squares in another, three in another, and so forth.) Have the children select an envelope and count out the number of items. Then, match this up with the month that corresponds to that number. (Example: 8 is August.)

4. Make a set of twelve cards. On each card, print the name of the month and its numeral. Place the cards face down. Have a student pick out a card and read the month. Then, see if the student can name the month that comes before and after that one, and the numeral that comes both before and after. Use a real calendar for checking the answers.

BOOK:

The Very Hungry Caterpillar
by Eric Carle. New York:
Collins Publishers, 1979.

THE BOOK—WITH A FOCUS ON ENDPAPERS

1. Endpapers. If you have a hard-cover edition of this book, be sure to call attention to the endpapers (the paper inside the covers and the first page and last page). Endpapers in this book have colorful, abstract shapes with little holes all over them that the caterpillar has eaten through. This could be a good starting point for exposure to endpapers in other books. When the children construct their own books, have them think about an object or shape that would make the endpapers synonymous with the story.

2. Using construction paper covers, ditto paper pages, and wallpaper for endpapers, make a whole set of little blank books. Then, let the children choose the endpaper they like that will stimulate their imaginations and motivate them to write, or dictate, a story. They can also make illustrations for an exciting book. This reverse method of focusing on endpapers first will encourage the children to look for endpapers in picture books.

3. Re-create the book. Have children make a ten-page book so they can retell the story. On page one have them print "Caterpillar," and draw one. On pages two through eight, have them print the days of the week and illustrate the food. On page nine, have them print "cocoon" and draw one. On page ten, have them print

"butterfly," and draw one. On the cover, have them print a title, the author's name, and an illustration. Of course, endpapers will give the book a special touch; be sure to have the children make them different from the ones in the real book. Now, they can retell their stories as they leaf through the pages of their books.

4. Make butterflies. Children can trace or draw a butterfly shape on black paper. Fold the paper in half and cut out two or three shapes. Open the paper up and glue the butterfly shape onto bright shiny colored paper, or cellophane, or tissue paper. These can be hung from the ceiling or hung in a window so sunlight can shine through them and create dancing colors in the room.

5. Make caterpillars. Young children can gain practice with eye-hand coordination by tracing large circles, cutting them out, overlapping them and pasting four or five together in a row. Add details (eyes, legs, and so on) with construction paper. Make pipe cleaner antennae.

6. Note the bold illustration of the sun in the book. Have the children paint large orange, red, or yellow suns at the easel. Also, have them paint hungry caterpillars and beautiful butterflies too!

CATERPILLAR MATH

1. Caterpillars have one dozen (twelve) eyes! What kinds of food come packaged in dozens that the caterpillar here would love to eat. Make a list and use illustrations.

2. Caterpillars have three pairs of legs; that would mean a total of six legs. When we speak about a "pair" we mean two. Let's think about our own body in relation to "pairs." Using butcher paper, trace around a child's body. Hang the tracing up. Then, let children identify and color in the "pairs" on the body (eyes, arms, legs, feet, hands . . .).

3. Caterpillar Measurement. When caterpillars are born, they are so tiny that you might not see them under the leaf, but they grow fast. By the end of three weeks, they are about three inches long. On a ruler, find the section from the left edge to the numeral three; that measures three inches. How many things can you find in the room that are three inches long? Keep a record. Also, keep the ruler straight on a piece of paper, draw a three-inch line, and label it.

4. Caterpillar Walk. The cocoon thread of the caterpillar, when unwound, is over one-half mile in length—that's 2,640 feet long. Using a trundle wheel and a pedometer, go for a caterpillar walk on the playground. You might go around and around, just like the caterpillar spinning a cocoon.

5. Caterpillar Farms. People who grow caterpillars for a living say that when caterpillars are ready to pupate (new vocabulary word) they are taken to trays of straw. First they rest, and then they turn from side to side, covering themselves with thick bags of silk, or the cocoon. It takes three days to spin this bag of silk, or cocoon. Chart this on the calendar in the room so that you know that on Day 1 the caterpillar is spinning, on Days 2 and 3 it is still spinning, and on Day 4 it is resting inside the cocoon. How many days will it rest before it

emerges as a beautiful butterfly? Find books in the library that will help locate the answer, and chart the days on the calendar.

MORE ABOUT CATERPILLARS

1. "Caterpillar" is from the French word chatepelose, or "hairy cat." The most hairy of the caterpillars is the woolly bear. Locate this in a book. Think up another name for hairy caterpillars.

2. Caterpillars are fussy eaters. They're born on just the right leaf and they begin to eat right away. A caterpillar needs the right food to grow. It can eat from a family of plants (for example, carrots, parsley, parsnips, celery, and Queen Anne's lace for the black swallowtail butterfly). Make a list of other butterflies and what they like to eat.

3. The Chinese discovered the secret of the caterpillars spinning their cocoons and the thread was carefully unwound and made into cloth that we call silk. Bring in samples of silk cloth so that children can feel it (handkerchief, tie, scarf, or a fabric sample). Have other types of cloth available so that students can make comparisons (texture, weight).

BOOK:

Bicycle Race
by Donald Crews. New York:
Greenwillow Books, 1985.

NUMBERS IN SPORTS

1. Identification. In this bicycle race, the riders have identifying numbers on their helmets so that you can keep track of them throughout the race. The numbers on the helmets don't change, but the position of the numbers keeps changing throughout the race. Make large number tags that children can put over their heads. Have half the class line up and half be the audience. As those who are lined up turn, twist, move around, and change position, ask the audience what number is first, last, in the middle, and so forth. Change places so that each child gets a turn being in the lineup and in the audience.

2. Number Sports. In what ways are numbers used for identification in other sports? Elicit responses from students. (Examples: numbers on football jerseys, baseball shirts, and jackets.) What about ski racing, running, hockey, horse racing, car racing, and the like? Where are the identification numbers located?

3. Rules. In what ways are numbers important in sports? Start with the games that children play during indoor and outdoor recess. Branch out to other sports (Examples: Football—yards gained/lost, downs, game is divided into four quarters...)

4. Time. How is time important to sports? Students can make a clock from a paper plate, and on the back list the ways that this instrument is helpful in sports. (You can use rule books to help.)

5. Keep track of the home team (school, city, state) during a season. There will be lots of number work here!

BICYCLES

1. Timing. Have students walk, run, and ride a bike a certain distance and record the time.

2. Have students design a safe "folding bicycle" that they could easily transport. Why would this be useful?

3. Students can design and make safety flags for their bicycles. (They can use cloth or 3×5 paper.)

4. Cut pictures of bikes from magazines, overlap them, and glue them onto a large piece of oaktag to make a photo montage. What can we notice about the people and the bikes that relate to math? (All ages, three wheels, and so on.)

5. Have students learn and demonstrate hand signals for bike riding.

MORE ABOUT BIKES AND SPORTS

1. Salaries in Professional Sports (Big Numbers). Get information from newspapers and sports magazines. Make a comparison chart for various sports.

2. Assignment. Listen to a game on the radio for five minutes. On a piece of paper keep track of the number of times and the way in which numbers are used. Watch a sports game on TV for five minutes. On a piece of paper keep track of the number of times numbers are used in speech and the way in which numbers are seen on the screen. Compare assignment lists. (Question: Does the type of game make a difference? Does the speed of the game make a difference? What other factors seem to make a difference?)

3. Let's Plan to Attend a Game. How much would it cost to go to a game this weekend? Have the children select their games. Have them plan for transportation, admission cost, program, refreshments, souvenirs. Have them compare notes with their classmates. Next, have them choose a big league game out-of-town, and include overnight accommodations and meals.

How much did each child spend? Have them compare notes with their classmates. Have them get set for the big trip—tennis at Wimbledon or bullfights in Spain. This time, have them show "receipts" for everything spent! (Both boys and girls like doing this; they're using math to solve problems and enjoying it! It's also a good vehicle for making math come alive for older students.)

4. Have a foot race, or a three-legged race. Assign numbers for individuals or teams. Make lanes with string or rope. Number the lanes. Have someone be the sportscaster; have someone be the timekeeper. Who is the scorekeeper? Who checks the scorekeeper? You're using math all the time.

5. Have student teams invent a Rainy Day Indoor Bike Math Game.

6. Athletes often endorse products. Have students look through magazines and cut them out as samples. Write and illustrate an ad that a bike rider is endorsing. Be sure to use math.

BOOK:

Moja Means One, Swahili Counting Book
by Muriel Feelings. Pictures by Tom Feelings.
New York: Dial Press, 1972

USING THE BOOK

1. Swahili is one language that is spoken in Africa, a continent where about 800 languages are spoken. It is difficult for children to imagine the enormity of this; it is not like having a separate language for every one of the 50 states of the United States. Even if 10 different languages were spoken in each of our 50 states, that would be only 500 different languages. When we understand other people and the problems they face in communication (including numbers), we gain a greater appreciation for our own unified language and number system.

2. Locate Africa on a globe or map. Go through the book page by page and learn to say the number names from one to ten. In the book, the names are spelled phonetically to help with accurate pronunciation.

3. Go through the book page by page to learn something about Africa—its marketplaces, storytelling customs, beautiful pottery designs, and so on. The mathematical concept of "highest" is communicated through the text accompanying the explanation for moja (one). The highest mountain in Africa is Mount Kilimanjaro. Have children locate it on the globe. What is the highest mountain in your state, or the highest hill or building in your community?

4. Mbili means Two. Mankala is a counting game played by young and old. It is played with a wooden container that has two parallel rows of six holes (similar to an egg carton), and little balls or beans or seeds. This game is well known throughout Africa and is called by different names. Village children have played the game by scooping dirt from the ground to make two sets of six holes, or

twelve holes. In some areas, the game boards have been cut into the big rocks so you just need your counters to play.

Look for information about how to play this game. Today there is even a computer version of Mankala. Perhaps your school has a copy, or can get one.

5. Tatu means Three. On this page the text deals with directionality, namely "east." Where is north, south, west, and east in relation to your classroom? Draw a simple map of your classroom and label the directions. Look for these directions on signs that have street names. How many live on a street that has a direction in its name?

6. Nne means Four. Four mothers are shown carrying babies on their backs. How do we carry our babies—back or front, or both? Name vehicles on wheels that we can use to transport babies. Divide a paper into quarters and draw four vehicles with wheels in which a baby could safely ride. Print the number of wheels.

ROTE COUNTING

1. Rote Counting with a Bouncing Ball. Have children bounce a big ball and count from one to ten in Swahili on each bounce. Children can take turns bouncing the ball while everyone counts aloud. Keep the ball bouncing. If you miss, begin again.

- Students can work in groups of two and bounce the ball back and forth as each one takes a turn at counting in Swahili.
- Echo Counting. Students can work in groups of two and bounce the ball back and forth. On the first bounce, one students says, "moja," and on the next bounce the student says, "one." On the next bounce, the first student would say, "mbili" (m.bee.lee) and on the next bounce the echo would be "two." This could also be reversed. When students become proficient at rote counting in both Swahili and English, they can mix up the numbers as they call them out to keep the partner alert. Keep the ball bouncing.

2. Rote Counting with Hand Clapping. Students can work in groups of two. Clap hands together for "one," clap hands with partner for, "moja," and so on.

- Student partners can do rote counting with hand clapping and see how high they can rote count using English.
- Students can sit in a large circle and rote count by clapping hands together for "one," and clapping hands on knees for "two," hands together for "three," hands on knees for "four," and so on. See how high the group can go. Next, start from the beginning but whisper the number every time hands clap together (one) and say the number out loud (two) when hands clap knees. What is happening? Students are rote counting aloud by twos. (This will help children when they have to write their numerals by twos. Many will refer to this rote counting game as an aid.)

3. Digits. Any single number is called a "digit." In English, "digit" means "finger" or "toe." Since people used to count with their fingers and toes at one time (and some still do) perhaps the connection is understandable. Children can count from one to ten using fingers. Work with the whole class or work in small groups or with pairs; have one person hold up a flash card showing the digit (numeral), and the other(s) must then hold up the correct number of digits (fingers).

4. Write Numbers with Hand Shapes. Just as a system evolved for using the alphabet to write words, a system evolved to use digits such as 1,2,3,4,5,6,7,8,9,0 to write numerals. Before the actual numerals appeared, there are some records of hand drawings that illustrate numbers. Early farmers and builders used hand signs and hand drawings for the terms "one," "two," "three" and after that the word "many" was used. Practice making the hand signs.

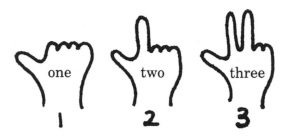

IN A TIME BEFORE NUMBERS

1. Pretend that we live in a time before written numbers. Students can put one hand down flat on the table and line up a row of toothpicks for each finger on their hand. How many are there? Scoop up the toothpicks and do this for the other hand. How many are there? How many are there for both hands? (Reinforcement exercise for numbers one to ten, and also five and ten.)

2. Base 5. People have been counting on their hands for centuries. In some languages, the word "hand" means "five." If you ask a farmer how many goats he had and the farmer answered, "hand," how many goats would that be? (Five.) Suppose you have not yet thought to use two hands but just use one hand for counting. You can use toothpicks for this, and put down one |, then another ||, and another |||, and one more ||||, until you have five |||||. Now, how do you represent six if you can't count on your other hand? (Maybe you could just use the same hand over again, or cross the picks like this ⟊⟊⟊⟊⟊ |).

Lead children to discover the following:

6	is	5 and one more
7	is	5 and 2 more
8	is	5 and 3 more
9	is	5 and 4 more
10	is	two 5s

3. Long, long ago, people did not use the clock as we do today. They kept track of the passage of time by the sun and the moon. During the day, they referred to time "when the rooster crows," or "when the waves come splashing to shore." Suppose that we were starting out without our system of clocks. What would be some ways to keep track of the time? (Focus first upon the seasons, and then the concept of morning, evening, and midday activities.)

BOOK:

Shapes and Things
by Tana Hoban. New York:
Macmillan Publishing Company, 1970.

PAGE BY PAGE

1. The Format of a Book. Look at the endpapers of the book. They are all shapes of alphabet letters. How many can we identify? Look at the title page and point out the title and the author's name. On the next page is the dedication with a pretty butterfly next to the names. Then, we have the book pages and, last, the endpapers again. Point out this format in all of the books that you read aloud until children become aware of the sequence of a book. This will help them to become authors/illustrators of their own books.

2. The process used to make this book is called photogramming. It looks like black and white negatives in photography. Bring in negatives so that children can see the similarity and can identify shapes in negatives.

3. Circles are very prominent on the first page. Some are solid white (positive) and some are solid black (negative) encircled with a white ring. Which two are alike? Are they all the same size? Which shape is not like the others? What is different about it? (three straight sides—triangle). On the next page, do you find any other shapes with three sides? Are the sides all straight? Can you find the one with four sides?

4. Have young children trace and cut out the basic shapes—circle, triangle, and square. As you call out the name of each item, children can hold them up (immediate feedback). Do this repeatedly until students can identify them.

5. Have the children form a big circle and sit down (bring chairs to the circle or sit cross-legged). Point out to them that together they have made the shape of a circle. Look around the room for objects that are in the shape of a circle. Have children take turns going to places in the room to touch an object that is in the shape of a circle.

6. Go through the book, page by page, and try to identify objects. Then, identify the basic shapes of the objects. Most objects are common ones that children will be familiar with.

7. Identify all of the objects (and shapes) from nature.

8. Identify the objects (and shapes) that are useful to you personally.

9. Identify the objects (and shapes) that are useful to people in certain occupations.

SHAPE BOOKS

1. Make a book about shapes. Some suggestions include a page devoted to the following shapes: zigzag, round, triangle, square, oval, cylinder, cube, squiggly shapes, and so on.

2. Make the books in the form of shapes. That is, make a circle book, a square book, a triangular book, and so on.

3. In your general shape book, include text and have the shapes talk about their qualities, and some of the things they're used for.

4. Have one shape claim to be superior to the rest and set out in the world to meet all of the other shapes and see just what they can do too. Have the shape return home feeling good, but not superior about what it can do!

5. Cut finger paint paper into shapes. With paint, trace around objects. You can do one, two, or three inner lines or rings. "Erase" and do it again. Try different shapes.

6. Everything has a shape. When we walk to school we create a shape. (Example: Walk down the street, turn to the left at the corner (angle), go two blocks to the intersection, turn right to cross, then turn left to cross, and walk along the sidewalk. Turn right into school.) Draw your "walk to school" shape.

7. Next time you go on a field trip, make a shape book not only of the place, but include the shape of your journey. (Include the shapes of traffic signals, traffic signs, the building, the route, and so on.)

MORE SHAPES

1. Squares. Make a variety of one-inch squares from different colored paper. Children can make a mosaic design or a mosaic picture of an actual object.

2. Save the circular shapes from the three-hole paper punch and give each child a handful. Sift through them, estimate them, count them. On 9×12 construction paper, make circles with the little circles. Paste them down.

3. Grocery Bag Shapes. Bring in a large assortment of empty boxes, cans, jars, containers from groceries. Sort them by shape. Also, look at the labels on the containers for shapes that are used in advertising

4. Shape Language. Make giant shape charts, and write directly on them the language that is generated by the children, such as: Round as a _____; Square as a _____; Thick as a _____; Thin as a _____; Oval as a _____; Squiggly as a _____; and so on.

BOOK:

Through the Year with Harriet
by Betsy and Giulio Maestro.
A Time Concept book.
New York: Crown Publishers, 1985.

GO THROUGH THE YEAR WITH HARRIET

1. The book begins with Harriet's birthday in the month of January. It will be a whole year before her birthday comes again, and that's an eternity for a youngster. Take twelve different colored pieces of construction paper and label each one with a different month. Tape white paper to the construction paper and print (or have children print) their name and date on their birthday month. Hang these above the chalkboard and keep them there all year for reference, or hang them below the chalkboard so that children can work with them to learn dates, students' names, names of the months.

2. From the illustrations, have children guess three presents that Harriet the elephant received. Which one would they like best? Make a graph that shows the favorites.

3. Make a Classroom Time Line. Divide a long roll of shelf paper into twelve sections. (This can be started any month. If you begin the time line in November, for example, the previous months can be reviewed and the information can be added.) Label the twelve sections for the months of the year. Under each month, put down dates and events that were important happenings in your classroom. For example:

SEPTEMBER	OCTOBER
6 – We started a new year!	3 – Today is Barrie's birthday.
12 – We got new reading books today.	7 – We're studying about Columbus.
15 – Our easel is set up.	12 – Mrs. B visited our class.
27 – Nathan is our new friend.	28 – We took a field trip to Apple Orchard.
	31 – Today we had a Halloween party.

Children enjoy reviewing the events and like to make accompanying illustrations. It's good for keeping a record of the highlights in class, and children can learn to identify the numerals and read the words. This can be hung under the chalkboard or along a side wall. At the end of the year, you can auction off the months of the year by having the children pick a number from 1 to 100.

4. January Art Projects. Have the children paint white snowmen on a dark blue background. Make the scarf, broom, and hat white too as if there were a big snowstorm in the night. You could make designer snowmen. Use three white construction paper circles as a beginning, and paste them onto a colorful background. Then have the children cut out construction paper hats, scarves, gloves, vests, boots, shovels, and so on. You could also use the three white circles to make a cowboy snowman, a dressed up snowman, a police snowman, a famous snowman, and so on.

5. For February, Harriet is painting a heart. The children could do the same for Valentine's Day. What other special holidays do we celebrate in February? How many days are there in this month? Check a calendar to make comparisons with other months. February has been called the Month of Presidents. Let's list the presidents born in this month.

6. Hot Cocoa! A quick way to make delicious hot cocoa is to heat chocolate milk. Children can add 1,2,3,4,5,6 miniature marshmallows for a topping and a counting experience. Making cocoa using the powdered form is a good math experience measuring dry and liquid ingredients, and timing.

MONTH BY MONTH

1. Use the calendar to learn the names of the months and the days of the week. Devote one bulletin board to the calendar in Pre K–Grade 3, so that children become familiar with it. Change the calendar monthly with a new theme. Numerals can be printed on by children, or identified by children and tacked onto the appropriate squares. The calendar is "math in action" since every day has a number, and with digital time we can get a readout of what the number is at every minute.

2. March finds Harriet still shoveling snow, but at dinner time it is lighter outdoors. Discuss hours of daylight with students. For younger students, the contrast can best be made when talking about summer days and winter days, and realization of the fact that in the summer, it's still light out after supper.

3. There is an old saying that "March comes in like a lion and goes out like a lamb." What exactly does that mean? Did it come in like a lion this year? In some areas of the country, March is known as the month of tornados. What are your plans for tornado safety, fire safety? Plan and carry out a classroom safety drill.

4. In April, Harriet is planting seeds. Can children tell from the seed packets what she's planting? Now is a very good time to try planting seeds in the classroom. Seeds can be planted and cared for in styrofoam cups, in pull-apart egg cartons, or in milk cartons. Try flowers that children will have success with, such as marigolds. Keep a record of the date planted, the date growth was first sighted, and appropriate illustrations. Measure growth with a ruler and record the measurements.

5. Note that Harriet is getting out her spring clothing. Is it getting warmer? Do we change to different clothing in our area of the country? Encourage weather

reporting and temperature notations that require using math (degrees, warmer than/colder than, warm/warmer/warmest).

6. How are the trees different in May than in January in this book? Make tree pictures that show a contrast between two seasons. (Concept: Time.)

SUMMER TIME, THEN SCHOOL BEGINS

1. In June, July, and August, Harriet is enjoying the outdoors. In what activities is she engaged? Take a survey to learn each child's favorite activity.

2. Plan a menu for a summer picnic with a friendly alligator. What would you take in the basket? Discuss number, size, and weight.

3. Discuss water safety rules for summer; list five.

4. September is... the Yellow School Bus. Do a "September is......" chart with students and have them individually suggest a word that pertains to school.

5. Harriet is shown at the easel. For Pre K–Grade 3, this is an excellent item to have in the classroom at all times. Use juice cans with plastic lids for paint so that paint won't dry out. Cut a small hole in the center of each lid so the brush can be inserted. Challenge students to paint a picture that uses math in some way.

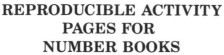

**REPRODUCIBLE ACTIVITY
PAGES FOR
NUMBER BOOKS**

2–1   The Elf and the Shoemaker Graph (graphing)

2–2   Go on a Shape Walk (getting in shape with numbers; body movement; body geometry)

2–3   Numbers Are Very Dependable! (creative mathematics; writing)

2–4   Number Concept Application Form (number concepts such as right, left, top, bottom, under, inside)

2–5   Help Bo Peep Count Her Sheep (using number words)

2–6   Number Book Illustrations (basic shapes)

2–7   The History of Numbers (number practice)

2–8   Taking an Inventory (counting; awareness of numbers and their use in everyday life)

2–9   Make a Number Book (using numbers; number correspondence; creativity)

THE ELF AND THE SHOEMAKER GRAPH

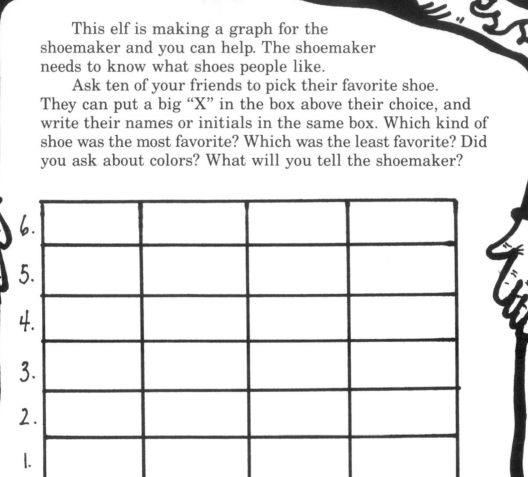

This elf is making a graph for the shoemaker and you can help. The shoemaker needs to know what shoes people like.

Ask ten of your friends to pick their favorite shoe. They can put a big "X" in the box above their choice, and write their names or initials in the same box. Which kind of shoe was the most favorite? Which was the least favorite? Did you ask about colors? What will you tell the shoemaker?

Two shoes are done for you. Make two more shoes.

Name _____   Date _____

Walk in a circle. 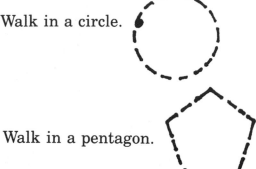   Walk in a square.

Walk in a pentagon.   Walk in this shape.

IN THE CLASSROOM

Draw your desk and label it "A." Then walk to another place in the room, draw it, and label it "B." Then walk from "B" to another place in the room, draw it, and label it "C." Now walk back to your starting point, or "A." Draw the shape that you walked.

ON THE PLAYGROUND

Walk a shape, and draw the shape that you walked. Some lines will be straight_____ some will be curved ⌢⌣ and some lines will have a turn (angle) ⌐_ .

Look Up! What shapes are the clouds? Draw the shapes on the back of this page.

NUMBERS ARE VERY DEPENDABLE!

You can count WITH numbers and you can count ON numbers to be dependable and constant. That is, unless one of them decides not to cooperate–then things can get confusing! Put on your thinking cap and write a funny story about a number that refuses to cooperate. It could be a mystery story, with things turning out all wrong! How do you catch the number that is pretending to be another number? Has it disappeared? This is going to be a thrilling story!

_____
(TITLE)

Name _____   Date _____

NUMBER CONCEPT APPLICATION FORM

We need an illustrator who can draw good shapes such as ○ , □ and △ . You also have to follow directions carefully. Fill out this application form. Use bright colors.

Make a ○ in the upper left corner.	Make a △ in the middle.	Color the top half of this space blue.
Make a □ in the upper right corner.	Make a □ in the middle. Make a △ under it.	Color the bottom half of this space red.
Make a ○ in the middle. Make a △ over it.	Make a △ in the lower right corner.	Make a □ in the middle. Put a ○ inside it.

Name _____   Date _____

Shhh! The sheep are asleep in their pens. Read the number word and draw that many sheep in each pen.

Then, use the number line at the bottom of the page to count the total number of sheep.

four

six

five

three

one

1 2 3 4 5 6 7 8 9 10 11 12 13 14 15 16 17 18 19

Total

Write the total number on the sheep. Did you count the one Bo Peep is holding?

Name _____   Date _____

NUMBER BOOK ILLUSTRATIONS   2–6

Pretend that you are going to be the picture book illustrator for a number book. In this number book, there are many shapes. As the illustrator, you will have to make a picture from each shape below.

Example: A circle can become a ball or a face or something else!

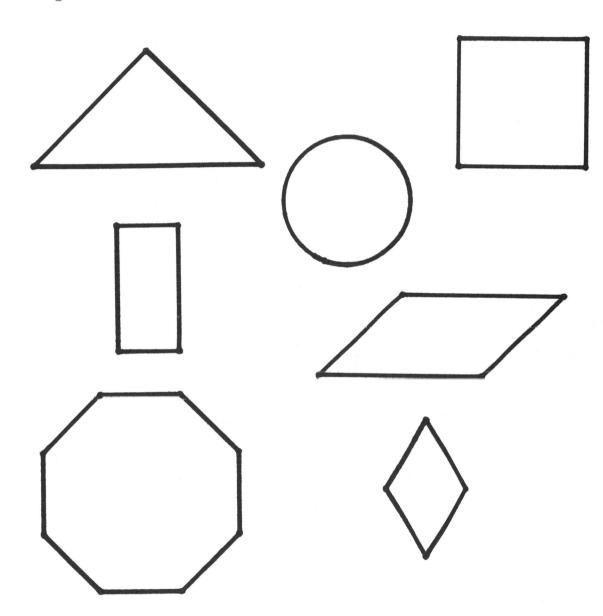

How many shapes can you identify by name? After you have made your shape into something, make comparisons with your classmates. How many different things were made from each shape? Keep a tally.

Name _____   Date _____

THE HISTORY OF NUMBERS

ARABIC NUMERALS: Gradually, Roman Numerals were replaced by Arabic Numerals. See how they looked at one time. They are the ancestors of the numerals we use today. This system is used throughout most of the world.

Practice writing from 1 to 10. See how the numeral used to look. Does it look similar today?

1	1	1	1	
μ	2	2		
μ	3	3		
ε	4	4		
o	5	5		
7	6	6		
V	7	7		
Λ	8	8		
9	9	9		
1.	10	10		

Using today's Arabic numerals, make up some addition problems. Exchange papers with a partner and record the answers. Check all work carefully. The first one is started for you.

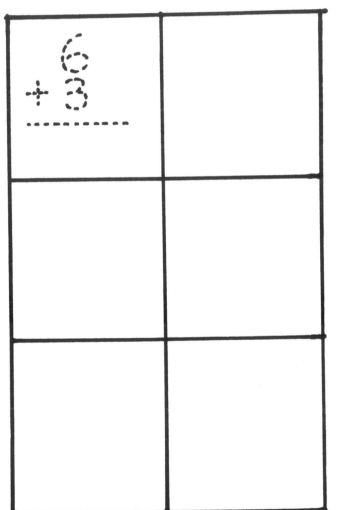

Do you know how to write the Roman Numerals? Write them on the back of this paper.

Name _____   Date _____

To take an inventory, you have to count. Count the number of each of these items that you have in your classroom. They are all items that help us with math. Record the total number in each box. Compare your inventory with those of your classmates.

When you have completed your inventory (total number), tell how each item is used to help us solve problems.

Why is an inventory important at the beginning of the year? At the end of the year?

Can you list people who take an inventory? Some examples are: grocery clerk, banker, and baker. How many can you list? What are they counting?

Do some people have to take an inventory more often than others? Why?

Take an inventory of the contents in your desk. Compare it with three others.

1. Think of what you will draw. Will it be animals, birds, fish, toys, trees, flowers, or something else? That is the theme of your book.

2. Your number book can go from 1 to 10, and even beyond 10.

3. Draw the items carefully and color them with bright colors! Practice.

4. Cut out the ten pages.

5. Make a cover from construction paper. Think up a good title. Put your name on the front.

6. Staple your book together.

7. Congratulations! You're an author!

1 one

2 two

3 three

4 four

5 five

7

seven

8

eight

6

six

9

nine

10

ten

Look through a lot of number books. Notice that some number books go beyond 1 to 10.

- Some number books continue with 11 to 20.
- Some number books go from 1 to 10, and then start counting by 10s and go all the way to 100! (20, 30, 40, 50, 60, 70, 80, 90, 100)
- What will you do with your number book?

SECTION 3

Picture Books

BOOK:

Hot Air Henry
by Mary Calhoun. Illustrations by
Erick Ingraham. New York:
William Morrow and Co., 1981.

THE BOOK

1. Students can work in teams and interview "Hot-Air Henry the Flying Cat" just as he lands. Tape record the interview, or write it up as an on-the-scene reporter.

2. Birds, bats, and insects can fly, but other animals can move through space too. There's the flying fish and the "gliders" such as the flying squirrel and the flying snake. Rewrite the part of the story where Henry meets up with a bird, and have him meet up with a different flying creature. How will it change the outcome of the story, or will it? What will the new illustration look like?

3. "We Interrupt This Program..." Make a headband with a big bird's beak on it, and have students give a bird report on the classroom "local TV news" about an invasion of a cat from space. Birds always must be on the alert for cats, and from the point-of-view of the bird this hot air ballooning could be a cat's scheme to catch birds in the air—a territory that they felt was safe from felines.

4. Make a picture story strip using five spaces. Spaces one, three, and five represent the beginning, middle, and ending of the story. In spaces two and four, draw your favorite parts in between. This time, include in the last space the exact words that the man said to Henry when he returned.

SPACE ADVENTURE

1. Students can list their special qualifications for working in a pilot training program; for example, having good math/science skills, being a serious student, liking roller coaster rides, enjoying stomach flip-flops on elevators, and so on.

2. The Futuristic Balloon! First make a sketch, and then, using a balloon, string, basket, and other materials, have students build a model of a hot air balloon of the future.

3. Coded Messages. Devise a code system so that a message can be sent back to the control tower. This can be a picture code, or a flag code.

4. The hot air inside the balloons is what makes them rise. The hot air is lighter than the cold air on the ground. The gas burner heats the air and it rises faster. Turn off the heat, and what will happen? (The air in the balloon cools down and it begins to descend, or land.) Using balloon shapes, put these instructions in simplified form for Henry, in case he should try again, or in case he decides to open up his own flying school for cats.

KITES ARE SAFER!

1. Kite flying originated in China. The Chinese made kites that whistled in the wind and made noises, sounds, or "music." Chinese name for kite, "feng cheng" means wind harp. Find other interesting kite facts at the library.

2. Message Kites. Kites come in all shapes and sizes—dragons, birds, bees, cats, animals. Have the students design and paint colorful kites and put kite information on the long tails. Hang the kite reports from the ceiling. (This can be confined to a corner of the room.)

Attach bulky yarn to the kites and let them hang from the ceiling. Teach the children to sing, "Let's Go Fly a Kite," and have them gently take the yarn and swing and sway as they sing the song. (This works surprisingly well for young children who are looking way, way up to the ceiling and imagining that they really are flying a kite.) Many kite flyers get launched this way.

3. Go Fly a Kite with Henry! Read to find out how a kite flies. The children can construct kites, and take them outside for flying on "just the right day." The children will have to be able to determine when this "right day" is; they can get this information from a book about kites. Have some commercial kites available as well, that Henry supplied.

4. Worker Kites. Thermometers are attached to some kites to test air temperature. Cameras have been attached to some to take pictures. NASA has experimented with kites to judge wind force. Write a report about kites on kite-shaped (diamond) paper.

5. Kite Flying Contests. In some countries, children take kite flying seriously. Have the children make their own kites and see whose can fly the farthest, the longest, and so on.

6. Creative Thinking/Writing. Create a story about a hot-air balloon that meets a kite in the sky. Henry is in the balloon and the kite is being held by the man (or another cat). Is the kite really talking or is the kite flyer sending messages up through the string? How? Put lots of lively conversation in the story, with a colorful picture of the meeting.

BOOK:

Babar's Birthday Surprise
by Laurent DeBrunhoff. New York:
Random House, 1970.

BABAR'S BIRTHDAY SURPRISE

1. As you read through the Babar series, make a family tree for Babar. What will your title be? What will its shape be?

2. Mold a statue of Babar from clay, just as Podular the famous sculptor did. Students can write and deliver a little dedication speech.

3. How clever to disguise the Babar statue with birds! Have students think of another clever but temporary disguise and illustrate it for the book.

4. Surprise! Babar's family is coming to visit your school for his birthday. Make a list of preparations for the guests. Who should be invited? Plan the menu. Role play the tour. The children can contribute illustrations for a class booklet of the visit. Show Babar at lunch, in the gym, in art class, doing arithmetic problems, in reading groups, and so on.

5. Surprise! Babar's family likes you and your city and plans to stay over-night for *your* birthday! Just think! You will have an elephant as an overnight guest. What exciting surprise would you like for your birthday? Help Babar to plan it!

6. Snappy Dresser. Babar likes nice clothes and is always well groomed. Design a suit for him or a dress for Celeste. Then draw them wearing these designer clothes. Put your drawing on the sports page, or the fashion page, or Section B page of the newspaper with headlines and a story. Include the byline that the clothing was styled by ____, or make it the main reason for the story.

ELEPHANTS

1. What is the name of the elephant at the zoo nearest you? Find books on elephants to determine how much elephants weigh, how tall they are, what they eat. Write an elephant report on a trunk, ear, or tusk shape.

2. Paint an African safari on rolled shelf paper. Each student can contribute an animal (single or in herds) and the animal can be repeated because you hope to see an elephant, giraffe, or lion more than once on your safari. Attach dowel rods at each end, for winding and unwinding the paper. A cardboard box could also be

used as the viewing station. Each student can write the narration for his animal, or tape record the safari information.

3. An Elephant Never Forgets. Is this true? What does this mean? Students can check a variety of library resources and share information that they find. For creative writing, compose "The Day the Elephant Forgot." Decide the characters, setting, and type of story (mystery, humor, adventure, and so on).

ANOTHER BABAR STORY

1. Bring in *The Story of Babar* by Jean DeBrunhoff (New York: Random House, 1933, 1961). Make a contrasting diorama that depicts Babar in the wilds on one side and Babar in the city on the other.

2. Babar liked riding up and down repeatedly in the elevator and had to be reminded that it wasn't a toy. What else in the city would appear to be a "toy" to Babar, but useful to people. Use your imagination, and show Babar in the city playing with a new "toy" (examples: gasoline pump, escalator, traffic switch control box).

3. Make a big cardboard cutout of Babar, and paint it gray. Dress him in fancy clothes with colorful paint. Staple it to a bulletin board. Put a book bag over his shoulder. Fill the book bag with more Babar books that can be read aloud or read in spare time. (You, an older student, or an aide can record the stories on tape, and young children can listen to the story and look at the book at the same time.)

4. Make your own Babar designer book bag. Use burlap or fancy cloth. Sew two square shapes together. Attach a shoulder strap made of macramé cord. Use it for all of your Babar information: Babar stories, Babar games, pictures of Babar in your city, school, home; a sheet to keep track of all of the Babar stories that you have read, and so on.

5. The Main Character. Babar is eventually made King of the elephants. What qualities does Babar have that make all of the elephants like him? Is he mean or friendly? Is he grumpy or cheerful? Does he get angry? If so, how does he handle his anger? Does he share or is he stingy? Is he a good listener or does he always have to do all of the talking? This is a good reason to read more books in this series, isn't it? (Young children are not only enjoying the story but also examining the main character so they are rereading or listening again for a definite purpose.)

BOOK:

Strega Nona
by Tomi dePaola. Englewood Cliffs, NJ:
Prentice-Hall, 1975.

GRANDMA WITCH

1. Strega Nona, which is Italian for Grandma witch, put up a Help Wanted sign in the town square. Students can make a Help Wanted sign exactly as they think it looked. Because she is a witch, she may have left letters out on purpose to trick us, or she may have written the sign in code, or in very fancy letters, or in "mirror writing" or it could be just plain and simple.

2. Stop Magic Pot! To stop the magic pot, Strega Nona needed to blow three kisses to it. There could be many special ways to stop the magic pot—ways that only the pots could know. Attend a Magic Pot meeting and let three magic pots tell you how they can be stopped. Be sure to write this information down (on magic pot shapes) so that we don't forget the special chants and movements. Then, share the information.

3. Design another cape for Strega Nona—one that she uses for special holidays. Also, make a paper apron for her, and print her grocery list on it.

EXPLORING PASTA

1. Check the word "pasta" in the dictionary. What does it mean? (Pasta can mean paste or dough, and is from the Latin "paste.") Some earlier dictionaries do not list it so look up under "paste" before you give up. (Pasta is dough made from flour and water and dried.)

2. Ask parents to send in one cup of unusual pasta. Also ask them to include their favorite pasta recipe and compile it into a book for children to take home.

Put the unusual pasta in different containers and note the different shapes and sizes. Have students categorize them.

3. Colored pasta? It's not only off-white, it's green, orange, and black. How did pasta get so colorful? (Some is made from flour flavored with spinach, bell peppers, beets, and squid ink to produce vibrant colors.) Be sure to have colored pasta included in your unusual samples.

4. Pasta Nicknames. Pasta seems to take on nicknames for its shape—such as stovepipe, elbow, corkscrew, shells, and the like. However, pasta has important

sounding names like "linguini," "fettucini," "rigatoni," "vermicelli," and so on. How many real Italian names can we list for pasta? Make a pasta dictionary with illustrations (and nicknames too).

LET'S EXPLORE PASTA SOME MORE

1. Big Anthony's Favorite Recipe. Big Anthony (you) can copy a pasta recipe from a cookbook on a reproducible activity sheet. Include the cookbook title, page number, and "copied by Big A." We know that Big Anthony does not pay attention to details and there are bound to be errors. Have the students find the recipe in the cookbook and copy it correctly directly under Big Anthony's recipe. To help him out, let's circle all of his mistakes. (There could be a number of recipe activities of this sort to assist students with location skills, proofreading, rewriting.

- Variation. Big Anthony could be copying a variety of plans and instructions from books. His interests could range from how to make model airplanes to how to make puppets. List the resource and the page number, and have the students help Big Anthony out with his written errors.

- Try to construct a model (of anything) using Big Anthony's plans. Where did he go wrong?

2. Suppose Strega Nona and Big Anthony opened up an Italian Ristorante; what would they call it? How many kinds of spaghetti and macaroni (pasta) would they serve? Make the titles of the dishes sound interesting.

Draw a picture of the restaurant—inside and outside. What is the shape of the sign that will hang outside their restaurant? Will the restaurant have awnings? Are there booths or tables? Do they use tablecloths or placemats? What do the hanging lamps look like? What pictures are on the wall? Maybe a diorama would help the class to visualize this gourmet pasta palace.

3. Pasta Party. For a tasty treat, have students help cook some pasta to see how it expands. Have a commercial brand of ready-made sauce cooking in a slow cooker so that it can be spooned over the pasta. What else will be served? (Math: timing, measurement, expansion.)

This special party can have waiters, waitresses, someone dressed as Strega Nona, someone dressed as Big Anthony, checkered tablecloths, and so on. Take colored photographs of the party. When they are developed, have students put them in sequential order on a chart. Together (or separately) write about this event on experience chart paper.

4. Other books. There are other books by Tomi dePaola about Strega Nona and her magic lessons and about Big Anthony. Be sure to include them in the theme box so that children can have more reading adventures with them.

5. Just in! Strega Nona and Big Anthony are so busy inside the restaurant that next month they will have a FAST FOOD DRIVE-THROUGH PICKUP

SERVICE. This means more specialties! Let's try to imagine them, and write up the menu. How many finger food items can we include? What magic way will Strega Nona and Big Anthony come up with for eating spaghetti in the car?

BOOK:

When the Sky Is Like Lace
by Elinor Lander Horwitz.
Pictures by Barbara Cooney.
New York: J. B. Lippincott, 1985.

A "BIMULOUS" NIGHT

1. Read the story once, then again. Then, go through it page by page and try to reconstruct the story using just the illustrations as a guide.

2. Have students describe a "bimulous" night in their own words. Maybe some students would prefer to do it with a KA-BOOM picture, similar to the style used in the book.

We know that a bimulous night is "strange-splendid and plum-purple" and there are certain rules about what should be done. Elicit a variety of descriptive, musical words from students (or have them use the dictionary) that could be applied to different nights. What colors would you associate each with:

Night	Colors	Rules
a _____ night	_____ and _____	
a _____ night	_____ and _____	

Students can select one of these descriptive nights and paint it. Make up rules. Compose a chant or a song or a special saying for the night

3. Plum-purple is great and wearing orange is taboo for "bimulous." How many purple and orange scenes or items can we find in this book?

4. Can we eat orange and purple? (They ate spaghetti.) Have peeled orange sections and big purple grapes for a "bimulous snack."

5. What colors mixed together make purple? What colors mixed together make orange? At the easel, students can paint a bimulous night scene using only orange and purple.

SKY WATCHING

1. Check the calendar. When will the next full moon be high in the sky? The full moon is known by different names at different times of the year, such as the

"Harvest Moon," and the "June Moon," and so on. Can we find any more special names for the moon?

2. How many children's rhymes use the word, "moon?" Do you know of any songs that use the word? Search through a Mother Goose book for moon rhymes.

3. Lunar or Moon. "Lunar" comes from the Latin word, "luna," which means "month." Long ago, the moon was used to measure time. There are many stories written about witches and werewolves appearing in full moonlight. Many people think that strange things really do happen when the moon is full. Do you? Pretend that the man in the moon just winked at you (as in the story) and off you go on an adventure. Write it down.

4. The story mentions keeping a penny in your pocket, just in case. There is an old saying, "If you have money in your pocket, turn it over at the very first sight of the new full moon and it will be doubled." How many sayings can we find that deal with money? (Some examples: "Money is the root of all evil," "Neither a borrower nor a lender be.") Make up a "money saying" for a special night.

5. *When the Sky Is Like Lace* is a very descriptive title. Think of other descriptive words for sky, using the same beginning words: For example, "When the Sky Is Like _____." Look through the book again, and this time focus upon the sky. This may help students with their descriptive titles.

6. Discuss lace. How many different samples of lace can students bring in? Is anyone wearing lace today? Can someone wear lace tomorrow? Have children take an inventory at home of where lace is seen on something and bring the information back so that it can be shared (lace curtains, lace ruffles on pillows, lace handkerchiefs, lace tablecloths, lace lining around placements, and the like).

- Are all lace patterns the same? Check them. How is lace made? Use descriptive words about lace so that everyone will know what lace is like even if they've never seen it. We can have a "sense" of lace. That's just like the word "bimulous" that's in the story. We have a real sense of the word! And we'll know a "bimulous" night when we see one.

- If the season's right, find some Queen Anne's lace, the wildflower that is also known as "wild carrot." Examine the design carefully.

CUSTOMS

1. Act out the customs for a "bimulous" night. Sway back and forth and forth and back like trees; slither like snails; wiggle your nose, but don't scratch it! (Does that make it itch?) Sing "The Katydid" song to your own tune. Record it on tape.

2. Look around the room for the color chartreuse. Can we find something? Describe the color. What gift of chartreuse would you give?

3. For creative play, pretend to be a helicopter, to juggle three peaches, to ride a camel, dance with an otter, and so on.

4. For an indoor recess project, turn a box over on its side, and make the inside of one of the rooms in the story; or use a larger box and make the upstairs

and downstairs. Using a cylindrical shape, plan to make a pavilion similar to one in the story where the girls ate spaghetti with pineapple sauce and where no rabbits were allowed inside.

BOOK:

The Snowy Day
by Ezra Jack Keats. New York:
Puffin Books, 1978.

PETER AND THE BOOK

1. After reading the book, go through the book quietly as though the snow is falling, and look for dark/light contrasts of colors.

2. Torn paper collage. This book was illustrated using torn scraps of wrapping paper, newspaper, wallpaper, construction paper, and cotton. Using only 9 × 12 or 12 × 18 paper as the background, have students gently tear (no scissors, please) a variety of papers and make a collage.

Gently tear three circular shapes for a snowman. Then tear his hat, scarf, gloves, broom, eyes, nose, mouth, and buttons.

Gently tear the papers and make a snowy day picture. You may want to work to background music.

Because tearing paper doesn't require precision, many children are able to have a successful art experience. Be sure to demonstrate the difference between a gentle tear using the fingers (you are guiding the tear) and a rip (random, no control).

3. Snowblindness. The glare of the bright sun on white snow can cause eye pain that is called snowblindness. In the arctic regions, people must wear wraparound glasses with small slits. Make a special pair of arctic glasses and look through the book again. Since it narrows the point of focus, what do we see that we didn't see before?

SNOW

1. After a snowy day, when the snow has drifted and piled high, take a yardstick outdoors. Poke it into the snow and measure the depth of the drifts. Find the deepest.

2. Playground Angels. Take the children outdoors and have them make the snow angel that was illustrated in the book. After the experience, make a snow

angel picture. Use 9×12 or 12×18 dark construction paper for the background, and white chalk dipped into water. By dipping the chalk into water, you get the effect of paint and you have no chalk dust.

3. Lay a thermometer on top of the snow for twenty minutes to get a reading. Record it. Find a snow drift, dig in, and place the thermometer on the ground. Bury it. Wait twenty minutes. Uncover it, and get a reading. (It should be warmer because snow acts as a blanket for the earth.) In our language, we even speak of a "blanket" of snow.

Cut a long strip of paper and fold it into four sections. This long strip could be made to look like a giant thermometer. Have children show the thermometer blanket experiment. In Section 1, show the snow with the thermometer on top. In Section 2, show the thermometer reading. In Section 3, show the buried thermometer covered with a "blanket" and in Section 4, show the reading.

4. Find weather maps in daily newspapers and keep track of the weather. (*USA Today* is an excellent resource.) Students can keep track of the daily weather reports by using a local newspaper, a portable radio, or battery-operated weather radio in the room. Have them record the information on their own "Weather Report" sheet.

5. Children can become radio announcers, and via tape recorder report a really big blizzard that's heading this way. How do we prepare for it?

6. Make a Winter Dictionary of Terms. Some starters are: avalanche, icebergs, glacier, icicles, jet stream. Some students may include Winter Facts in their books that include information about giant blizzards (1885, 1977). What shape will this book be? Will it be illustrated?

ANIMALS THAT LIKE WINTER

1. What animals would be likely to appear in *A Snowy Day* when Peter goes out again for his next walk? List them, show them, illustrate one with Peter.

2. What animals are hibernating in *A Snowy Day* that Peter will not see? Make up a three-part riddle about them: "I'm thinking of an animal that has _____ and that _____, and _____." (Clues can include body shapes, body covering such as fur or feathers, sounds that animal, bird, or sea life do/do not make, coloring of animal, and so on).

3. Track Record. (Playground, neighborhood, or under bird feeder). Go outdoors and look for animal tracks. Study them, using a magnifying glass. Illustrate and label samples.

Make a "Track Map." Where do animals appear and disappear on the map? Make a legend for the track map. Also, study animal paw shapes and tracks in library books, and see if you can locate any.

4. Paw prints. Using library resource books, make a glossary of paw prints. Study the shapes carefully. Then, using small cards, make a set of the shapes (one per card) using a felt-tip pen or construction paper, and put the name of the animal on the reverse side. On another set of small cards, print the name of the

animal that matches the paw print. Put all of the paw print cards in a row, and turn the name cards over. Take one name card at a time and match up the sets. (Check answers on reverse side.) Each student can construct his own Paw Print Game, and make up variations on the procedure.

BOOK:

Town and Country
by Alice and Martin Provensen.
New York: Crown Publishers, 1984.

TOURING THE CITY

1. This is a picture storybook of contrasts. Point out to the students that this book is divided into two equal parts. Part One deals with the big city and Part Two deals with the country.

- As in all picture books, there are two modes of storytelling—visual and verbal. Notice that when dealing with the city, both the pictures and text have a vertical quality, like walking among the tall buildings. Similarly, when dealing with the country, the visual and verbal emphasis is on horizontal lines and one gets the feeling of land and space. Be sure to discuss this with the students.

2. Go walking slowly through this detailed book in the city section looking for the following: bridge styles, methods of transportation, building and architectural styles, machinery, workers on the ground, workers above the ground, neon signs, and advertisements.

- What activities are taking place under the bridge where the construction signs are displayed? How has the built-up bridge helped traffic congestion underneath? What do the international signs mean? How many students have gone through a traffic tunnel in a car?

3. What can students find to do in the city on Saturday and Sunday? The text and illustrations are rich with ideas. Make an indoor and an outdoor choice of city activities.

4. Cities are usually filled with restaurants and this one is no exception. What ethnic foods can be purchased? What countries are represented? Take a vote—where would students like to stop for something to eat? What makes it look "busy?" (See Section 3, number 1 to help students make a busy picture.)

5. Street vendors. How many students know what a street food vendor is? How many have purchased food from a street vendor? (Pretzels, chestnuts, hot dogs, ice cream, soda pop, and so on.) How do these people advertise? (Signs, and calling out.) Have students set up shop as street vendors and line up calling out their wares.

6. Theatre Section for Listening. Is there a Mozart Symphony No. 5? Find out. If so, obtain a copy from the city lending library record collection and listen to it as if you have stepped inside that theatre. Then, visit a rock session for contrast. Stop to listen to the musical comedy *Oklahoma,* and then on to the ballet. What sights can students conjure up in their mind's eye as they listen? Illustrate what is happening inside of one of the theatres.

7. City Sounds. Look at the pictures for sounds and listen to the text for sounds. Everyone can become a city sound, and at a given signal make the sound for the cacophony of the city. When the page is turned, new sounds are heard. Rehearse.

TOURING THE COUNTRY

1. Have the children get the feeling of space as you go through this section; note the sky, the hills, the trees, the fields. Especially enjoy the two-page spread that shows four horizontal pictures.

2. Name the different animals and count them. What are the people busy doing?

3. If you go to school in the country in this book, what will you see at recess on the playground behind the school that you definitely would not see in your city school? Do you think the schools would be different? In what way? Would the teachers be any different? In what way?

4. On Saturdays and Sundays, what would you do in the country on a rainy day, or on a sunny day?

5. In the country, when you go to the city to do the shopping, where will you eat? Does the picture show this? What does the text tell us about food?

6. "The city never sleeps," but does the farm sleep? Would you get up earlier if you lived in the city or in the country? Does it make a difference? Do the children have more responsibilities for helping out in the city or in the country? Is there a difference?

VERTICAL, HORIZONTAL, AND CONTEXT CLUES

1. Make a tall city mural. Take a long sheet of butcher paper and hold it vertically. Students can make skyscrapers from construction paper and, starting at the top of the paper, paste them on in an overlapping manner, so that all the space is filled with buildings at least three-quarters of the way down the mural. Then, fill the remaining one-quarter with people, vehicles, traffic bridges, smaller buildings, sidewalks, and streets. These can be painted on, or made from construction paper and overlapped.

2. Make a horizontal farm mural. Using the idea from the book, make several long pictures on the mural, with text or title underneath. The mural could show morning, noon, and night on the farm; or activities in different types of weather, or seasons.

3. Make vertical city books. Compile ABCs of the city, and illustrate them.

4. Make vertical and horizontal bar graphs. Make a "forced choice" question so that the graphs will show an either/or response and, thus, will result in a very tall (vertical) or very long (horizontal) graph. (Forced choice means being given only two choices and having to make a selection, such as "Would you rather ride on the subway or on the traffic bridge?" "Would you rather go to the Italian restaurant for pizza or the Chinese restaurant for egg roll?")

5. Context clues for reading. How can we tell that there is an Italian restaurant in the Food Section of the city page? Do we always have to have all of the letters in a word to know what it might be? The context is important, too. If we saw "zza" and "orante" and "erria" on a machine page, would we be as apt to figure out the word? (No, because the words would be out of context; but in the Food Section, we can fill in the rest.)

- Work with context clues by having students cut colorful advertisements from glossy magazines. Have them cover up part of a word—the first letter, the last letter, or slice the word right in the middle of a letter so that we see part of the letter. Try slicing the word horizontally, so that we don't see the "tails" of the letters that fall below the bottom line. We are, in a sense, reading what isn't there; filling in the necessary part of the information to enable us to read the words. Practice doing this.

BOOK:

Where the Wild Things Are
by Maurice Sendak. New York:
Scholastic Books by arrangement with
Harper & Row, 1963.

ABOUT THE BOOK

1. After reading the book aloud to the children, go through it silently just looking at the pictures. What happens? As Max has a monster of a temper tantrum, the pictures get larger and larger until his rage fills the page. As Max simmers down, his anger recedes and so, too, do the monster illustrations. Finally, Max is in control again.

Point out the relationship between the temper tantrum and the size of the pictures. The temper tantrum took over the book, didn't it? Just as the temper tantrum took over Max. There is an expression, "I got so mad I couldn't see!" and another expression—"blind with rage." As the readers, we were allowed to "see" this anger. In this instance, the rage and the illustrations are choreographed, as in a dance. If we, the readers, are the audience, the illustrations allow us to see Max before, during, and after his temper tantrum; we're peeking in on the build-up, the explosion, and the simmering down again.

2. Acting Out. During play time, encourage the children to role play the experiences in the book. For a cast of characters we will need: Max, the monsters, a boat, the moving water, trees swaying, plants, a King's crown, the bedroom.

Make a videotape of the reenactment of the book. Play it back for the "audience." Now, using a cassette tape, make up words and music to go with the video.

Make a "shadow stage." You will need a hanging sheet, and a bright light focused behind the stage. Have three or four "wild monsters" dance at one time while the audience watches. Take turns being actors and audience.

3. Children have consistently voted for this particular book as their favorite picture book. Ask them why they like it.

Encourage children to discuss their temper tantrums. How did they feel before, during, and after? Did they get scared? How is it possible to tell if one of these moods is coming over us? What are the warning signs? What can we do to help prevent a really big explosion?

4. "Go to your room!" Do we like to hear those words? When do parents send their children to their rooms? Think of other things that we don't like people to say to us, or to each other. What can we do to avoid this?

LET'S GO VISITING

1. Let's go to the Land of the Wild Things. Besides the monstrous looking creatures, what other things would be wild? (Examples: Wild flowers, wild cats, wild horses, wild Indians, wild pigs, and so on.) If everything was "wild" who would be in charge? They wanted Max to be King. Have students draw their own King of the Wild Things.

2. Make a calendar of Wild Things Holidays. What do they celebrate? Do they get dressed up? Draw a special holiday picture for an individual calendar this month.

3. Make a Wild Thing hat. Decorate an old hat with a variety of items brought in for this purpose, or make one from paper.

4. "Sailing Off Through Night and Day." Make the private boat using a cardboard box, and a plain cloth sail. Children can each draw a wild thing on the sail with fabric crayons or water crayons. Then set sail for the Land of the Wild Things. The boat could have a prop box that stores a map, life preserver, swim fins, swim goggles; the children can scribble messages that only the wild things will be able to read, since they're really very bright and can read scribbling even though adults can't.

MORE WILD THINGS

1. The technique used for the illustrations in this book is called "cross hatching" and is usually done with pen and ink. However, it could also be done with felt tip pen or crayons. Here are some samples of cross hatching:

Have children make a wild thing—one that we didn't see in the book. They all seem to have horns, big eyes, and pointed teeth. Use the cross-hatching technique on some part of the wild thing.

2. Have other books by Maurice Sendak in the theme box, and read them. First, point out the very different styles that the author uses for his illustrations. *In the Night Kitchen* is almost in cartoon style drawing with bubbles for the conversation. *Outside Over There* has a dreamy quality that looks like pictures in some of the old-fashioned children's books. This particular book is just like something out of the Brothers Grimm Tales, and yet it was written not long ago.

When children see that an artist uses various techniques and not the same one over and over again, it stimulates them to try other techniques themselves.

REPRODUCIBLE ACTIVITY PAGES
FOR
PICTURE BOOKS

Name _____   Date _____

Some colorful words to use

yellow

red

orange

violet

green

blue

brown

Colorful Title: _____

You can be an artist with WORDS and with PICTURES. Make a painting on another page to go with your colorful story.

ARTIST AT WORK

Name _____   Date _____

A POTATO PRINT

I drew a design on a potato. My teacher cut it out.
I painted it with a long-handled brush. Press—look how it turned out!

Name _____   Date _____

HELP WANTED AT THE EASTER EGG STUDIO   3–3

This Want Ad was just cut out of the paper. What does it say?

HELP WANTED. Artist/illustrator. There are thousands of eggs to decorate. Need artists who will use bright colors, and who can make lines that are wavy ⌇⌇⌇ or bumpy ⌒⌒⌒ or pointed ⋀⋀⋀ . NO TWO EGGS CAN LOOK ALIKE. Use your imagination. Remember: There are no right or wrong Easter eggs! Good Luck!

APPLICATION FORM. Make each one different. Yes, you may also draw pictures on the eggs.

Name _____   Date _____

Using crayons, felt-tip pens, or colored pencils, illustrate below a part of the story that did not have a picture to go with it. Plan carefully.

Story Title _____

Author/Illustrator _____

Name _____   Date _____

When you open up a picture book with a hard cover, the paper that is attached to the inside of the book cover is called the endpaper. Sometimes the endpaper is very colorful, and often the design or pictures go right along with the theme of the book. The endpapers can prepare you for what's coming.

Look through many picture books just so that you can see how the endpapers relate to the story. Which ones do you like? Why?

Look at the endpaper illustrations below, and tell what you think the story is about.

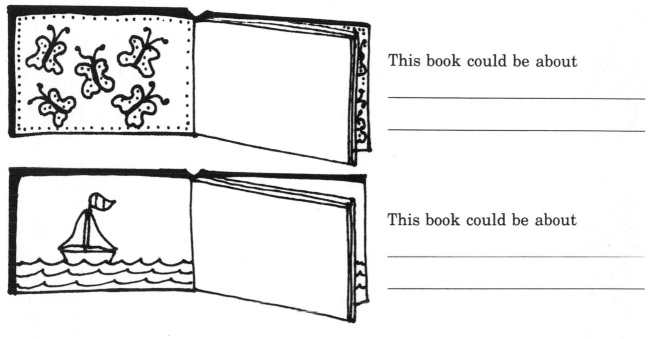

This book could be about

_____

_____

This book could be about

_____

_____

In the space provided below, draw and color the endpapers for a picture book. When we look at them, we should have some idea of what the book is going to be about. Maybe the endpapers will inspire you to write a story, and to use them in your book.

Name _____   Date _____

THE PUPPET BOOK ENDPAPERS   3–6

Endpapers are important in many picture books because they are the first things you see when you open the covers. The endpapers are attached to the front and back covers.

This is the beginning of an endpaper design for a book on puppets. You can finish the illustrations. You can keep going with the same repeat design, or change it. You can color and decorate the puppets any way you want to. You can color the background of each square different colors, or choose just two to use over and over again.

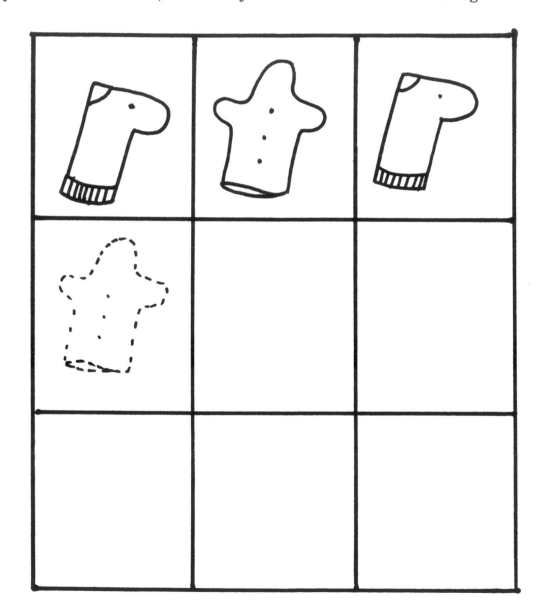

When you finish your endpaper, you can write a story about a little puppet who could talk by itself. Use your endpapers for the inside covers. Make a fancy title page.

Make a sock puppet. Use a big, old sock. Cut out material for features (eyes, ears, nose, mouth) and glue them on. Use your puppet for story telling.

Name ______________________________ Date ______________________________

INVITE YOUR FAVORITE STORYBOOK CHARACTER TO VISIT YOU 3–7

NAME OF FAVORITE CHARACTER ______________________________

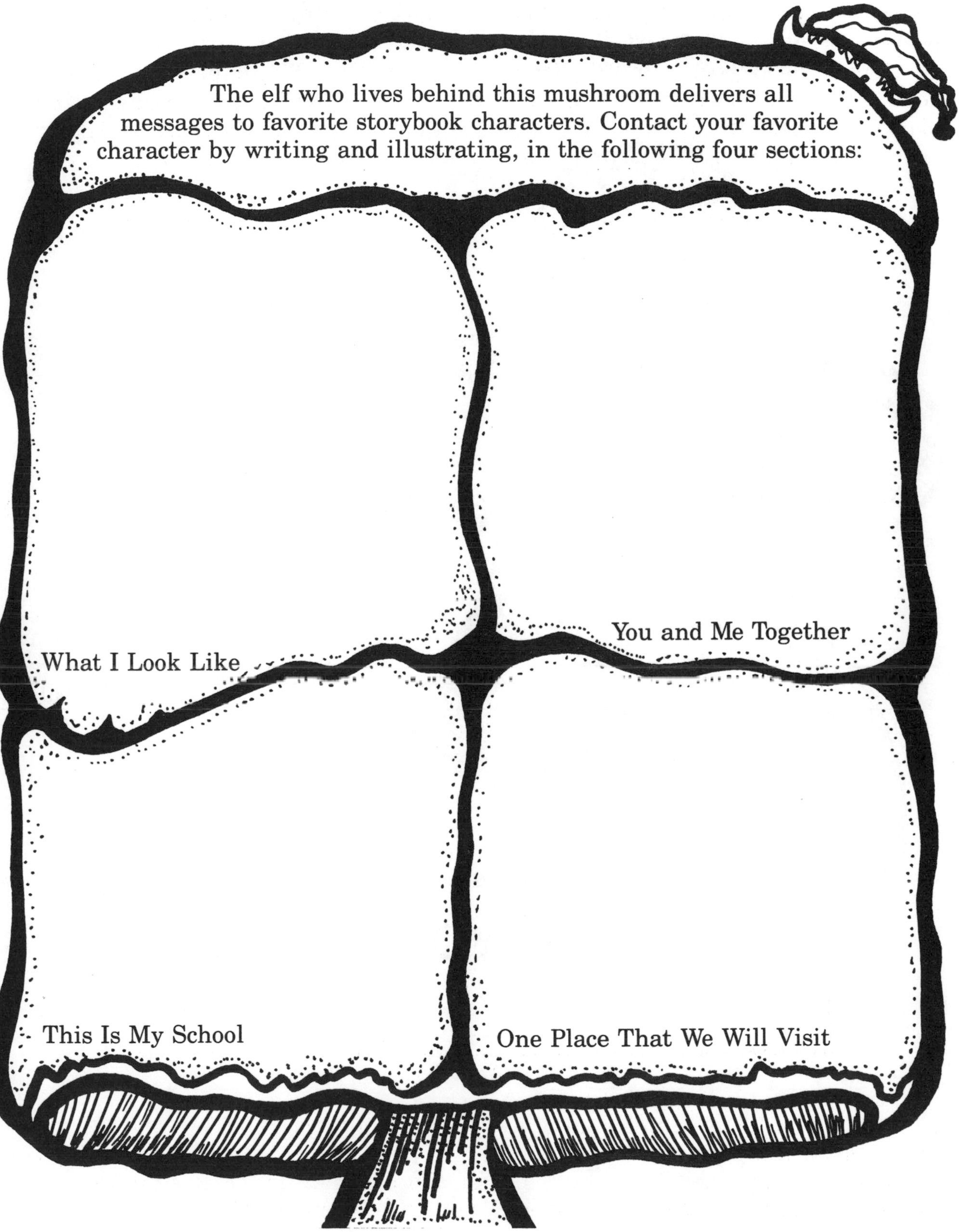

The elf who lives behind this mushroom delivers all messages to favorite storybook characters. Contact your favorite character by writing and illustrating, in the following four sections:
What I Look Like
You and Me Together
This Is My School
One Place That We Will Visit

Name _____   Date _____

There are many books that get medals. Perhaps the two best known are the Caldecott Medal (best illustrations) and the Newbery Medal (best story). Not all books get medals. Maybe your favorite book didn't get a medal. The GINGERBREAD MAN MEDAL is the children's award. You can give it to your favorite book.

The Gingerbread Man Medal

title: _____
_____
_____
_____

Cut out your medal and wear it around your neck by attaching a piece of yarn. Become a "walking advertisement" for a good book that you like!

Learn the name of the author and of the illustrator too!

Name _____   Date _____

Picture books communicate VISUALLY (illustrations) and VERBALLY (story). Illustrators often use an emotional part of the story to get the message across to the reader in the form of a picture.

Use the following story part to make an illustration for the reader that communicates the FEELINGS of the character (and the dog):

Andy didn't know whether to laugh or cry! There, scratching at the door, was his pet dog Snuffy. The dog was covered with sticky tar and feathers piled so high that Snuffy looked like a giant duck.

"Wow!" exclaimed Andy, "_____

_____."

MAKE A WORDLESS PICTURE BOOK   3–10

Read a story. Then, tell your story in picture form; or make up your own picture story. Draw the beginning (1) and the ending (6), and then go back and draw the important events that happened in between. Congratulations! You are an author/ illustrator.

1.	2.	3.
4.	5.	6.

There are many Wordless Picture Books. How many can you find at the library?

THE PICTURE BOOK HOUSE

Look through many picture books. Read them. Decorate each room of this house with an item that you like from six different books.

Why do you like this item? What part did it play in the story?

What colors will you use to make your picture book house look pretty?

1. Title _____
   _____

2. Title _____
   _____

3. Title _____
   _____

4. Title _____
   _____

5. Title _____
   _____

6. Title _____
   _____

SECTION 4

Animal Books

BOOK:

Angus and the Cat
by Marjorie Flack. New York:
Doubleday & Company, 1931

ABOUT THE BOOK

1. Angus is a Scottie dog. Have students find information about Scottie dogs to determine what their characteristics are, and why they make nice pets. What other types of dogs make nice house pets? Make a list of a variety of types of dogs that students have actually seen. Name the biggest and the smallest.

2. Ask students to describe a dog in their own words (oral or written). Suppose they are talking to a creature from outer space who has never seen a dog. Have them explain exactly what a dog is and why people take dogs indoors into their homes and make them into pets.

3. Examine the two-page picture spread of Angus looking out of the upstairs window, while the cat is hiding on the roof. If the cat could talk, what would it be saying at this particular moment?

4. Have students go through the book page by page and retell the story from the point of view of the cat.

5. This story has a happy ending, because Angus realized that he liked having someone to share his home with. Discuss sharing and its importance when it comes to friendships (Angus could have been glad to be rid of the cat so that he could have everything for himself). Suppose that Angus and the cat decide to share their home with still another pet. What would the pet be? (Try to make it very different, and create a new story entitled "Angus and the Cat and the _____.")

CATS AND DOGS

1. Discuss the difference between cats and dogs. Basically, dogs aim to please people and cats are independent; but they both need love. Discuss the different level of care required by cats and dogs (food, bathroom habits, grooming, attention).

2. Grooming. Angus no doubt needs to be groomed occasionally. He would need to have a haircut and perhaps his nails would have to be cut since he is a house pet. If we were to set up a Good Grooming Shop for pets, what supplies would be needed?

Children enjoy role playing in a busy grooming shop, with attendants working on toy dogs, the phone ringing for appointments, people and dogs waiting, dogs with ribbons being picked up by owners, and so on.

3. Oral Language Development. Make an Angus puppet and a cat puppet and have them discuss these topics: (a) Their upcoming trip to the boarding kennel, (b) Who is responsible for keeping the toys picked up, (c) Eating only from their own food dish, since cats often like to leave some of their food for later.

4. Make designer leashes and designer tags for Angus and for the cat. Use real materials such as belts, rope, twine, yarn, leather, rickrack, ball fringe, and the like. When someone asks about these items, children can tell the story of Angus.

MORE ABOUT CATS AND DOGS

1. Fleas are a problem for both cats and dogs. There is such a thing as flea powder, collars, and spray, but they're different for dogs and cats. Boys and girls should be cautioned to stay away from these items. Check some labels and see what they advise.

2. The cat will need a scratching post for his claws and to stretch and get exercise, if he stays in the house. What will Angus use the scratching post for? Make up a very funny story about the dog and cat at the scratching post.

3. For dog care and cat care information, send a self-addressed stamped envelope to The Humane Society of USA, 2100 L Street, N.W., Washington, D.C. 20037.

4. Design a Toy. Using an old sock, string, ball, or the like, design a toy for a cat or dog. Try it out on your pet.

5. Cats say "meow" and "mroo" and make other sounds like "hiss." Some dogs make sounds like "woof," or "grr-r-r" or "bow-wow-wow." Turn this story into a "participation sound story." Reread it, and every time the name "Angus" is mentioned have the children bark. Every time the word "cat" is mentioned have the children meow. Make it an enjoyable time for all.

6. Compose a catchy title for a dog food or a cat food. Design a label, list the ingredients, and put the label around a can with a lid. Write a thirty-second TV commercial for your product. Thirty seconds is not long, so children may just want to hold up a big sign showing the name of the product, and happy cats or dogs eating it, or just show the product and have happy cats or dogs repeat a slogan for the food. Put the cans on a shelf. Which ones would we be attracted to, and why? (Discuss color, size, neatness, design, and so on.)

Role play. Leave a sample of the food on the doorstep of the home of Angus and the Cat. Knock on the door and hide behind a bush. Have Angus and the cat come to the door and find the food. What will they exclaim! (Example: Holy Cats and Cuttlefish! Jumping Jellybeans! Well, if that's not a delicious looking treat, I'll eat my collar!) This will require talking about exclamations that people make. Think of some. Make up some for both the dog and the cat!

BOOK:

Chickens Aren't the Only Ones
by Ruth Heller. New York:
Grosset & Dunlap, 1981.

PAGE BY PAGE

1. At first, go through the book by reading it aloud to the children so that they can catch the rhyme. Promise to return to the pictures. Then, go through the book page by page, again reading it aloud, and also pause to enjoy the lovely illustrations. There is a wide variety here.

2. With the students, examine the book page by page and look only for the shapes and sizes of the eggs. Note the snake eggs. What is that shape? On the page that shows the ostrich who lays the largest egg and the hummingbird who lays the smallest, how many eggs can we count? How many colors can we identify? Introduce the vocabulary word, "marbleized," which is how many of the eggs look.

3. Look at the two pages of birds, both wild and tame. How many can be identified? Note the brilliant reds and tones of red (pinks, fuchsias), and see just where they are located on the bird (entire body, throat feathers, under the long bill, tail feathers, crown, head feathers, beak, and so on).

A BOOK THAT TEACHES

1. Note that the author/illustrator has drawn the life cycle of the frog; be sure not to miss it. Also a new vocabulary word is introduced on this page—amphibians. Have the children find out what it means.

2. Note the variety of fish. Some have little spots all in a row, some have big spots; the brown fish with the white spots has rings around the white spots; note the whirling lines and design. Have the children examine this page with a magnifying glass. Children can make the outline of a large fish and then with paint, chalk, water crayons, or oil crayons create a beautiful fish!

3. Count the legs on the spider. How many are there?

4. On the insect page, how many look familiar? How many look vaguely familiar? Go through the colors of the rainbow (red, orange, yellow, green, blue, violet) to see if all of the colors are represented in the insect family. Locate a

resource book that includes pictures of insects in order to help with identification. Note that this page leads directly to the metamorphosis of the caterpillar. A new vocabulary word "chrysalis" is introduced on this page.

5. More vocabulary: Everyone who lays an egg is "oviparous." Teach the children to say their new word. On these two pages, we are reintroduced to many of the animals, birds, and so forth, that were on previous pages. Have the children identify them. Where were they located?

On those two pages, have students identify the extinct animal, the amphibian, the eight-legged creature, the ones that came from the chrysalis, the one who hangs all of her eggs up with tiny threads, and so on. Students can check through the book for answers.

MORE ABOUT EGGS

1. Coloring eggs at Easter is a very old custom. We celebrate Spring by coloring the eggs (a symbol of fertility and new life, just as Spring brings forth new life). In years gone by, people gave and received decorated eggs at Easter time. Just as mother nature puts on new colors for spring (tulips, daffodils, crocus, forsythia, lilies, lilacs...) so, too, do children dress up in new clothes (or new shoes, hat, pants, dress...) at Easter time. It's a tradition that has been handed down from one generation to the next. This may be a good time to discuss this tradition and other Easter customs.

2. In Greece, red was the favorite egg dye long ago, because people thought red was a magical color. Purple is thought to be a color of royalty. Here are some natural egg dye recipes: Take five plastic containers; place 2 cups of water and 1 teaspoon of vinegar in each. Add dandelion blossoms for yellow, outer onion skins for dark orange or light brown, crushed blueberries or grapes for blue, mint leaves for green, and beets or beet juice for red.

3. Designing Eggs. On 12×18 sheets of white paper, have children make a huge oval shape with black crayon. Then, using the black crayon, have them make a variety of designs on the eggs—lines, circles, flowers, and so on. Next, have the children carefully paint their egg designs using water colors. Allow these beautiful eggs to dry, then cut them out. Display them in a huge construction paper basket on a bulletin board or in the hall, and pile all of the eggs high inside (tape) for an egg celebration.

4. Eggshell Planters. Fill eggshells with dirt. Place two or three seeds inside. Little fingers are very adept at poking the seeds gently into the dirt. Water. When plants are about two inches high, poke holes in the bottom of the egg shell and plant them outdoors right in the shell.

5. A resource story book to accompany this book: *Who's in the Egg?* by Alice and Martin Provensen. A Big Golden Book. New York: Golden Press, 1970.

BOOK:

Bedtime for Frances
by Russell Hoban. Pictures by Garth Williams.
New York: Harper & Row, 1960.

BEDTIME

1. Take a sheet of 12 × 18 newsprint and fold it in half the long way. Label it, "Getting Ready for Bed." Flip the top up, and have students make three or four pictures inside that show what procedures children regularly follow when getting ready for bed (brushing teeth, taking a bath, having a story read to them, and so on).

2. Have each student make a clock from a paper plate or a pizza circle. Put numerals on the clock, cut out two hands, and secure them in the middle with a paper fastener. Have children show bedtime, wake-up time, lunch time, and so on. Discuss the importance of sleep. Perhaps a short message for parents could be written on the back of the clock by the students: "Frances says to keep me healthy and happy, tuck me into bed at ___o'clock so that I can have ___hours of sleep every night."

3. Frances is a badger. We use the word badger in another way—as a term that means "to pester," or "to harass." Frances was a true "badger" at bedtime. Discuss all of the delay tactics that she used. Move from the badgers to the students, and ask if they every use "delay tactics" or pester at bedtime. What tactics do *they* use, or what do younger brothers or sisters do at bedtime?

Badgers are nocturnal animals, so it's no wonder they're having trouble putting Frances to bed. What is the meaning of "nocturnal?" Do we know of any other nocturnal animals? (Cats prefer this life style.) What about people? Some people are "morning glories" (they love the early morning and go to bed early) and some are "night owls" (they love the late hours and prefer to stay in bed late). Conduct a "Morning Glory/Night Owl" Survey of class members and record results.

4. How could bedtime be made extra "special?" This is a problem that we have to solve. The students can brainstorm for ways to make bedtime so appealing to children, that they just can't wait to jump into bed. They will come up with lots of ideas. How will they "sell" the health-conscious parents and children of America on their ideas?

MORE ABOUT BADGERS

1. Print "Badger News" at the top of several large pieces of newsprint. That is the newspaper that father was reading in the story. Turn the newsprint sheets into a newspaper, and have a front page, society page, food section, and so on.

Children can be the reporters and write in the badger news items. Use the reference books to help with some of the information.

2. A real badger is a meat eater who burrows underground. It has short legs, long claws, and a shaggy, grizzly coat. It has a white mark (badge) on its forehead. What other Badger Facts can students find and record on badger shapes?

3. The Australian wombat is related to the badger. Write a letter from the wombat in Australia (locate it on the globe) to the badger in your town.

Children could be divided into two groups—the Wombats and the Badgers. One group writes the first set of letters; the other group answers. This could also be done with two different classrooms at the same grade level.

4. Wisconsin is called the "Badger State." Why? Find Wisconsin on a map of the USA. How far away are you? Does your state have a special name? What is it? Let's learn it.

FOR BEGINNING READERS

1. Develop an "I Can Read" Badger Book with simple sentences and illustrations. Print on the chalkboard:

> Frances is a badger.
> Frances is a little badger.
> Is Frances a badger?

Have the children read it as you put your hand under each word.

Ask the children to circle the word "badger" in the first sentence, in the third sentence, in the second sentence.

What is different about the little marks at the end of each sentence? Which one asks the question? Erase the periods and question mark. Have children replace them.

Point to a word and have children spell it. Do this regularly.

2. Write or print the phrase "Frances is a badger" three times in big letters, very low on the chalkboard. Using chalk, children can trace it. (Three children can work at a time on just one phrase.) This can be done before they write it on their own paper.

3. Establish a "Badger Tracing Station" on your chalkboard. Children benefit from tracing letters again and again. Also, have children print on the board using a paintbrush and water. It soon dries, and there's no chalk dust.

4. Circle Time. Let's all think of a word that begins like the sound of badger, or words that begin with the letter "b." The chant and rhythm will be important here. Say this three times until children pick up the tempo: "B-b-b-b   b-b-badger." Go around the circle, and have each child add a word that begins with the badger sound. If they can't think of one, they can say "badger."

Variation. Everyone says, "B-b-b-b   b-b-" (and remains silent until the one person whose turn it is calls out a "b word" that begins like "badger."). By hearing all the words—bird, Billy, Betsy, bubbles, big, brother, but, best, biggest, bunny, baby...), children will expand their repertoire of "b words." They will learn from each other. Children need much praise for this. They also need constancy in their environment. Young children would benefit from doing this type of activity daily. Begin to add more letters; "F for Frances" could be next. (Eventually, children can clap in unison six times to the rhythm of the sound of "b" and be silent so that they can hear the word. You can introduce a new one too!)

5. Make Badger Badges. Make an "I Can Read" reading badge pin for children. When someone asks them about it, they can tell about Frances, or tell three words that begin like "badger," and so on. (Arrange beforehand with the school secretary, aide, custodian, librarian, or a parent volunteer, to ask a child what the badge means. For a little person who could use an extra heap of praise, send him to the office with a note that says "PS. Ask ⎯⎯⎯⎯⎯ what his badge is for.")

6. *Bread and Jam for Frances* is another in the series of Frances books. Have it available for the children to enjoy. Serve bread and jam, and learn to set the table with Frances.

BOOK:

Swimmy
by Leo Lionni. New York: Pantheon, 1963.

SWIMMY'S WORLD

1. Sea shells can be kept in a little bucket of the type that children use at the seashore. Encourage students to handle the shells and to note their sizes, shapes, colors, and designs. Students can categorize them (sets, subsets, intersecting sets). Bring in unusual coral, starfish, sea horses, and other skeletons of sea life. Set up a sand table using a large shallow box with sand. Rope off a section for Swimmy, and have the children use it to act out the story.

2. Add to written and oral vocabulary these "S" words: spotted, swirl, symmetry, symmetrical. The terms symmetrical and asymmetrical provide another way to categorize. Students can make a Sea Dictionary in the shape of the sea creature of their choice.

3. Language Development. Bring in a large conch shell and have the children put it to their ears and listen to the "sound of the sea." If the sea could actually speak, what would it say? What would make an ocean happy? Why would an ocean become sad? Does the ocean like to be rained on? Does it like fish and other sea creatures? Do boats tickle the ocean when they pass through? Have you ever dunked your foot into the ocean, or a river, or a pond, or a swimming

pool, or a puddle? What rules should we have for visiting the water? Do you think fish have "rules." What rules does a baby fish need to understand?

4. From the library, get a record of sea sounds, such as *The Sounds of the Humpback Whale*. Play it and have the children imagine Swimmy in that environment. Later, play the record as children paint their favorite part of the story using tempera paint and small sponges for the foamy sea.

SEA SOUNDS

1. It's noisy! All is not dark and quiet beneath the deep waters; fish make noise! Swimmy might encounter snapping shrimps who make sounds like "popcorn popping" and a "campfire crackling." He might meet up with crabs who hiss to frighten enemies. There are croakers who croak and sea urchins whose spiny points make a sound like two sticks being rubbed together. Noises have been recorded that sound like fingers snapping, playground whistles, the crinkling of cellophane, and barking, mewing, shrieking, moaning, and snarling.

Create an orchestra of the sea, using all of the sounds listed above. Have the children compose "Swimmy's Song." Use musical instruments such as rhythm sticks, triangle, sandpaper blocks, and so on, for the sea compositions. For variety, they can use instruments instead of making the sounds.

To help get the singing started, sing this song (to any melody) and make accompanying sea sounds:

> I saw a fish and a fish saw me (grunt, grunt)
> I liked the fish and the fish liked me (grunt, grunt, eeek, eeek)
> We got married, now we're three (grunt, grunt, eeek, eeek, mew, mew)
> 'Cause we have a family!(grunt, grunt, eeek, eeek, mew, mew, whistle, snap fingers)

There is an "Echo Fish" of the sea. Divide the class into two groups; have the first group sing the tune and make the sound, and have the second group echo the sound.

2. Fish Week at the Easel! This message from out of the deep means exactly that. Have a sign-up sheet in the shape of a giant sea creature. Students can paint with glossy colors and make striped and spotted fish. (Use magenta, aqua, chartreuse, fuchsia, as well as iridescent paint.) Display fish all over the room for a sea world effect.

GOING FISHING

1. Make separate "Going Fishing" activity cards that tell the students to "go fishing in the library" for books about: fish, shells, porpoises, lobster traps, sea fans, coral, whales, boats, and the like.

When children go fishing in the library, they can find instructions printed on cards (shaped like fish) that have been hidden in specific places; for example,

"Look in the big dictionary for the word 'porpoise,' " and in the big dictionary, on the porpoise page, there could be a card that states, "To find your next clue about lobster traps, look up 'lobster' in the Encyclopedia Americana." Also, a fish shape with written instructions could direct students to the card catalog, to a specific book number, and even the book *The Biggest House in the World* by Leo Lionni for more information about sea creatures.

Vocabulary booklets could be made in fish shapes and looped together at the mouth like a day's catch.

2. Catch of the Day. Get a huge net (perhaps from the gym) and tie it to a pole. Explain to the students that in seashore area restaurants, "catch of the day," means the specialty of the day. You can use the "Catch of the Day" motif for catching all kinds of information or things. It may "catch" such things as lost and found items, good work papers, or messages from the deep about what's going to be special in the classroom today.

The net could be used to catch goldfish-shaped crackers and some tuna fish for a special snack. It could catch a variety of bite-size seafood treats. It could catch another Leo Lionni book entitled *Fish Is Fish*.

BOOK:

Curious George Goes to the Hospital
by H. A. and Margaret Rey.
Boston: Houghton Mifflin, 1966.

CURIOUS GEORGE

1. Discuss the meaning of the word "curious." This curious monkey, George, wants to know about a lot of things, and gets into mischief. It is a fact that monkeys are intelligent and learn quickly. The more intelligent they are, the more curious they are. They also have good memories. Babies and young children are also very curious. Have children tell what they're "curious" about and what they'd like to learn more about in school. Begin an "I'm Curious About...." list, and use the word "curious" in spoken language.

2. Curious George Puzzle Area. Set up a jigsaw puzzle in the room, and let children work on it in their spare time. Some children can't seem to get enough of this type of problem solving, and other children can be assigned to work on the puzzle for five- or ten-minute periods, depending upon their age level. (This focus on shape and configuration is a prerequisite skill for reading.) Cut out colorful pictures or advertisements from magazines, laminate them, and then cut them

up into puzzle pieces. Did you know that monkeys like to work puzzles? They enjoy finding solutions to problems.

3. Curious George had to go to the hospital, and this experience will be helpful for children who might be fearful of hospitals or doctors. Make Curious George Identification Wrist Bands. Print the child's name on a strip, with a little picture of Curious George. Laminate. Use transparent tape to hold it together on the child's wrist. The bracelet may help children remember parts of the story, and may help them to remember their new vocabulary word: "curious."

4. Story Starters. "I'd like to be a doctor (nurse, x-ray technician, and so on) because . . . ."

STAYING HEALTHY

1. Examine a real thermometer. The ideal body temperature is 98.6 degrees Fahrenheit. There are wrist thermometers that can be applied to the skin and fastened with velcro that turn colors according to your temperature level. Bring in several if possible, so that children can examine them. Perhaps the school nurse could be involved with temperature taking.

2. "Shots" are given to help prevent disease. Did Curious George get a shot? What other instruments did the doctor use to examine George? Have the children list them, draw them from simple basic shapes, and tell their purpose. Then, when children have to go to the doctor they'll know something about the doctor's job.

3. "You Are What You Eat!" Staying healthy requires eating right, and eating good food and regular meals. There are four basic food groups from which to choose nutritious food. What are the four food groups? Children can plan a balanced breakfast, cut the items out of magazines, and paste them onto a paper plate.

Curious George Junk Food. Since George is so curious, he will want to know what "junk food" is. Is it all bad? Is it all good? Let's take a look at labels and see what the food contains. Would a steady diet of junk food be good for helping us to grow healthy bones, teeth, skin, and so on? (The term "junk food" has been applied to many foods that have a high calorie/low nutritional value.)

4. Garlic. Certain foods are said to contain natural ingredients to help ward off illness. Some people used to wear garlic on a string around their necks to help avoid colds. It has been discovered that garlic contains a natural antibiotic that is useful in warding off germs. Have garlic cloves available so that the children can smell them. (If wrapped in colorful nylon netting, and tied with a pretty ribbon, these might be nice cold-weather necklaces to try for an experiment.)

MONKEY TALK

1. Real monkeys spend a lot of time grooming themselves and other monkeys. They know the value of being germ-free. This might be a good time to talk about good grooming before coming to school (combing/washing hair, clean-

ing nails, washing hands, knees and elbows, and so on, and taking pride in the way we look).

2. Monkeys go to college! Capuchin monkeys are actually being trained at the Albert Einstein College of Medicine to serve as aides for people who are bedridden or confined to wheelchairs. Monkeys have been trained to take food from a refrigerator, place it in a given spot, turn out lights, dust furniture, and even spoon-feed people. Capuchins were chosen for this experiment because they are very intelligent. Ask the children: Do you think Curious George could learn to do this job? What would you like him to do for you at your house when you don't feel well? Talk about it, make a list, illustrate it.

3. There are many types of monkeys—the rhesus, the macaque of Japan, the dianas, the capuchins, and many more. Let's be just as curious to find out something about them, as George was curious to find out something about the hospital. We can begin in the library by looking at *Ranger Rick, World, National Geographic,* and other sources that show vivid pictures.

4. Puppet Show Time. George gave a real puppet show with a dragon, a clown, a bear, and a policeman. Make these four puppets (use paper bags, paper plates, cylinders, socks, or pictures on a stick). Four children at a time can put on a puppet show that they develop. (Does anyone want to try to put on the puppet show the way George did it, using all fours?)

5. Have other books available about George such as *Curious George Rides a Bike, Curious George Learns the Alphabet, Curious George Takes a Job,* to name just a few in this series by H.A. and Margaret Rey.

BOOK:

Anatole and the Cat
by Eve Titus. Pictures by Paul Galdone.
New York: McGraw Hill, 1957.

ANATOLE THE MOUSE

1. Anatole lives in France and is a cheese taster by night in the Duval Factory. He prefers to remain anonymous, so Monsieur Duval has never met him, but Anatole does a splendid job. Have students sample three different types of cheese and write up a little report card for them, just as Anatole did. (Write the report using the same format that Anatole uses. Students can write funny reports, as Anatole did when he was frightened by the cat, or they can be realistic.)

2. Ask students where they would like to work if they could be a food or drink sampler. They can compose a letter to the manager asking for work, listing their outstanding qualifications for this type of work. Who will answer?

3. Night Shift. Make a list of the occupations of people who work by night (baker, police, firefighter . . .). Alphabetize the list and learn to spell the words.

4. Around-the-clock. Look in the yellow pages of the telephone book for companies that advertise around-the-clock service. Make a directory.

CATS AND MICE

1. "Chat." Anatole lives in France and the word for cat is "chat." In other countries, the word for cat is different too. This is how the word "cat" sounds in other languages; perhaps students can learn them: Gatto (Italian), Katze (German), Gato (Spanish), Kot (Dutch, Polish). Do students know any others?

2. Historically, cats have been rewarded for catching mice because mice eat grains, eat paper with writing on it, and in general can do damage. Students can each compose one of Anatole's famous memos: "To: Le Chat From: Anatole," explaining that he is a working mouse and very special. Collect the memos and put them in a wire basket labeled "IN." Then, each student (not having seen Anatole's memos) can write a response memo: "To: Anatole From: Le Chat." Put all of them in a wire basket labeled "OUT." Then, each student can randomly pick one memo from the IN basket and one memo from the OUT basket. Read the two memos aloud; first Anatole's and then the reply. Are these two communicating?

Try the communication process again. This time have each Anatole write a memo and put all of them into the IN basket. Children can randomly select a memo and write the response from Le Chat. This time, there may be some communication. Review: What is necessary for real communication to take place?

3. Compose a class story about Anatole and Le Chat where there is a happy ending and another story where they are still at war with each other.

4. "Nocturnal." Anatole has a night job at the cheese factory. Cats are night creatures or nocturnal animals. They like to sleep by day and explore by night. Anatole will not work days (when the cat is sleeping) and insists on working at night. Try to work out a new solution to this problem.

MORE ABOUT ANATOLE

1. This book is one in a series of stories about Anatole. Anatole is married, has a wife and four children, and loves music. He is the conductor of the Mouse Orchestra. Create a special tune for Anatole using hand bells. Several children could ring the bells and one could conduct.

2. Since Anatole loves music, have a concert time. Listen to records of famous composers for quiet time, for rest time, for writing time, for listening time, for drawing time, for "getting ready to go home" time.

3. Let's suppose that Le Chat has a family as wonderful as Anatole's. Draw a scene (or create a diorama) that would allow Anatole to get a peek at Le Chat

with his family. Show Anatole in the picture too, but make him very small and inconspicuous. Use the word "inconspicuous" for language development and have children get used to saying it when they tell about the picture that shows Le Chat and family.

4. Pretend that you are the president of the Duval Company that makes the famous cheeses. You have never met Anatole, but you like his memos. The telephone rings, and someone on the other end of the line is telling you that your newest cheese is absolutely superb! The best ever! While you're listening, "doodle" on your memo pad and make a picture of what you think Anatole looks like. Also, print the fancy new name for the cheese.

5. Have other books about Anatole available for children to enjoy.

BOOK:

Pelican
by Brian Wildsmith.
New York: Pantheon Books, 1982.

WORKING WITH ILLUSTRATIONS

1. The technique used in this picture story book is different. The illustrations are on a two-page spread, with a little turnover page in the middle. This is a unique way of showing the next action in the same setting.

After reading and enjoying the story, go through the book page by page for the sole purpose of examining the little page in the middle of the big page. Have children note that the general scene remains the same, and then note what is different when the page is turned.

This technique requires a lot of skill, because the story needs to keep flowing. Some older children may be ready to try the type of illustration that the author is presenting because it is challenging and unique. Some children may be ready, not for a book, but for one illustration using this technique. Some action has to take place within the confines of a little bit of space. Have students plan and do a practice page first, and then from this model, make their illustrations.

2. For Younger Children. Some of the larger objects seem to delight the younger children—the large speckled hen, the enlarged illustration of the pelican who is carrying groceries on the other side of the illustration. For the young children who are excited by this type of illustration, working with larger objects will be more successful. (Examples: Something inside of a trunk in an attic setting, ingredients inside of a refrigerator in a kitchen setting, something inside the closet in a bedroom setting, and so on.)

3. Watercolor Wash. The last illustration looks wet and runny; watercolors lend themselves to this type of illustration. It is difficult for children to work with watercolors and not have the picture become runny. For a real treat, have children work on watercolor paper that real artists use.

THE STORY

1. Language Development. What do children think the hen is saying or thinking to herself as she sees the pelican breaking out of the gigantic egg? For the hen the egg is "gigantic" (new vocabulary word). Also, the hen looks gigantic on the page. What else can we find in the book that is gigantic?

To illustrate gigantic, make a very large white hen. Have the students put her spots or speckles on by dipping a drinking straw into black paint and then dabbing it all over the hen. Add a yellow beak. On the back, with crayon, draw the gigantic egg with the crack and the beak sticking out. Also, print the word "gigantic" on the back.

2. At the end of the story, the author has put an illustration of a bird hatching from an egg, and has written "the beginning." What does this mean? Usually, we find the words "the end" at the ending of the book. (It's the beginning of life for the bird, and children who are familiar with the words "the end" take delight in this situation. Be sure to point it out to the students.)

3. Sayings. The pelican in this story is "like a fish out of water." He is out of place and doesn't fit in. Think of other sayings that would describe the out-of-place pelican: "Like a bull in a china shop, or an elephant in the grocery store, and so forth.

REAL PELICANS

1. The tremendous bill of the pelican can be as long as eighteen inches. It uses its bill to catch fish, spear fish, and it also uses it as a hammer. Have children measure eighteen inches (one and a half feet) on a yardstick. Find things in the room that are as long as a pelican's bill.

2. A totipalmate swimmer. The pelican is in this class of fish—those whose feet are completely webbed. In fact, the pelican is the largest of the web-footed birds. Let's do some research to find some of the others.

3. The pelican has a wingspan of about nine feet. Measure a nine-foot long piece of string and have two children, one on each end, hold it taut. The children will certainly be impressed!

Getting a ten-pound pelican with a nine-foot wingspan off the ground takes a lot of energy. That may be why the pelican is a nonstop eater! It eats tons of food each year. It likes fresh fish (it will not eat fish that have been washed up on shore) and likes to catch them with its bill and flesh bag that sags under its bill.

4. Water pollution. The pelican has fallen victim to water pollution and in some areas is considered an endangered species. Because the pelican eats the fish that swim in polluted waters, it too has had problems—mainly not being able to produce an egg with a hard enough shell to enable a new baby bird to be born.

5. Locate Pelican Island, Florida, on the map (south of Cape Canaveral). It is a national wildlife refuge. How can we find out more information about Pelican Island?

6. Locate the state of Louisiana on a map of the USA. The pelican is the state bird of Louisiana. What is your state bird? Arrange for them to "meet" and exchange information about themselves. (Write fanciful letters or make puppets.)

7. The pelican in the book layed one egg, but more are no doubt on the way, because the pelican usually lays two or sometimes three. Both the male and female are nest builders on the ground or in a tree. (It would have to be a sturdy tree.) The nest can be two feet in diameter and measure ten inches deep—that's like a big washtub made out of sticks, reeds, straw, grasses. Try weaving a pelican nest (around a plastic tub) as a class project. Maybe it could be a "Pelican Information Station." Broadcast a fact a day from the station...about other birds too.

8. Have other books by Brian Wildsmith available, such as *The Little Wood Duck, Squirrels, Daisy, Owl and the Woodpecker, Lazy Bear, Goat's Trail, Give a Dog a Bone, Brian Wildsmith's 1, 2, 3's,* and *Brian Wildsmith's Birds.*

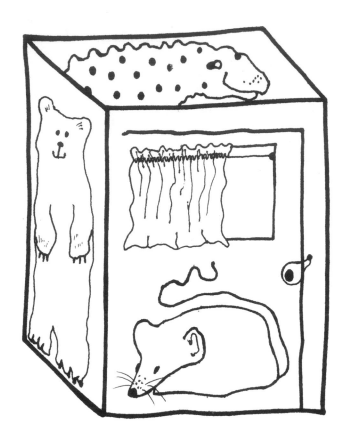

REPRODUCIBLE ACTIVITY PAGES FOR ANIMAL BOOKS

MRS. P. BUNNY THE STORY WRITER

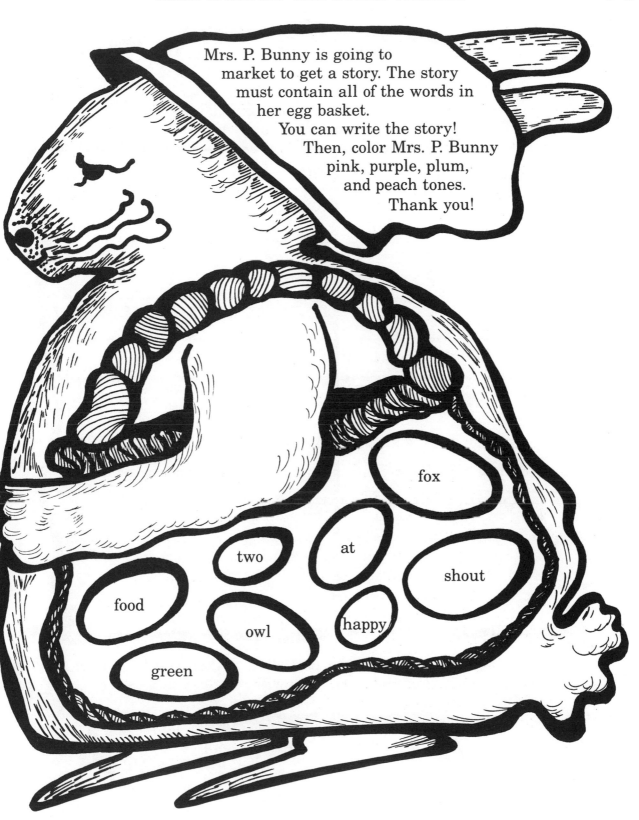

Mrs. P. Bunny is going to market to get a story. The story must contain all of the words in her egg basket.
You can write the story!
Then, color Mrs. P. Bunny pink, purple, plum, and peach tones.
Thank you!

fox

two   at   shout

food   owl   happy

green

Name _____   Date _____

Ren Bear read a book about Abe
Lincoln. He learned that President Lincoln kept important
papers and information under his tall hat.
    Ren Bear can help you to do the same thing. Read four animal story
books and keep the following information under the hat!

Title: _____

Author: _____

I learned that _____

_____

_____

_____

_____

_____

Title: _____

Author: _____

The reason I liked this story is _____

_____

_____

_____

_____

_____

Title: _____

Author: _____

I will list three colorful words

from the story and tell what

they mean: _____

_____

_____

Title: _____

Author: _____

I would tell a friend to read this

book because _____

_____

_____

Ren Bear says, "Good books are to be shared." When you have read four
books, share the information under your hat with your classmates.

Name _____ Date _____

There are many fanciful stories about animals
and how or why they are the way they are. Can
you think of any of these
stories or fables? Here is a
chance to write one
about the rooster
and his bright, red
"comb." Did he
get it by doing
a good or
bad deed?

MAKE A DOUBLE PUPPET

Color the Teddy Bear hand puppet. Carefully cut it out around the edges. Next, trace around it on a sheet of construction paper. Make a different animal face on that shape. Put the two pieces together back-to-back. Your teacher can help you staple it together.

Use the back-to-back puppets for story telling.

Name _____   Date _____

These two mice are having a long talk. They have not seen each other in one month. Felix lives in the city and Fritz lives in the country. Fill in the conversation balloons with their stories. Remember to use punctuation marks, such as " " ! , ? and .

<u>Helpful City Words</u>

    traffic light
    noise
    fire alarm
    soot
    high rise

<u>Helpful Country Words</u>

    grass
    flowers
    bees buzzing
    breeze blowing
    blue sky

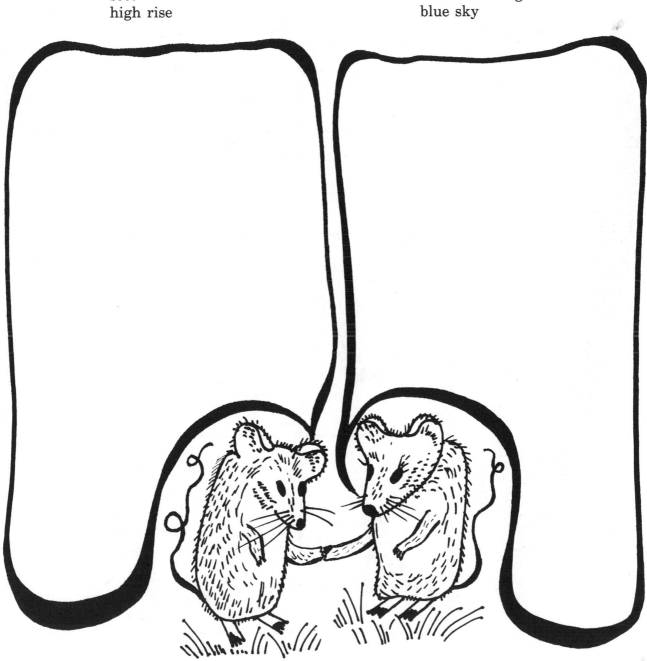

Name _____

Date _____

BEAKS, CLAWS, AND ANIMAL PAWS

Birds, animals, and insects SEND and RECEIVE sounds in many different ways. Some sing, some grunt, some thump the ground with their tail or foot; but animals don't write like people do. Make a Secret Animal Code using beaks, claws, and animal paws as symbols for the alphabet. Then write a word or message using the Secret Animal Code. Some letters have been done for you to get you started.

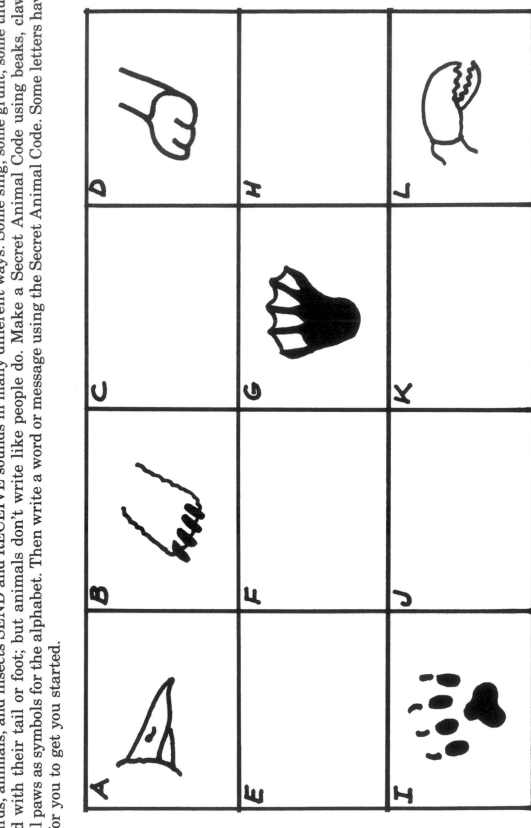

© 1988 by The Center for Applied Research in Education

BEAKS, CLAWS, AND ANIMAL PAWS

M	N	O	P
Q	R	S	T
U	V	W	X
Y	Z	Quotation Marks Exclamation Mark	Period Comma

Name _____   Date _____

THREE CHEERS FOR GOOD BOOKS!   4–7

Pretend that you are a cheerleader standing in a crowded stadium surrounded by hundreds of loyal fans! They are cheering for good books! You can make them very happy by the illustrations that you choose for your cheerleader sweater. Think carefully! What book characters will you paint on your outfit?

Book Character 1	Book Character 2
Book Character 3	Book Character 4
Book Character 5	Book Character 6

Make up a cheer that you think one of your favorite characters would act out. Act it out in that character's voice.

STORY TRACKING   4—8

Use the animal paws to help you track your way through a good animal story. Use words or colorful drawings on the paws.

Make a Story Tracking Book-let for several characters in the same story; or, make a booklet of the favorite animals that you have met in several books.

FAVORITE CHARACTER

TITLE:_____

_____

AUTHOR: _____

_____

ILLUSTRATOR:

_____

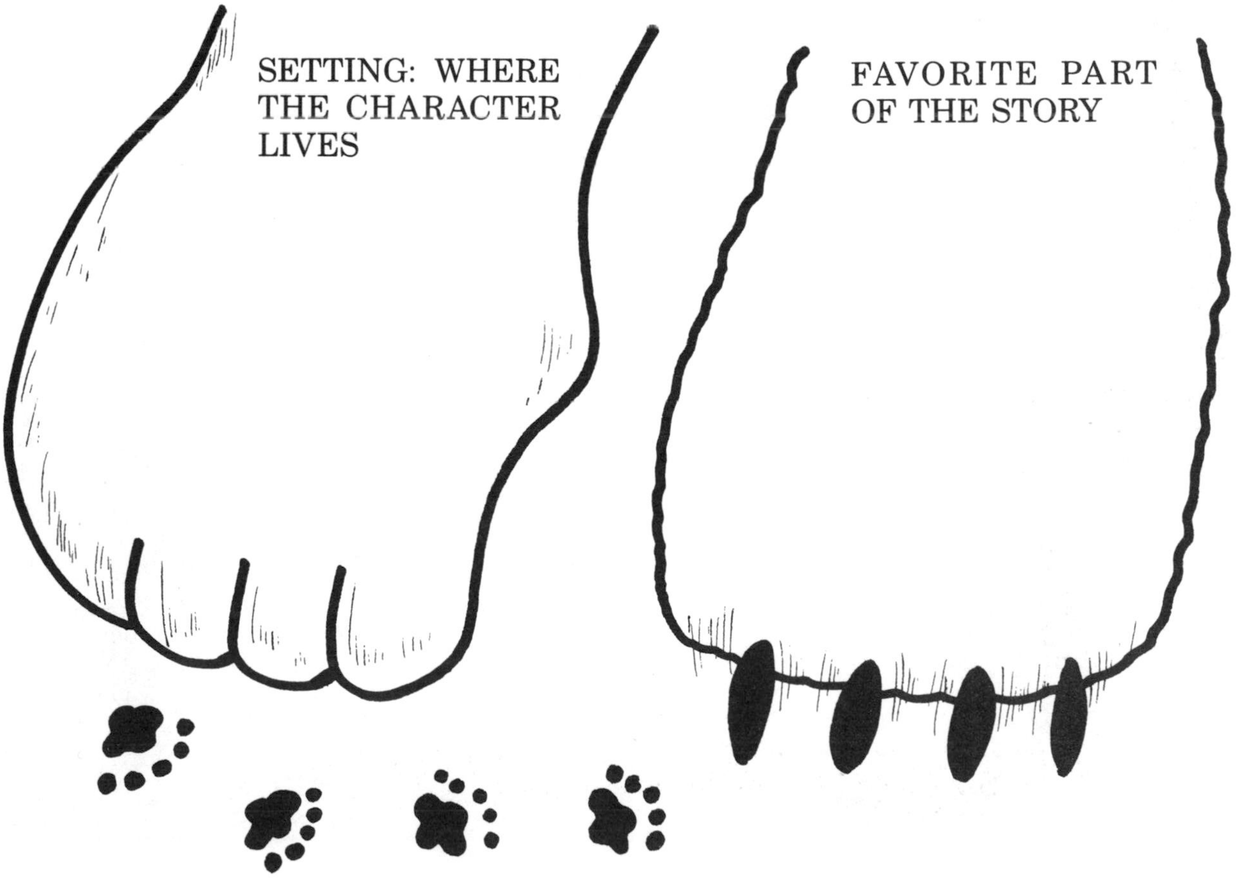

SETTING: WHERE THE CHARACTER LIVES

FAVORITE PART OF THE STORY

Name _____   Date _____

Hold this paper still and look into the eyes of each cat. (You just moved, or "exercised" your neck.)

Keep your head still and move the paper so that you can see into the eyes of each cat. (You just moved, or "exercised" your arms and wrists.)

The cat had you exercise without your realizing it. That's his magic!

Now, you can write an exercise for the cat. List three things for the cat to do. Then, you do the exercise.

1. _____

_____

2. _____

_____

3. _____

_____

_____

Helpful words: roll
jump
crawl
stretch
twitch
spread

Name _____   Date _____

Draw and write your story on this bunny shape. Cut out the shape, and trace around it to make more pages for the bunny book. Then staple the pages together.

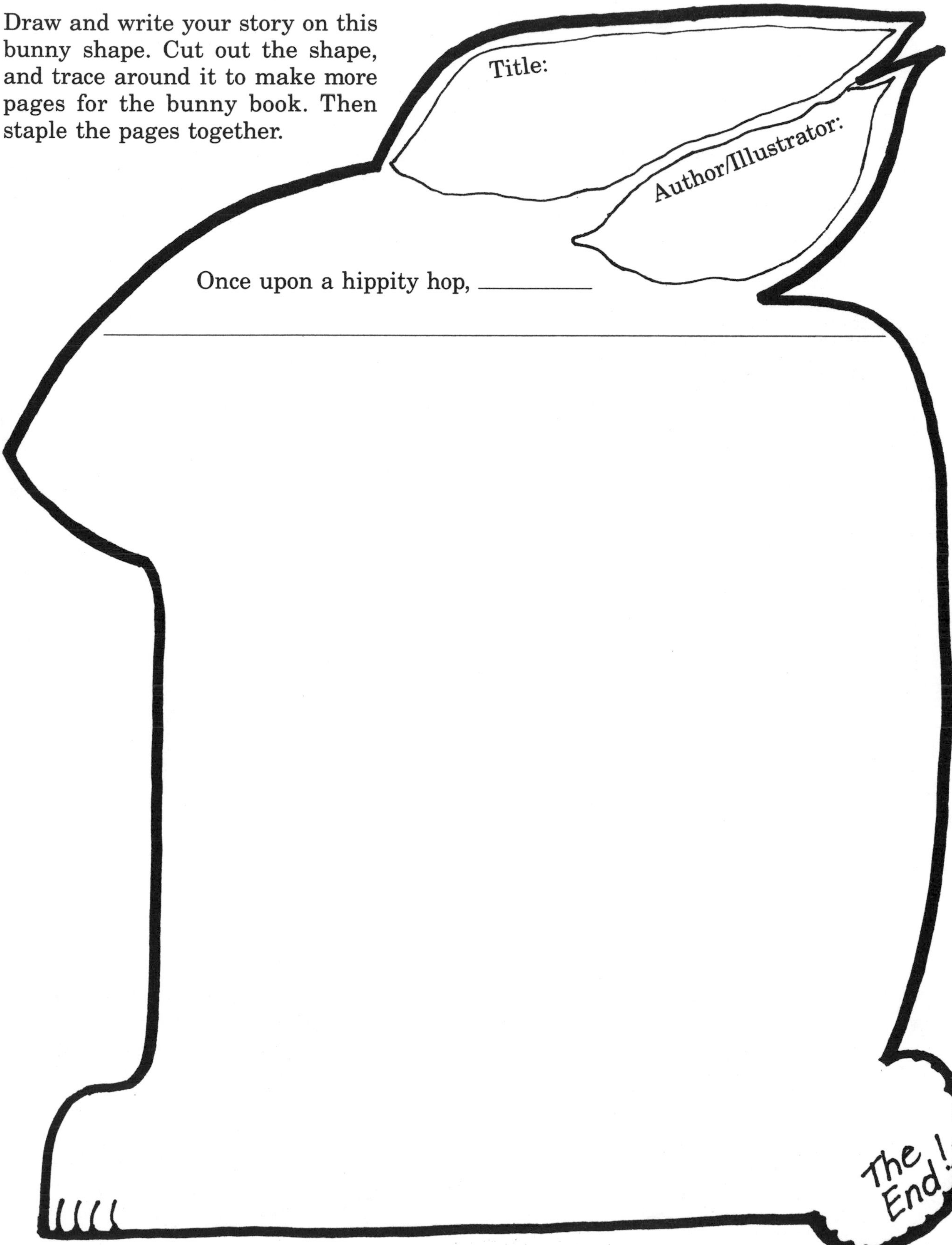

Title:

Author/Illustrator:

Once upon a hippity hop, _____

_____

The End!

Name _____

Date _____

4–11

MAKE A DUCK SHAPE BOOK

Draw and write your story on this duck. Cut out the shape, and trace around it to make more pages for the duck book. Staple the pages together at the duck's neck, and tie a pretty ribbon around its neck.

Once upon a quack quack, _____

Title:

Author/Illustrator:

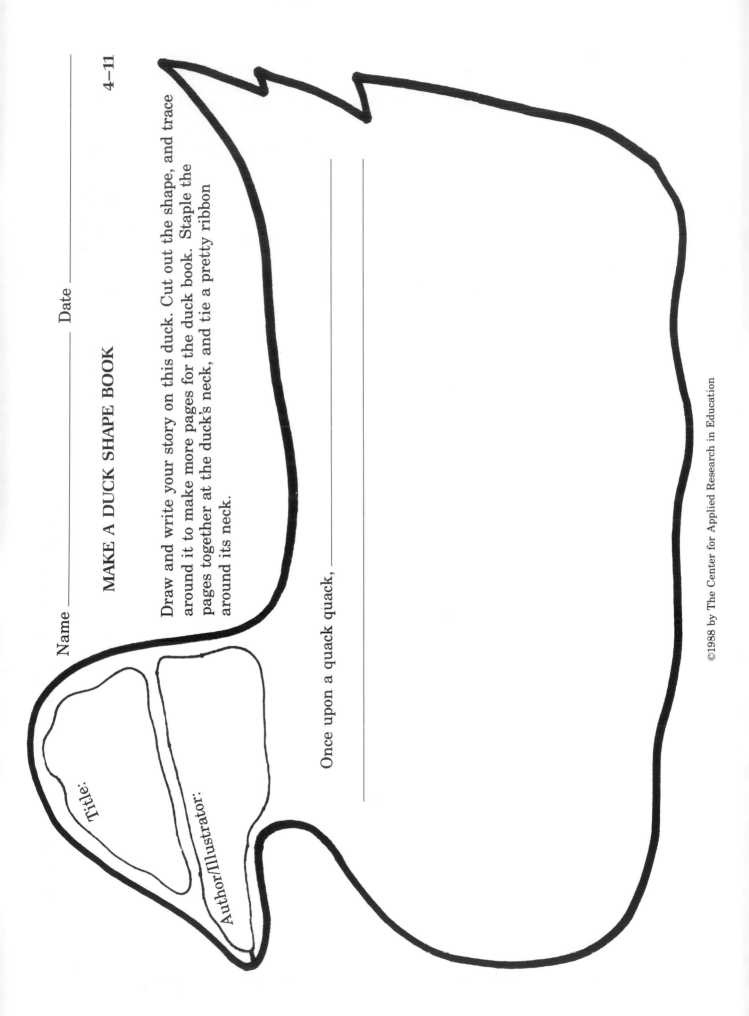

MAKE A BIRD SHAPE BOOK

Draw and write your story on this bird shape. Cut out the shape, and trace around it to make more bird book pages.

How do you plan to make the feathers bright and beautiful?

Once upon a tweet-tweet,

_____

_____

Title:

Author/Illustrator:

SECTION 5

Fantasy Books

BOOK:

Mike Mulligan and His Steam Shovel
by Virginia Lee Burton. Boston: Houghton
Mifflin Company, 1939, 1967.

SHOVELING OUT

1. The diesel motor shovels, electric shovels, and gasoline shovels all replaced the steam shovel. Today there are nuclear, solar, computer, and geothermal shovels. Have students design a shovel of the future and label the parts, just as they are labeled in the endpapers of this book.

2. Popperville might be called an old-fashioned town. Look carefully at the pictures of the milkman, farmer and family, and the fire department. How have they been changed? Since this is a "town that cares" what did the people do for them when modern methods took over? Where is the old fire engine and the horse-drawn milk wagon? Draw them as they are today—just as productive and useful as Mary Anne.

3. What would it be like to feel unwanted like Mike Mulligan and Mary Anne? What other machines have "felt unwanted" in the past few years? Are there any that are about to "feel unwanted" in the future?

Write the story from the point of view of Mary Anne. Other obsolete machines may come to her for advice. What could she tell them?

"JUNK" AND MODERN TECHNOLOGY

1. Look through an old-fashioned Sears Catalog to see what items were in style many years ago. What items have replaced them? Draw a "before and after" picture of some of them.

2. What are some new kitchen appliances that we are enjoying today that our great grandmother just dreamed about? Help the children list some. (Examples: Plug-in iron (she warmed hers on the stove); electric stove; microwave oven; electric knife; refrigerator with ice-maker; electric dishwasher; electric toaster; kitchen machines for peeling, slicing, dicing vegetables; blender.) Notice what has made a lot of difference possible in the kitchen—electricity. Some students may be interested in books about this topic; find some in the library at their level of understanding.

Invite someone who has antique or outdated kitchen gadgets to bring them to the classroom so that children can see what apple peelers, pie crimpers, old strainers, egg beaters, and so forth, looked like and how they worked.

Is it any wonder that in Mary Anne's day, Mondays were for washing, Tuesdays were for ironing, and so on? Each day of the week had a special task assigned to it because it took just about all day just to do that task. Now, someone can do a load of wash in the electric washer, be baking a frozen pie in the microwave oven, and be doing a load of dishes in the dishwasher at the same time! Running water, as well as electricity, has made this possible. We no longer have to carry our water in from the well, or collect it in a rain barrel. Modern technology is still working for us. Robots are the "wave of the future" in the kitchen. Have the children design a big "Kitchen of Tomorrow" and explain it.

3. In the workshop, we have benefited from a variety of new tools. We can work with an electric saw, electric jigsaw, and sharpen electric scissors and electric blades for the power mower. Interview one or two parents to see how tools, automobiles, and so on, have been "updated."

4. Start a collection of "Mary Annes." Bring three or four "old" items that young children probably would not know about. Have them examine them to decide: (A) What they could be used for today and (B) What they might have been used for.

5. Write a story, with conversation, between a pencil sharpener with a handle that ended up in the junk pile, and a brand new electric pencil sharpener that is considerate and kind. (This will provide practice with quotation marks and noting exactly what people "say" in print.)

MACHINES

1. Take Mary Anne on a tour of modern-day construction equipment. Some resource books would be helpful for finding the lift crane, transporter, earth movers, and so forth. The back hoe (excavator) can reach out almost 40 feet and dig down over 25 feet to scoop out dirt. Have Mary Anne draw and label them, or construct three-dimensional models.

The big tires on dirt-hauling machines weigh over 3,000 pounds each. Some trucks have six tires that are each 12 feet tall! How tall are the students in comparison to a 12-foot tire?

2. Bring in machine parts from small, worn-out appliances and have children examine them. (Remove all plugs first.)

3. Have an assortment of nuts, bolts, screws, ball bearings, nails, and let children identify, sort, and classify them.

4. Work Area. Have supplies such as a lever, pulley, inclined plane, and the like for examination. Have string, spools, and cylinders available. Students can design a pulley system for a specific reason and implement the design.

5. "The New Mike Mulligan." Tower crane operators work 700 feet up in the air. How do they get up into the crane? They use a ladder, climbing hand over hand, one rung at a time. This is demanding work because the operator has to pick up loads and put them down in precisely the right spot. If the wind is blowing too hard, the operator has to stop because the work becomes too dangerous.

Some crane operators work twelve hours a day, seven days a week, and they are all alone in "the cab in the sky," or their very own Mary Anne. Mike Mulligan would have probably made a good tower crane operator because he had "stamina." Discuss this new word. What qualifications would a person need to have to make this a career? Find out what careers interest students and discuss some.

BOOK:

A Pocket for Corduroy
by Don Freeman. New York:
Scholastic Book Services, 1978.

THE LAUNDROMAT

1. After reading the book, discuss laundromats. How many students have been inside of one? Have the students close their eyes and pretend to be inside a laundromat. What are the sounds? sights? smells?

2. Role play: Interview the bags of laundry (students wrapped in bulky pillow cases) and discuss "feelings"—before, during wash, rinse, dry cycles, and when clean.

3. The machines are coin-operated. They "eat coins" in order to operate. List other machines that are coin-eaters. How do these machines help?

4. "Swan Flakes" was the name on the soap box. Have students design a new soap with a clean, fresh name and an attractive box. Wrap the new covers around used soap boxes, and line them up. Which one would you buy? Why? Which colors appeal? (What colors are used on the real soap boxes?)

Conduct a "Person on the Street" survey right outside of your own classroom or get permission to do this in the main hall. Have all of the boxes there and ask the "consumers" which box they would select and why. "Producer" and "consumer" could be the new vocabulary words of the week.

5. Students can write a forty-five-second radio or TV "pitch" for their soap. Point out that one is a visual medium and one is an aural medium, so the commercials will be quite different, but in what way? (Radio ads will have to describe what the box looks like, color, and so forth.) A singing jingle would be a good technique for both radio and TV.

6. Many laundromats have bulletin boards where they put messages and ads. Make a "Laundromat Bulletin Board" for the classroom and have students, storybook characters, and teacher communicate (real or fantasy).

THE BOOK

1. The laundromat is crowded with people. Look through the busy book again and find the most crowded page, the least crowded page. (Concept: Most/ Least.)

2. Pockets must be emptied before laundering. Have students ever "lost" anything to the machine that they left in their pockets? Discuss. Write a class story about a favorite item left in a pocket.

3. Have students describe Corduroy's rescue from the dryer by the artist, in their own words, as though they were right on the scene.

4. Finger paint the swirling clothes in the dryer.

5. "Pandro's" is the name of the laundromat and the worker calls Lisa "Senorita." What does Senorita mean? What would he call a boy? What nationality are they? Learn some other names in this laundry.

6. Why is "Corduroy" a good name for a bear? Bring in samples of corduroy so that children can feel it. Are any other pets named after material? List some types of material (velvet, cotton, calico, gingham, denim) and bring in samples for touching. What animal could be named "Velvet?" or "Cotton?" (Remember the story of the Gingham Dog and the Calico Cat?)

7. Find other Corduroy stories by this same author, and have them available for children to read and enjoy.

POCKETS

1. Describe the texture of corduroy. The term "corduroy" may have been derived from French "corde du roi" or "cord of the king." The heavy fabric is known to have been produced in England. Have a "royal corduroy day" where children wear something corduroy and become princes and princesses.

2. Make pockets from real corduroy swatches. Fold them and sew up the sides. Then, students can print their name (directory style), address, and phone number on a little card. Tuck it into the corduroy pocket and then tuck that into a jacket pocket, or lunch box.

3. Discuss pockets. How do they open? (Zip, flap, snap.) Do we always get into a pocket from the top? side? Where are pockets located on clothing? Bring in a hidden wallet used by travelers.

BOOK:

Blueberries for Sal
by Robert McCloskey. New York:
Viking Press, 1948.

THE PARALLEL STORIES

1. This book contains a parallel plot; two similar stories are going on at the same time—that of the mother/daughter out picking berries and the mother bear/

cub out looking for food. The action takes place on the same hill, but on different sides (pages 38, 39).

2. Draw parallel lines on the chalkboard. Explain "parallel," in terms of two streets going in the same direction but never meeting, two people talking at the same time with neither listening to what the other is saying, playing side by side in the sandbox but not together, and so on. Have the children give additional examples of "parallel."

3. The parallel plots meet. On page 42 of the story Little Bear's mother turns and sees Sal. What might a "real" bear do? In the story, the mother bear turns with a grunt and is only interested in finding her baby. On page 48, Sal's mother turns and sees Little Bear instead of Sal. The point that the author is making is that both mothers are experiencing the same feeling about the loss of their babies. The story doesn't end there, but goes on in its parallel form until both mothers find their offspring.

4. More "parallels." Sal's mother is planning ahead for winter, to take the blueberries home for canning. Bears eat and grow fat to plan ahead for winter, which is just what the mother bear is instructing Little Bear to do.

Also, there is a parallel in conversation on page 42 and on page 48, when the two mothers see their strange companion for the first time. Example: "She was old enough to be..." (see page 42 and page 48).

5. After this book has been read and discussed in terms of mothers and their babies, get a copy of *All Those Mothers at the Manger* by Norma Farber (New York: Harper & Row Junior Books, 1985). This tender picture book deals with the magical bond between Mary and the Christ child and all the other animal mothers in the manger.

THE BOOK

1. Notice that all of the illustrations and print are done in blue; so appropriate for a picture book about blueberries. This might inspire students to print or write creative stories with colors that relate to the story line. (Use pencils or felt-tip pens.)

2. Note the "country kitchen" of Sal's home at the beginning of the book before the story begins. Which items look old-fashioned? Using the same kitchen scene as a model, draw the kitchen of today.

Sal is playing a game with rubber ringed jar lids and a wooden spoon. Make up a counting game using these same items.

3. Call attention to the egg beater in the drawer. How many children have seen one of this type? If possible, borrow one so that children can use one to whip up "potatoes" (water and soapsuds). (Be on the lookout for kitchen items of this type at garage sales and barn sales.)

4. Get some fresh blueberries and have the children count them, using a "kuplunk!" pail.

5. Play a listening game. Use a "kuplunk!" pail and purple beads, and have children close their eyes and listen for the total number of beads (berries) being dropped into the pail. Take turns listening and dropping berry beads.

MORE BOOK ACTIVITIES

1. Make blueberry jam using this simple, all natural recipe. The measuring could be part of a math lesson one day, and the jam could be used for snack time the next day.

Ingredients: 1½ c. blueberries; 1 Tbsp. lemon juice; ¼ c. honey

Procedure: Combine all ingredients in a saucepan. Bring to a boil and let boil for 20 minutes. Stir occasionally to prevent scorching. Pour into a clean (sterilized) jar. It will thicken on cooling. Yield: About 1 cup. Serve on crackers, using a blue-checkered napkin.

2. Artists in Blue. Fold a 9 × 12 piece of light blue construction paper in half. Using only blue crayons, draw Blueberry Hill in the middle of the fold. Make Sal and her mother on one side of the hill and Big Bear and Little Bear on the other side. Using this folded picture as a guide, flip back and forth between the action on either side of the hill to retell the story. As "artists in blue" the students are doing as the illustrator did with the pictures in the book.

3. What other mothers and children are represented in this story? (Crows, page 29; partridge, page 35.) What others could there be that we just don't see in the illustrations?

4. Mothers and babies were reunited in the story. Discuss the feeling of being lost and what children can do when they lose their parent or sitter in a shopping mall, in a large store, at a picnic, and so forth. Make a plan.

5. Young children enjoy acting out this story during play time, and need very little in the way of props. If the story were recorded on a cassette tape, children could listen and role play at the same time. Several groups of children could act out the story at one time.

6. Discuss the color blue. How many are wearing blue? How many different shades of blue are we wearing? How many children have blue eyes? When we eat blueberries or blueberry jam, what happens to the color of our tongues? How many blue items can we name in the room? How many shades of blue are in our crayon box? Have the students fingerpaint their favorite part of the story with blue.

Discuss "blue" in language. What does it mean when we say that someone "feels blue?" Is blue a sad color? A warm color? A cool color? What other sayings can we think of for the word blue? (Examples: true blue, it's a blue world without you, blue is forever, blue blood.)

7. Read other Robert McCloskey books to children such as *Make Way for Ducklings, Time of Wonder, Lentil, One Morning in Maine.*

BOOK:

The Pooh Story Book
by A. A. Milne. Illustrations by E.H. Shepard.
New York: E.P. Dutton & Co., 1965.

BUILDING A HOUSE FOR EEYORE

This book contains three separate Winnie-the-Pooh stories. Children can be encouraged to bring in their stuffed Pooh bears, other stuffed bears, or stuffed animals so that the animals can "listen" to the stories and enjoy them too.

Also, have a big jar of honey available (a small jar could be placed inside of a huge round container which has been covered with colored paper and with big letters that spell HONEY printed on the outside). Spread it on crackers for snack time, or after story time.

1. Using sticks and clay or plasticene, students can build a suitable house for Eeyore.

2. Teach children the "Tiddely Pom" rhyme. Say it. Sing it. Chant it with hand motions. (On the last part work with a partner or with three students together.)

3. Students can make up their own "Outdoor Hum for Snowy Weather." Practice. Then record it on a cassette tape.

4. For practice with upper and lower case letters, students can write three favorite Pooh Bear snack recipes for "elevenses." (List ingredients and procedure for making the snack.) Perhaps students can vote on the favorites and make one or two.

PIGLET—SURROUNDED BY WATER

1. Students can build Piglet's house in miniature, using a tiny box, plasticene and a sturdy tree branch. Accessories can be added.

2. A Sequential Diorama. A diorama of a scene from this story is fun to plan and create. Older children can work in teams of three, so that three dioramas in a row could depict the beginning, middle, and ending scenes from the story.

3. Write a "HELP" message for a bottle, just as Piglet did. Put it in a wide mouth jar, cover it, and float it in a tub of water, or have the jar "washed up" on a shore of sand. Have students take turns sending and answering the message. Now we have a sender and receiver, and so communication is possible. This type of writing and responding could go on until the sender has made very clear to the receiver the "Who? What? When? Where? Why?" of the message.

4. Using this story (or even the book) make a list of the happy words, scary words, quiet words, funny words, sad words, noisy words, and so forth.

5. Construct a different boat for Pooh from styrofoam and cardboard and sticks. Give it a name that has "Honey" in the title.

6. Compose a different ending for the story. Suppose the message in the bottle was not found. The ending can be mysterious, magical, amusing, but it can't be tragic because we know Piglet lives on.

POOH INVENTS A GAME

1. Have the children paint a big Pooh Bear by dabbing a sponge into paint the color of honey. Then, using the same dabbing motion for a "fuzzy" effect, make a circular shape for the head, oval shape for the body, and then add arms and legs and ears. Allow these to dry and add other features later with a felt-tip pen.

2. Have a Celebration Day for Pooh Bear and his friends. Invite all Teddy Bears, make name tags for them, set a table for the bears and have them all sit along in two rows (or around a table). Students can "listen in" on the conversation periodically and then, at the end of the day, tell us what the bears and stuffed animals were talking about, and what they learned at school.

3. Have a "Show and Tell" Day (the original oral report) where children can introduce their stuffed bear or other stuffed animal that is spending the day (or two) at school. "This calls for a celebration," as Pooh would say and sharing a good snack of "Honey Milk Punch for a Friendly Day," or having a "Honey Oatmeal Cookie" would make everyone feel good. An excellent reference book for these and other delightful Pooh recipes is *The Pooh Cook Book* by Virginia H. Ellison, with illustrations by Ernest H. Shepard (New York: Dell Publishing Co., 1976).

4. Using the recipe from the above mentioned cookbook, make "colored honey" using drops of food coloring. A dab of colored honey on a cracker makes a snack taste oh, so delicious! Have young children smack their lips and think up "delicious" words that can be listed on honey-pot shapes.

5. Invent a variation of the game that Pooh and his friends play. Challenge: It must be played either in the classroom or on the playground.

6. Children can make paper puppets on a stick of Pooh Bear, Eeyore, Tigger, Piglet, Owl, Christopher Robin, and reenact the stories.

7. A.A. Milne, the author of the Pooh Bear stories, used to tell these stories to his son, Christopher, at bedtime. They were so delightful that he was urged to write them down. They grew into a collection of books that young children enjoy hearing again and again. Read more to the children, such as *Winnie-the-Pooh, The House at Pooh Corner, When We Were Very Young, Now We Are Six.*

BOOK:

Amos & Boris
by William Steig. New York: Penguin, 1977.

A FRIENDSHIP CORNER

1. When Boris "sounded," Amos fell into the water. Amos was "crazy with rage." Discuss this colorful phrase. Extend the discussion: Have students ever been very angry at someone? Why? When? For how long? What do they usually do with their anger? (Discuss helpful ways of dealing with anger—talking about it and explaining why we are angry, doing something physical like walking, running, or swimming to use up all of the extra energy.)

We use the word "crazy" in a variety of ways: "crazy with rage," "she's crazy about him," "Joey's crazy about double-fudge nutty ice cream," and so on. Try substituting other words for crazy.

2. Friendship. Boris speaks of Amos in glowing terms—gemlike radiance; and Amos admired Boris for his rich voice and "abounding friendliness." Picture one of your good friends in your mind. What nice words would you use to describe your friend?

3. Amos and Boris had to "part." Have children ever had to part, or say goodbye to a good friend? Discuss feelings. Stress the making of new friends. Perhaps students could write a letter to an old friend (or relative) and let the person know that they are thinking about them. Maybe they could become pen pals.

4. Helping a friend is sometimes called "doing a good deed." Have students recently done a good deed for a friend? Ask them to tell about it. Can they give an example of doing a good deed for someone they didn't know very well? How could this be shown in a picture?

5. What other books has the class read together (or have students read) where someone needed help? List them. What are some telltale signs when someone needs help?

6. Find a good song about friendship and teach it to the children, (Example: "Make new friends, but keep the old, one is silver, and the other is gold.") Perhaps you could begin or end each day with the friendship song (very young children), or sing it just before playtime as a gentle reminder to share.

7. What could Amos do for the two elephants who helped save Boris' life to show his appreciation? What are the names of the elephants?

PLAYING AROUND WITH WORDS

1. Make a chart listing the colorful words or phrases for the story. Use colorful felt-tip pens to print these colorful words:

phosphorescent sea,   whales spouted luminous water
enjoying his trip immensely   worn to a frazzle
Holy clam and cuttlefish!

Learn some of these interesting, musical words. What do they mean? Let's try to use these words. Let's keep listening for more unusual words, and add them to the chart.

2. "Fooling Around." Amos was "mousing around" and Boris was "whaling around." What would your pet dog be doing? your cat? fish? turtle? gerbil? What about zoo animals? farm animals? What about you when you're playing sports like baseball, football, tennis, or games like hide-and-seek or tag? (Encourage children to enjoy working with the language as they make up new words.)

3. "Message in a Bottle." Suppose Amos had a pencil and paper, and a bottle? Ask students what message they think he would write? Remember, someone could find it who might not speak the same language as Amos. This calls for lots and lots of pictures next to (or instead of) the words.

4. The story doesn't tell about this, but what happened to Amos' boat? Did it sink? Was it discovered still floating along? If so, who discovered it? (Let the children come up with some ideas. They might think of pirates, sea creatures, and the like.) When it was found, where was it put? Is it being used for something else now, and if so, what? (Suppose it was found by a squid, a hermit crab, or a jellyfish?)

TAKING A TRIP

1. Amos set sail in "The Rodent" and took food, necessary equipment, and two play items to help pass the time. Suppose students were setting out on a long journey. Have them pack their suitcase with food, clothing, necessary items, and two entertainment items.

Use a real suitcase for this activity so that children will be able to see how much space they have. They could also pack it. Bring in specific items that could be taken along on a trip.

2. Students can construct another boat for Amos, using such materials as wood, cardboard, string, tape, cardboard cylinders, cloth for the sail. What will they name this sailing vessel? What is the meaning of "vessel?" Let's look it up in the dictionary under "v" (will that be toward the beginning or the end of the dictionary?), then vote on a name.

3. Amos was well prepared for his trip but he forgot himself and rolled overboard. What list of rules would students make for taking a boat trip? A car trip? An airplane trip? An overnight trip to stay with a friend or relative?

Do some of the rules remain the same regardless of our mode of travel or destination? Encourage students to make a list of basic rules. (Some children may want to take the list home and place it in their overnight kit or bag for handy reference.)

4. Have each student design a colorful book jacket or book cover that shows Amos and Boris (the two main characters) taking another trip together.

BOOK:

The Garden of Abdul Gasazi
by Chris Van Allsburg. Boston:
Houghton Mifflin, 1979.

THE MAGIC GARDEN

1. After reading the book, go through it page by page and notice that the garden bushes and hedges have been trimmed to make animal shapes. Using green cutouts of circles, triangles, ovals, and rectangles, students can become gardeners and make another garden scene of fascinating animals that are around the back of the house—the garden we didn't see.

2. Pretend that the animal bushes come to life at the stroke of midnight. What goes on in the garden? (Have students read their stories in hushed voices. Turn out the overhead lights, and have only a reading lamp on for this.)

3. What special tools does Abdul Gasazi's gardener keep in the shed in order to keep the garden so well manicured? Draw a chart showing these special tools and their special functions/uses/names. Catalogs may be helpful.

4. What is the magic formula that is sprayed on the plants to keep them green and happy all year long? Design the bottle label and list the ingredients. It's the bottle that we spied in the gardener's shed.

ABDUL GASAZI, THE GREAT

1. Suppose Miss Hester was upset because Fritz really didn't come home? Write a different (but magical) ending to the story.

2. Make a three-dimensional model of Gasazi the Great's home with trap door, fake food, and other tricky items.

3. The word is out! Mr. Gasazi is looking for an assistant. Let's write to him telling why we want the job and why we think we'd be especially good for this job. Work in teams.

4. "Gasazi's Greatest Goof!" Pretend that we overheard Abdul Gasazi talking about the day when, right on stage, his big trick didn't work. What trick was it? How did he cover it up? (Write and illustrate.)

5. Try to change a dog into a duck by folding and cutting paper. Is it possible?

THE MAGICIAN

1. Start a Prop Box. Students can bring in a cape, top hat, robe, fake moustache, and so on. Put on the Abdul Gasazi outfit and be interviewed by the press after a hat trick.

2. Get books from the library on magic tricks. Students can learn to do one. Practice before a mirror! Wear the robe and hat when the performance is polished. and perform as "Gasazi the Great!" (This time, don't reveal any secrets.)

3. Book of Tall Tales. When someone is believed to have magic powers, stories get started and they grow bigger and bigger and more and more unbelievable. Make a tall tale book using a cutout of a tall magician's hat. Have students write something unbelievable that Magician Gasazi did. Staple the hat together at the top as a flip-up book. Then, make very big hat shapes as the tales get bigger and more preposterous. Maybe these can be held together by making a hole in the upper left-hand corner with a paper punch and putting a ring through it. Perhaps inside pages can be stapled so that they can flip this way and that.

4. Just suppose that Gasazi the Great was in disguise when he opened the door to let Alan inside. Have the students draw a passport photo likeness of the "real" Abdul Gasazi. Compare the students' versions.

5. Using glossy paper and printing from magazine advertisements, construct a "billboard" that advertises Gasazi the Great's next performance. (Who, What, Where, When, a clever title, adjectives on star shapes or rabbit shapes.) Have the children use words like "mind-boggling," "dazzling," "splendiferous." This billboard could become a large book cover.

6. Make "combination" words to describe Gasazi the Great! (Example: Put "wonderful" and "marvelous" together and create a new word like "wonderlous," or "marvelful." "Fantastic" and "Entertaining" can come out like "Fantaining" or "Entertastic".) Children enjoy "playing" with the language and should be encouraged to do so. It is a good exercise for making children more comfortable with words and with reading.

BOOK:

Charlotte's Web
by E.B. White. New York: Harper & Row
Junior Books, 1952.

CONSTRUCTION AREA

1. For a class project, make giant, stuffed, cloth shapes of Charlotte and Wilbur. Materials needed: Red burlap, brown burlap, blunt needles, yarn, as-

sorted felt pieces, stuffing material. Procedure for making Wilbur: On a giant sheet of paper have the children draw the outline of a pig. Cut it out. Pin it onto two pieces of blushing red burlap. Cut. Using blunt needles and yarn, children can sew around the edge, sewing the two pieces of cloth together. Stuff. Put the "blushing" Wilbur in the reading area, so that children can use him for a cushion.

Procedure for making Charlotte: Cut two giant circles from brown burlap. Have the children sew around the edges with colorful, bulky yarn. Stuff. Using bulky yellow yarn, braid Charlotte's eight long legs and sew four onto two opposite sides. Glue on eyes and mouth. Place her on a table top, or hang her from the ceiling so children may touch and talk to her.

2. Using clay and pipe cleaners, children can mold Charlotte and Wilbur. Encourage them to form other barnyard animals. Have them construct a cardboard barnyard. Use this area to reenact scenes for the story.

3. Make a red "Construction—Do Not Touch" sign to use when working on class projects. Some of the items that are in process cannot be readily dismantled and moved.

4. Have children construct felt and burlap book marks.

5. Help the children make a felt board and have them design felt cutouts of story characters to reenact the story during their creative play time.

TEMPLETON'S TERRITORY

1. Feeling—No Peeking! Using a shoe box, make a messy interior using straw or paper strips. Have children reach inside and by feeling try to guess what Templeton brought back from one of his nightly escapades. Elicit descriptive words from the children (scratchy, smooth, sharp, squiggly, and so on). Keep changing the objects and make them unusual (orange rind, apple core, twine, limburger cheese, half a sandwich of salami and rye with a big bite out of the middle, old jewelry that children could "borrow" and wear for a day).

2. Write a letter to Templeton suggesting a slogan for the web. Include a diagram. Then, construct a web design using a ball of white yarn or string, glue, and dark construction paper as a background. Children can tuck written messages (torn from a magazine, perhaps) inside.

3. Make Treasure Maps. Materials: 9×12 paper, felt-tip pens. Procedure: Have children decide what the treasure will be. Talk about map symbols, store sign symbols, traffic sign symbols. Draw a map to the hidden treasure. On the reverse side, explain how to find the treasure.

Variation. Students could pretend to be Templeton and draw the treasure maps to one of his gastronomical delights from his point of view. His symbols could be sewer pipes, gutters, old buildings, and so on. He would surely have a "Beware of Cat" symbol too!

4. Templeton's Tasty Treats. Just suppose that Templeton, with his interest in food, opened up a restaurant for rats? What would appear on his breakfast, lunch, and dinner menus? What would some of his week-old "specials" be? What are some interesting shapes for Templeton's restaurant menu? Have children

make the menu, or make several menus (breakfast, lunch, dinner, midnight snack).

5. Comparison of Characters. Compare Templeton's personality traits with those of Wilbur and Charlotte, and some of the other barnyard animals. Be sure to remind the students that all of them have redeeming qualities; after all, Templeton did help save the day!

WILBUR'S PIG PEN

1. "Self-Help" Booklet. Make a blank booklet with a page for each student. Since Wilbur is so very shy and blushes easily, they can suggest ways to help Wilbur gain more self-confidence. Draw or paint him in positive situations and print helpful messages in the book. What should the book be called?

2. A "Dear Fern" Mailbox. Bring in a big country mailbox and have pencils and small pieces of notepaper available; or, decorate a shoe box to look like a mail box, and put a slit in the top. Have children write a "Dear Fern" letter from Wilbur, telling about his thoughts and feelings, and asking for advice. (Fern should answer.) For a variation, have children write their own personal "Dear Fern" letters expressing their feelings, thoughts, and questions. (Fern should answer.)

3. "Blue-Ribbon Winners." Cut circles from gold foil paper and paste them onto a larger white circle. Glue blue ribbon streamers on them. On one blue ribbon, make a complimentary statement about Wilbur and pin the ribbon on him. On the others, each student can make a complimentary statement about himself, and wear it. (Examples: "I am honest," or "I like...," or "I like to....") Make up a set of blue-ribbon winner statements and see who gets to wear them today. Some sample statements are: "I am helpful to others," or "I picked up litter today," or "I tried not to talk out today."

4. Create a cheer that the cheerleaders at the Fair might use for the competitions. Do a special one for Wilbur complete with body movements to go with the cheer. Use words and phrases such as, "Rah!, Rah!", "Go Wilbur, Go!" and spell out W-I-L-B-U-R...Wilbur!" These will help to spur Wilbur on if he begins to feel faint!

REPRODUCIBLE ACTIVITY PAGES
FOR
FANTASY BOOKS

INGREDIENTS FOR A FAIRY TALE

MAGIC

FAIRY TALE

Color the ingredients that could be used in a fairy tale

COLORFUL WORDS

1 2 3

THINGS HAPPEN IN THREES

"ONCE UPON A TIME"

ANIMALS THAT TALK

TRUE FACTS

GOOD AND BAD CHARACTERS

HAPPY ENDINGS

OLD MOTHER HUBBARD'S FULL CUPBOARD GAME 5—2

In each box below, there is something from Mrs. Hubbard's cupboard. Color each item to make it look delicious! Cut the cards apart on the lines.

Now you are ready to play the game. It will help improve your memory. (Two or three can play.)

1. Lay the cards face down.
2. Turn over one square, and then another square. If they match, you may keep them.
3. If the two cards do not match, turn them back over. TRY TO REMEMBER WHERE THEY ARE.
4. Now it is the next person's turn. (Look back at Number 2 for directions.)
5. The winner is the person with the most matching pairs.

doughnut	pear	bread	cheese
muffin	peanut butter	pear	carrots
apple	bread	doughnut	peanut butter
cheese	muffin	apple	carrots

Name _____   Date _____

Princess Tootie says that nobody likes to hear someone brag a lot, but that every once in a little while it is nice to share something nice that you have done. You have that opportunity right now!

Greetings! I am Princess Tootie from the Kingdom of Good Deeds. We have read about many kind things that people have done for someone else. We're waiting to hear from you.

The best deed I ever did was

It made me feel

I wish that

Name _____   Date _____

The story setting is where the action takes place (in a house, on the roof, under the bridge, at the swimming pool, and so on).

Select a book: Title _____

Author/Illustrator _____

Show the different settings where the action takes place. What do they look like? Pay special attention to details, and show the reader as much as you can!

1. Beginning Setting.	2. Where do we go next?	3. Then where are we?
4. Show the prettiest set.	5. Your favorite setting.	6. Ending Setting.

THE FOLK TALE PROBLEM-SOLVING RECIPE

As you read many folktales, you will notice that there is a "formula," or a recipe for them. The recipe consists of three things: (1) Setting, (2) Characters, (3) Problem. The problem is always solved and the tale ends on a happy note. Below are some samples of the three necessary ingredients:

SETTING

In the land of the setting sun
In a place where it never rained
At the edge of the world
Halfway between north and south
In a land far, far away

CHARACTER(S)

king and queen
wicked stepmother
farmer and his wife
three sisters or three brothers
a fool (who wins in the end)

PROBLEM

the hens stopped laying eggs
the princess would not laugh
the prince was turned into a rock
the trees refused to grow apples
the crops would not grow tall

Select your three ingredients and become a folk tale problem solver. Make up your own ingredients, too! Begin at the ●

● _____
(Setting)
there lived a _____ and a _____
                  (character(s)   (character(s)

who _____

Now, one day _____
                              (problem)

_____

_____

_____

(Use the back of this sheet if you need more space to write.)

What is your title? _____

Name _____   Date _____

COMMON ELEMENTS IN FOLK TALES

COMMON ELEMENTS IN FOLK TALES   5–6

5–6

You can find out much information about different countries by reading folk tales. Select a country (Japan, Russia, Germany, Kenya, . . .). Read two or three folk tales from that country. Look for things such as colorful sayings in the language, holiday customs, special foods, pet animals and work animals, and houses.

Write down the information about your country in the spaces provided below. Compare it with folk tale information that a classmate wrote about another country.

Let's go traveling to _____
                              (country)

1. Customs	2. Special Foods
3. Animals and Their Uses	4. _____

©1988 by The Center for Applied Research in Education

EATING YOUR WAY THROUGH A GOOD STORY

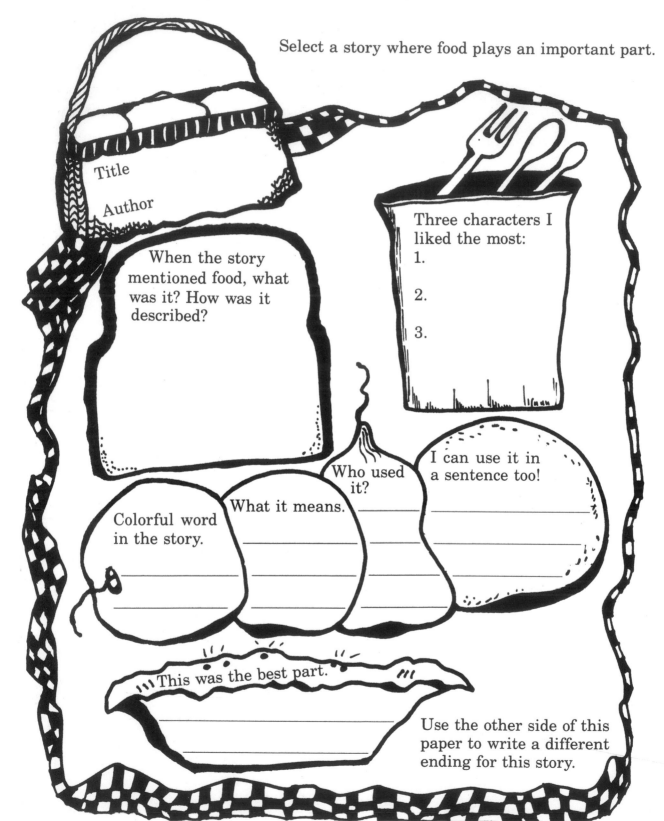

Select a story where food plays an important part.

Title

Author

Three characters I liked the most:
1.

2.

3.

When the story mentioned food, what was it? How was it described?

Colorful word in the story.

What it means.

Who used it?

I can use it in a sentence too!

This was the best part.

Use the other side of this paper to write a different ending for this story.

Name _____ Date _____

ONCE UPON A TIME

Pretend this is magic writing paper that will help you write a story. In your story, include: a magic item, a magic animal, a beast, and a kind little elf who has lost its magic powers. Close your eyes and start daydreaming! The magic is beginning to work . . . .

Name _____   Date _____

Pack this bag with six magic items found in fairy tales.

Many objects that have magic powers are used repeatedly in fairy tales. Identify each object, and the story where it was used. Use bright colors. The first one is done for you.

1. The magic wand in Cinderella.

2. _____

3. _____

4. _____

5. _____

6. _____

SECTION 6

Humorous Books

BOOK:

Cloudy with a Chance of Meatballs
by Judi Barrett. Illustrations by Ron Barrett.
New York: Atheneum, 1984.

MY TOWN

1. In this book, Saturday is a special day because grandfather fixes pancakes. Do students have a special Saturday or Sunday menu that they like? Draw the family on the weekend during breakfast, lunch, or dinner, identify the family members, and describe them in writing.

2. Evening time is special because Grandfather tells stories. What are three of your favorite bedtime stories? Students can practice telling their favorite story from beginning to end in front of a big mirror, using hand gestures. Have them tell it aloud to a small group or to the class. Record them on tape, and use them for special occasions.

3. Check the morning and evening weather reports in the newspaper for one day. "Translate" it into a Chew and Swallow weather report.

4. Check through the newspaper ads, looking for dry cleaners and "specials" at the grocery and drug stores. Then, make a typical newspaper ad for a dry cleaner, or a different store in Chew and Swallow.

5. Grandpa told a "tall tale." Find the section in the library that deals with tall tales and read several. There is usually a "grain of truth" in a tall tale. Compose a group tall tale local weather report.

6. Compare your town with Chew and Swallow. What would be the best reason for living in each town.

THE TOWN OF CHEW AND SWALLOW

1. If the weather report is "Cloudy with a chance of meatballs," complete the following reports: "Sunny with a chance of... ," "Windy with a chance of... ," "Rainy with a chance of... ," "Snowy with a chance of... ".

2. In Chew and Swallow people just grab for food (note Ralph's Roofless Restaurant). Do the people have any restaurant rules? Have students list three that might help.

3. It's remarkable to have a restaurant that doesn't know what it's serving and that gives the food away. Is it a food station? Students can make up an amusing menu for Ralph's Roofless Restaurant.

4. Crayon Resist is a method of illustration where items are drawn and colored with crayon and then painted over with a watercolor wash. The crayon "resists" the paint and gives a textured effect. Students can use this method to

illustrate their version of the following phrases taken from the book: (a) A salt and pepper wind accompanied by a tomato tornado; (b) Fifteen-inch drifts of peanut butter and jelly sandwiches; (c) Hot dogs in rolls blow in at five miles per hour.

5. From scrap materials, students can construct a sanitation truck or garbage pickup truck for the town.

MORE FUN IN CHEW AND SWALLOW

1. One day cheese, another day pancakes and syrup. Students can cut out magazine pictures showing their favorite day in Chew and Swallow.

2. Nutrition Weather Reports. When we hear or read real weather reports, the weatherman uses terms such as "dry spell," "we really need the rain," "this is the hottest month in history," and so on. Chart the food (nutritionally) for a week, and see if you're in a "carbohydrate spell" or if you could "really use the protein," ....

3. What career would students choose in this town? Create a mural of the town at work.

4. Look through several copies of cookbooks. During a stalled weather pattern of eggs, how many different ways could you prepare them? Divide a paper into four squares and show them. (There could be a spell of ground hamburger, or french fries, and so on.)

5. Check the yellow pages of the local telephone book and list five stores that would do a heavy business in Chew and Swallow. List stores that would go out of business. Explain.

BOOK:

Madeline's Rescue
by Ludwig Bemelmans. New York:
Viking Press, 1951, 1953.

THE MADELINE STORIES

1. The *Madeline* series is still popular today because the young children identify with her as she triumphs over adult authority. Young Madeline wins and she is not unruly or bad, but she is headstrong when she believes in something, and it usually turns out all right in the end.

2. Be sure to point out the endpapers at the beginning and the ending of the book; they show a very detailed aerial view of Paris. (Older children may want to make such detailed endpapers for their next book.)

3. All *Madeline* stories (there are several in the series) are told in rhyme; read the story first so as not to break the rhyme and the story line, and discuss it later.

4. Dogs go to Obedience School. Dogs do go to school to learn to obey commands and to please their masters. There are also dogs who do work, such as seeing eye dogs, police dogs, and so on. What could a school dog be trained to do? (Examples: Guard children from straying on the playground, growl at unwanted strangers if children are crying out, be in the office to greet children when they deliver messages.) Pretend that Madeline lends one of the dogs to your classroom, and write a story about the event.

5. Vocabulary. "Gendarmes" are French police. Have students learn the new word. What are other names for police?

MADELINE

1. After reading several *Madeline* stories, encourage students to tell the funniest. Read *Madeline, Madeline and the Gypsies, Madeline and the Bad Hat, Madeline in London.*

2. Make up a tall tale about Madeline and the girls at the school. Record it on tape.

3. Pretend that a friend has never heard of Madeline. Draw a picture and write a description of Madeline.

4. Students can pretend to be Miss Clavel and make out Madeline's report card. Also, they can print a general message about Madeline's behavior at the school.

MADELINE'S PARIS

1. In most of the books, the setting is Paris. Help students locate Paris, France, on the map or globe. Note the book illustrations of the Eiffel Tower, Notre Dame, the Tuileries Gardens, and so on. (These are pointed out in the book entitled *Madeline.*) Find books about Paris and read about these well-known places.

2. Bring in picture books of Paris; note the Eiffel Tower, Notre Dame, and the Tuileries Gardens. How do they compare with the illustrations in the *Madeline* books?

3. Paris is the capital city of France. What is the capital city of the United States? (Learn this.) What famous buildings or monuments are located in Washington, D.C.? Get books about this great city. Learn to identify five monuments and draw and label one of them. (How is France linked to the United States through one of our monuments, or famous statue of a lady in New York harbor?)

4. Write and illustrate a class book entitled, *Madeline Visits Washington, D.C.* Will she meet the president? What will happen when she goes to visit the

Lincoln Memorial, or the Jefferson Memorial, or the Washington Monument? Share the book with another class.

5. Write and illustrate a class book entitled, *Madeline Visits Our School.* Will she meet the principal? Will she like the school lunch today? Will she bring her dog? Will she want to see the city or town where we live? Where will we take her—the zoo, museum, fast-food restaurant, shopping mall, department store, shopping center? Arrange an appointment for three students to read the book to the principal.

BOOK:

Jim and the Beanstalk
by Raymond Briggs. New York: Coward,
McCann & Geoghegan, 1970.

THE BOOK

1. Have a copy of the familiar tale, "Jack and the Beanstalk" available so that children can see similarities and differences between the two tales. Children thoroughly enjoy this retold tale. Have them decide which part is the funniest, and then the next funniest.

2. Anticipation. Can children begin to anticipate what is coming next, as this is read aloud to them? Since there is some patterning, they do begin to catch on. The giant's words, "Get 'em!" can be said in a chorus.

3. Glasses, Wigs, and Teeth.

Make fancy designer glasses, using various colors of sturdy oaktag. Have children role play trying on these "Giant Jim" glasses.

Make Giant Jim wigs (or another name children can choose), using string mops or yarn as a beginning. Also use these for role playing.

Teeth. Scientists are working on a microchip that could be permanently attached to a back tooth for identification purposes. The chip would contain information all about you. Have students make an identification chip for Jim's giant, and also an identification chip (I.D.) for themselves. This will be a new futuristic item to show Jim's giant.

4. What else is the giant in need of? Note his shoes and clothing. What happened when he shaved his stubble of a beard? Students can make a Giant Designer Catalog for the giant, complete with order forms, sizes, and so forth.

5. "I look about 100 years younger!" said the giant. Try to project your thinking into the future 100 years. What will Jim have to offer to the giant during that trip up the beanstalk?

RETOLD TALES

1. Have children perform or read aloud both versions of the beanstalk tale. Record it on cassette for playback and listening enjoyment.

2. What else grows very tall that could be used in the story instead of a beanstalk? (Examples: cornstalk, sunflower, tomato plant, banana tree, bamboo tree.) How would the story be changed if the plant were different?

3. Make a giant construction paper beanstalk for the bulletin board, that goes over the top and up the ceiling! Use a measuring tape like the one Jim used on the giant, and have children measure themselves (for example, around the head, from hip to ankle, around the waist, from elbow to wrist, and so on). Record the information on the stalk in graph form.

4. Giant Good Spelling! Make a giant bulletin board head of the giant, with his great big white teeth made from styrofoam squares, his hair made from red yarn, and his big glasses made from clothesline rope. List spelling words for the week, and have students teach them to the giant. Does he get 100% on each paper? Is he getting better each week? Does he need more study time?

RETELLING OF OTHER TALES

1. This book can serve as a kickoff for retold tales. Have children select an old favorite short tale for retelling. Work in small groups, with everyone working on the very same tale. Then share the story and the fun.

2. Have students update a tale in the form of a modern newspaper story. What section of the paper are they writing it for—business, front page, society, help wanted, comics? Don't forget the catchy headline.

3. Interact with a Tale. Have children store their retold tales in plastic food containers. They can make labels and put artifacts (items) in the container that the person in the story might have used. Perhaps the reader could use the materials to perform some task.

4. Mixed-up tales. Have students put characters from two tales together and rewrite the story. (For example, Goldilocks and the Three Little Pigs, or the Three Billy Goats Gruff and Hansel and Gretel, and so on.) Students enjoy the writing, spelling, reading, speaking, listening—all communication skills—and they are gaining practice during this exercise.

5. Make cutouts of famous characters and put them in an envelope. Have children reach in and select two or three characters, or items, and weave them into a fanciful story.

BOOK:

Petunia
by Roger Duvoisin. New York: Pinwheel Books,
Knopf/Pantheon, 1973.

THROUGH THE BOOK WITH PETUNIA

1. Read the story aloud and let children enjoy it. This is an excellent book for reluctant beginning readers, because from the story message they learn the value of being able to read. Discuss with the students the "value" of reading. Explain that reading is a process of "deciphering" or "decoding" a message from print to talk; and this is all done with twenty-six letters of the alphabet used over and over again.

Visual Discrimination. Make a large vertical alphabet chart. Children can work together in pairs to go through printed material in the book (a designated page), or in their own reading books, and keep a tally on a small vertical alphabet chart of how many times the letter "a" appears, the letter "b," the letter "c," and so forth. Transfer the tally marks from the small sheets to the large chart. Are there some letters that "work harder" (appear more often) than others? Which ones are they?

Give each child a page from the daily newspaper and have him or her circle a particular letter every time he or she finds it (location skills). Encourage children to use discarded newspapers and junk mail for finding letters, words, phrases, sentences.

2. Petunia is referred to in the story as a "silly goose." What things does she do that make her a silly goose? Have children recall the information from the story. At what point in the story does she stop being silly?

3. King, the rooster, was told by Clover, the cow, that his comb was "as red as the barn." Have students compile a list of other comparisons for red. Make a chart labeled AS RED AS A .... Work through other colors too.

4. Petunia told King that his comb was plastic, which was "silly." What other silly answer could she have given? Let's brainstorm.

5. Petunia Math. Where did Petunia go wrong when she talked with Ida the hen about the number of chicks she has? Why should Ida learn to count? How can we teach Ida to count? Make nine cutout baby chicks from yellow construction paper. Have a small jar of popcorn kernels and take one out for every chick (one-to-one correspondence). Take the chicks away and just count the corn. How many? Could Ida keep nine kernels of corn in an apron pocket, and match them up with

her own chicks to keep track of them? Would the corn get lost? Should she use pebbles? Can we teach her to make tally marks with her beak? How can we help Ida?

MORE MISCHIEF

1. Straw, the horse, is referred to as a "poor forlorn horse" when Petunia is finished with him. Make a big set of upper and lower horse teeth from glossy, white paper, and tape it to the chalkboard or bulletin board. Use a brush broom with a small handle to teach Straw to brush up and down, up and down. Children may want to discuss trips to the dentist, x-rays, fluoride, brushing, flossing, and so on.

2. Use a felt board and cutouts so that children can reenact the story. They especially like the part where Petunia suggests that in order to rescue Cotton the Kitten from the tall tree, they will have to do it together, so "Donkey climbed on top of Clover, Pig on top of Donkey, Goat on top of Pig, Sheep on top of Goat," and so on.

3. Danger, Firecrackers! How would the story be different if the box really did contain candies, as Petunia said, instead of firecrackers? Draw a picture to show some or all of the animals enjoying a giant box of chocolates. (Discussion: What will that do for Straw's toothache? Will it make Ida's chicks sick?)

4. Identify all of the animals after the "BOOM" page. If they all lined up in alphabetical order to obtain help, who would be first? last? fifth?

PETUNIA LEARNS TO READ

1. Petunia has learned the importance of opening up a book to help her to gain "wisdom." How does the author describe this moment in words? One element of wisdom is certainly knowledge, which can come from books and experience. Have children begin to share something that they learned from a book (even a picture book).

2. To help Petunia learn to read words, you can make identification name tags for items in the room, such as "desk," "clock," "sink," ... and tape them on or next to the item. Make another set, so that children can go around the room and match the sets.

3. Typewriter. An old typewriter is an excellent teaching/learning tool for the classroom. Children can locate the letters and numerals , and also type their names, spelling words, reading words, stories, and so on. (Old typewriters are often donated to classrooms when the "call" is sent out to parents.) Also, old typewriters can be purchased for a nominal fee at garage sales, or from the Business Education Office in large school districts, or from used office equipment companies and the like.

4. Children can make individual word banks for Petunia. Use a recipe file box and 3 × 5 cards. Have several section tabs, such as: "Words Petunia Knows," "Words Petunia Needs to Work On," "Words Petunia Would Like to Know."

Students can print the word on the 3×5 cards and, when they know it, they can use the other side to spell the word, to write a sentence using the word, to make a picture of the word, and so on. Also, ABC tabs can provide another way for students to begin to build their word banks, and to begin to learn alphabetical order, which leads to working with the dictionary.

Students can play word games using the word bank cards, such as "Petunia is thinking of a word that begins with the letter ____ and it _____." Or, "I'm thinking of a word that begins like bird, and _____." Since each student's word bank can be different, (for example, "Words Petunia Would Like to Know") many new words are introduced informally by the students.

5. Be sure to tuck some other good books about Petunia into this box, such as *Petunia Beware, Petunia's Treasure, Petunia Takes a Trip,* and *Petunia and the Song.* Let's not forget the *Veronica* series by the same author, such as *Our Veronica Goes to Petunia's Farm, Lonely Veronica,* and *Veronica.* These books make children giggle and grin and send out the message that reading is fun.

BOOK:

Amelia Bedelia
by Peggy Parish. Illustrations by Fritz Siebel.
New York: Harper & Row, 1963.

MEET AMELIA BEDELIA

1. Children will get the giggles from this book because Amelia Bedelia does *exactly* as the words in a note command, or she follows directions *exactly* as she hears the words. We say that she takes things "literally." Amelia Bedelia does not "read between the lines," nor does she try to "make sense" of what someone tells her to do. She just does it as she hears it.

2. One reason that children like these stories so much is that *they* bring understanding to the words and put them in context, where Amelia Bedelia does not. Therefore, reading or listening to the story makes children feel good. They are in a position of knowing more than she does. If the story were a movie, it would be called "slapstick" humor.

Children love to "talk to" Amelia Bedelia and to explain things to her in their own words, so the books (there are several in a series) call for puppet making. Each child can make an Amelia Bedelia puppet.

Trace Amelia Bedelia. A student volunteer can lie flat on a double piece of brown butcher paper, and one or two others can trace around the outline of the child's body. It is good eye-hand coordination practice to cut out the outline of the shape. Then, have children work in small groups—one group can cut out construction paper shapes for her face and paste them on, another group can make her construction paper dress, another can make an apron and shoes, another can make her construction paper hat and hair. (Use crayons minimally.) Everyone can have a turn to work on the large figure. Then, staple around the edges and gently stuff with small paper pieces. (Repaste where necessary.) We now have an Amelia Bedelia for a quiet area where children can go and sit with her (she is as big as they are) and read to her and explain things to her. Some children will want to show her things in the room, special building blocks, how to make towers, and so on. They will even have her sit on their laps and guide her hand. It is good for children to be able to instruct her informally during free time; some have an amazing amount of patience for this.

3. Look at the directions that are listed on the classroom chalkboard. How would Amelia Bedelia carry them out?

4. Students can go through magazines and cut out advertisements and slogans about soap, traveling on airlines, fast food and the like that might be very confusing to Amelia Bedelia. Put them in a magazine scrapbook for her so that she can "read" it in her spare time. Children and the puppets can help her.

KITCHEN ILLUSTRATIONS

1. Spoons. Long ago, the first spoons were made of wood. Later, iron and silver spoons were made. If a family had enough money, a silver spoon was given to a new baby at christening time. That's where we get the saying, "He was born with a silver spoon in his mouth." Try explaining that one to Amelia Bedelia.

2. Have children draw Amelia Bedelia's example of a toothpick. Before there were toothpicks, some people used to pick their teeth with the sharp end of the knife. What kind of a pick will Amelia Bedelia draw? (For younger children, a demonstration of things that we use to pick up objects might be helpful, such as tongs, tweezers, and so on.)

3. Sometimes at holiday dinners or special parties, people make a "toast" (short speech) and clink glasses with the person next to them. Write or draw an illustration of Amelia Bedelia's "toast to good health!"

4. Draw a cartoon picture of Amelia Bedelia with a cartoon bubble overhead showing just what she is thinking when she hears us say, "Amelia Bedelia is a good egg!"

5. Have children come up with their own kitchen sayings that could confuse Amelia Bedelia.

COOKING WITH AMELIA BEDELIA

1. Cooking with young children affords many opportunities for doing math and for children to learn that math is a useful and necessary tool for measuring (liquid and dry), classifying, timing, and controlling temperature.

2. Look through several cookbooks for "confusing directions" such as: "add a pinch of salt," or "a drop of oil," or a recipe that calls for "tail onions," and so on. There are plenty of examples in cookbooks.

3. To follow through on this, some children might want to make a simplified picture cookbook for Amelia Bedelia to follow so that she does not become confused. Divide the page in half. On one side, draw an illustration as she would do it, and on the other side, draw or write the correct interpretation. Cookbooks have plenty of really good examples, such as:

Bake until bread leaves the side of the pan.

Place dough in a greased bowl and turn once.

Strain and cool.

Beat butter until soft.

Dry with a paper towel or drain.

Roast until done.

4. One of Amelia Bedelia's specialties is lemon meringue pie, and that's not easy! How many children have ever had the experience at home of watching someone make meringue? Look up the recipe for meringue in a cookbook. Have the children make it, and drop it onto lemon cookies or lemon pudding.

5. For a real treat, make "pigs in blankets" for a party snack (frankfurter fried in an electric fry pan, and hot dog roll, with a "dash" of mustard or ketchup). How would Amelia Bedelia make them?

6. Have other books available for children to read that are in this series, such as *Amelia Bedelia and the Surprise Shower,* and *Come Back, Amelia Bedelia.*

BOOK:

Mr. and Mrs. Pig's Evening Out
by Mary Rayner. Baltimore: An Aladdin Book,
Atheneum, 1976.

REVIEW OF "THE THREE LITTLE PIGS"

1. Review with the children, or reread "The Three Little Pigs" because this book is a spinoff or a "spoof" of that story.

2. Review of the story shows, again, the use of the number three in tales. There were three pigs and three tries by the wolf to huff and puff and blow the house in. Are there any other threes in this book?

3. In folk literature, there are many tales from different lands that deal with "blowing the house down." These tales have been handed down by the storyteller before the stories were recorded in print. In some cultures, for example, the three little pigs are three little rabbits, and the wolf is a fox.

4. "Be prepared to be out in the world" is one message of this story. In some versions, the parents tell the three rabbits how to build their house so they will be safe from harm; and, in an effort to establish themselves as knowing just as much as adults do (a familiar theme in folktales), the two oldest rabbits build their house as they want it, not as they were advised. They meet with disaster when the fox arrives. The youngest child obeys (again a familiar theme in folktales) and builds the house exactly as the parents teach, and is a survivor when the fox comes.

Discuss this with children. Why is it that we will take advice from some people but not from others? Why is it that some children will take the advice of older people but other children want to do things their way? What is meant when we say, "Some people have to learn the hard way!" What is the "magic key" here for taking suggestions and yet trying out new things?

AN EVENING OUT FOR THE PIGS

1. Children take delight in this turned-around tale, where the pigs are established in a safe home with their piglets. (Can children predict the number of children? In this case, we can't, and that is why we find the tales so delightful. Just when we think we have them figured out, something is changed.)

2. List the piglet names in alphabetical order.

3. What is the first reaction of the piglets when they learn that they will have a baby sitter from the agency? What does "agency" mean? (This baby sitter has filled out an application, given references, been approved,....)

4. Surprise! The suspense and tension begin when Mrs. Pig opens the door for the baby sitter. (Children will squeal with delight!)

5. Describe the way the piglets slept in the bunk beds exactly as Mrs. Pig described the pattern.

6. In this updated tale that uses "The Three Little Pigs" as a basis for the humor, have the children compare the two stories. Do they think the children were brave? Do they think that the wolf got what she deserved?

7. Discuss baby sitters. Should we have a number to call where the sitter (or the children) can reach the parents? What should we know about the baby sitter? What information should the baby sitter know about us? (Favorite bedtime story, favorite late night snack, bed time,....)

8. Read *Mrs. Pig's Bulk Buy* by M. Raynor. Also, read *Garth Pig and the Ice Cream Lady.*

TAKING A LOOK AT REAL PIGS

1. Pigs are really very intelligent animals. Many years ago, in some countries, they were used to help hunters, much as we use dogs today, because of their very keen sense of smell. Hunting dogs replaced hunting pigs.

2. In the past, pigs were trained as circus animals. Just like dogs, they can do tricks such as jumping through a hoop, dance, pull or push a cart. They can

even figure out how to do things that dogs don't do, such as lifting the bolt and getting out of their cages. Illustrate a circus pig, in costume, performing a trick.

3. Pigs are good natured. If treated kindly, they can become nice pets. Remember Wilbur, in *Charlotte's Web?* Can we think of any other stories where pigs are pets?

4. Domestic pigs are raised and cared for and entered in county and state fairs for prizes (best coloring, best form, best spots, all white,...). Perhaps the children living in rural areas know more about pigs that they can share. More information is available from the local Farm Bureau.

5. Pigs in the laboratory. The heart of the pig is amazing in its similarity to the human heart, and many surgeons who perform heart operations on humans have used valves from the pig's heart.

6. A football is sometimes called a "pigskin." That's because at one time the pig's strong bladder was filled with water, closed, and used as a ball for tossing.

7. Find out more about this misunderstood barnyard animal. Have a "Let's Hear It for the Barnyard Pig!" class report, and have each person contribute a bit of information on pigs.

BOOK:

I Can Read with My Eyes Shut
by Dr. Seuss. New York: Beginner Books, A
Division of Random House, 1978.

THE CAT IN THE HAT CAN READ

1. Go through the book page by page to enjoy the rhyme and the concepts presented.

2. Glue an assortment of 9×12 pieces of cellophane on oaktag frames. Then, one by one, lay them over the pages of the book and "read in red, read in blue, read in pickle color too."

3. Language development. If green is referred to as "pickle color," what can we call red, orange, yellow, blue, violet? Make up similar names for these colors and use the cellophane frames in number two.

4. Make several circular rings, such as the one on page 3, print the ABCs on one ring, print numerals on another ring, and print words or phrases on another ring. Have the children try to read them without moving them or their position (they will have to try to read sideways and upside down).

5. Try reading first with the left eye, and then with the right eye. Is there any difference? Can we really read with both eyes shut? Why not?

6. For younger children, make a big tall hat shape with red and white horizontal stripes. On the red stripes list words we know, and on the white stripes list the words we're working on. Then, make the cat's umbrella shape and list three words from the book that are new to us that we would like to learn (meaning and spelling). The Cat in the Hat is really a teacher, isn't he?

HAVING FUN WITH THE BOOK

1. One picture shows "bees" on the numeral "threes." Using this rhyming pattern, what would be on top of the numeral one? two? four? five through ten? On a heavy paper strip, have children draw the numerals one through five on one side, and six through ten on the other side. Then, color the rhyming picture of the item on top, just like bees on threes. Using this method might help some children in numeral identification and rote counting.

2. Foo-Foo the Snoo is dressed all in blue. Make another designer outfit for Foo-Foo. Perhaps wallpaper samples will help.

3. Design a three-dimensional musical instrument for the Cat in the Hat using cardboard boxes, string, cylinders, gadgets for twisting and turning, and so on. Where will the music come out? Have an accompanying rhythm band with cymbals, rhythm sticks, bells, drum, sandpaper blocks, and make up your own version of the Cat in the Hat Dance.

4. Let's take a vote. What is the funniest part of this book? Graph the results.

READING

1. On the double-page spread just before the last page, how many picture signs can the children "read?"

2. Children can "read" pictures before they come to school. Many are wearing T-shirts that display a message, and they can read it in that context. They are picking up visual/verbal clues from TV and from their own environment. Have students go through the local Sunday newspaper and cut out ads that show the logos or signs for familiar stores.

3. Make traffic lights. Children can use long paper strips for the light. Cut out three circles—red, yellow, green. What does each one mean? Where are they to be pasted on the traffic signal light? (This can be done in two lessons so that children get an opportunity to observe the traffic light after school.) We can all "read" the message which the brightest color is giving out. What other traffic light signals are there for turning and for pedestrians?

4. Arrange a field trip to the local library. Call in advance so the librarian can arrange for a tour, a story, filmstrip, or movie. Also, send a copy of the

children's names to the children's librarian so that she can have library cards ready for them. They can take the cards home and arrange for a family member to take them back for a book (to look for some of those books that the Cat in the Hat mentioned). Encourage parents to take children to the library via a newsletter.

5. There are many, many more books by Dr. Seuss that children enjoy. Have a "Cat in the Hat Book Celebration Week" and read lots of them. Students can make very tall Cat in the Hat (red and white striped) bookmarks. On one side, keep track of the stories that were read for this special week.

**REPRODUCIBLE ACTIVITY PAGES
FOR
HUMOROUS BOOKS**

Name _____   Date _____

Pretend that you just finished reading your favorite book to date, and you can't wait to tell your best friend about it, so you will have to make a phone call to tell all about it.

Title: _____

Author: _____

1. "Hello _____.

This is _____ .
I just finished reading such a good book, I've got to tell you something about it!"

   It's a _____ story.

2. The story takes place in _____
_____

3. The main characters in the story are _____
_____
_____
_____

4. And the problem is that _____
_____
_____

5. Oh! One part that I really liked was when
_____
_____
_____

6. I'm not going to give away the ending but I will tell you this much.
_____
_____
_____

Use the back to write more about this good book. Draw a picture to go along with number 2, 3, 4, or 5.

BOOKMARKS FOR CHILDREN'S BOOK WEEK

Children's Book Week is always in November. This rabbit has made a bookmark for you to use. Color it, and cut it out. Use it to keep track of your place when you are reading or looking through a book. Also, design your very own bookmark.

Name:

read   read
read   read
read   read
read   read
read   read
read   read
read   read
read   read
read   read
read   read
read   read
read   read
read   read
read   read
read   read
read
read
read
read
read
read
read

CHILDREN'S BOOK WEEK
November

Name:

Name _____ Date _____

This lion is roaring with good news about a very funny book that he read. Write about the book on the lines below.

Title _____

_____

_____

Author _____

_____

_____

_____

_____

_____

_____

_____

_____

_____

_____

_____

_____

_____

_____

_____

_____

THE EVER-POPPING POPCORN POPPER

We had a popcorn popper in our classroom
and it made lots and lots of popcorn
for us! Let me tell you about it.

Popcorn Recipe

Words to describe the smells

Words to describe the sounds

This is my story about the ever-popping popcorn popper that wouldn't stop popping!

(over)

READING IS A SALAD BAR

Try a little taste of everything for a balanced reading diet. Color in each area on the plate as you read a book from that category. On the back of this sheet list the book title along with a sentence that sums up the story. Learn to enjoy all kinds of stories!

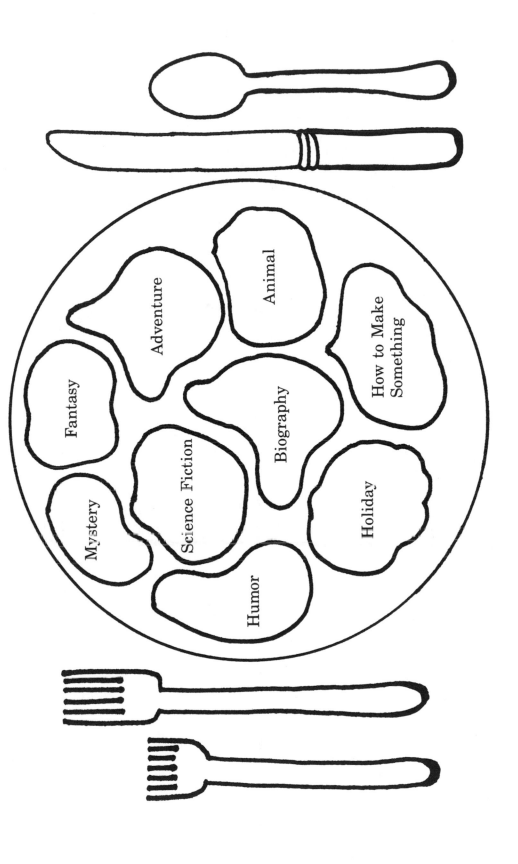

THE FUNNY BUSINESS

Sam and Jo Funny have been in business for many years. They laugh eight hours a day. If you like to be happy, and enjoy laughing, fill out the application below.

Draw an illustration to go with the words.

Ho
Ho
Ho

Ha
Ha
Ha
Ha

Draw the Funny Business Logo here ⟶

It's raining cats and dogs!

"Lettuce, pickles; hold the onion."

Mike has on his running shoes.

Pass the pizza, please.

The dog is crying.

Answer the telephone.

Name _____   Date _____

You can write a humorous ending to this story starter. After all, B.J. and T.J. don't want to fight over a simple thing like a delicious jar of honey!

B.J. Bear and T.J. Bear are the best of friends. At the County Fair they both won the same jar of honey, or did they? When the announcer called out, "And the winner is #4765219, both B.J. and T.J. jumped up onto the stage with the winning tickets. Just then, the wind blew them out of their hands and the tickets were never seen again.

Write a humorous middle and ending to this story. Draw an illustration of the funniest part on the back of this page.

Some helpful words are:
sticky   stuck   slipped   divide   spill   crash

Name _____   Date _____

MAKING A BOOK JACKET   **6–8**

A book jacket is the colorful paper covering on a book. Take a good look at many book jackets to get an idea of what they contain. Mackerel the Cat wore a big jacket today so that you could make a book jacket just for him. Use colored pencils and crayons, and write and draw on his jacket.

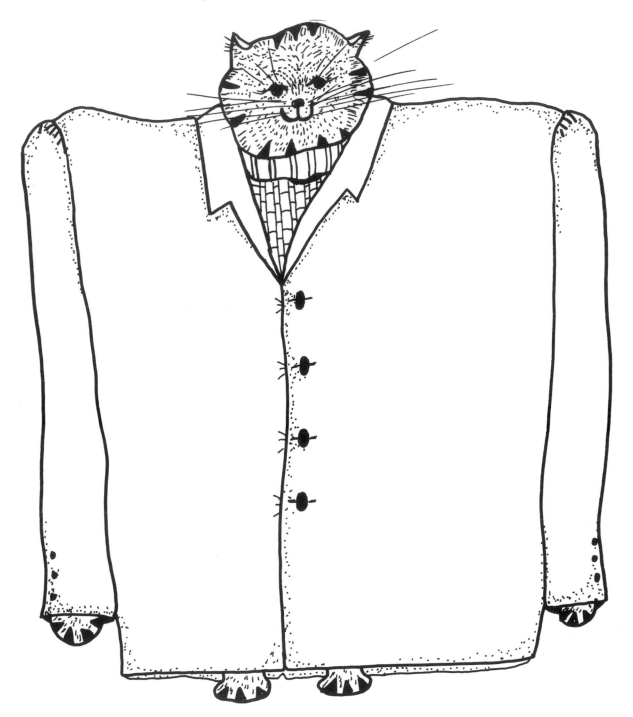

After making Mackerel's book jacket, try making a real book jacket for a book in your room that has no jacket.

Name _____   Date _____

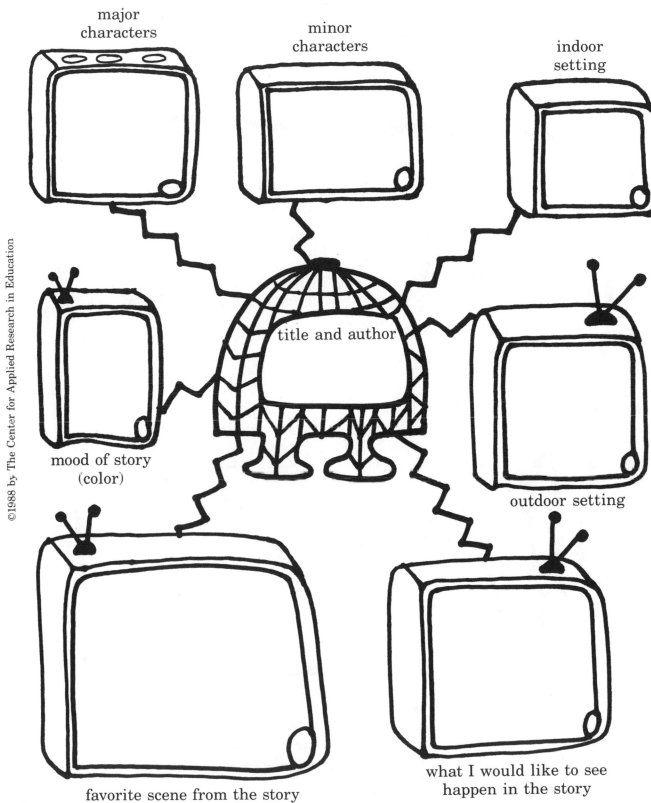

major characters

minor characters

indoor setting

mood of story (color)

title and author

outdoor setting

favorite scene from the story

what I would like to see happen in the story

AN ELEPHANT STARTER STORY

This *adventure* story is started for you. This elephant has wandered away from the circus and finds himself in a shopping mall. He decides to go inside. What adventures await him as he visits the china shop, the flower shop, the hat store, and finally the stuffed toy store? Write your story on the elephant and read it to the class just like a reporter on the six o'clock local news show!

Title:

"Oh! I must be seeing things!" exclaimed the store clerk at the new shopping mall called _____ _____. "I thought I just saw a huge elephant looking in the window." Just then there was a loud BOOM! _____ _____ _____ _____ _____

Author:

Monsters, Ogres, and Scary Things

READ AT
YOUR
OWN RISK

BOOK:

Wobble, the Witch Cat
by Mary Calhoun. Illustrated by
Roger Duvoisin. New York:
William Morrow & Co., 1958.

MAGGIE THE WITCH

1. Maggie the witch is described as "fat," and a "chuckling old lady with short, gray hair." What other descriptive words do we have about Maggie? Read just the descriptive words and have students draw her, concentrating on them.

2. Vocabulary: Maggie and her cat, Wobble, live in a "teetery" little house. Students can show us with their bodies what "teetery" means to them. (Example: Climb the teetery stairs.)

3. Wobble is grumpy and cross, but he wasn't always that way. What is it that is making him so fearful? Discussion: When students are fearful what are their reactions; are they sometimes grumpy and cross? Should we consider being grumpy and cross as signs of being fearful? Let's talk about it.

4. Find a recipe in the cookbook for simple sugar cookies and make them, using the measuring and timing as a math lesson. Make a big experience chart and label it "Maggie's Magic Wish Cookies" and record, sequentially, what the class did. (This is good for recall of information in logical order.) For some children, this will be the first time they have seen cookies baked from beginning to end. If there is not enough time to bake cookies, buy wafers or plain cookies and make a simple confectioners sugar and water frosting, using orange coloring. Spread this on the cookies, making them look like pumpkins. Decorate with raisins for eyes, nose, teeth. Have the children make a wish and eat the cookies.

HALLOWEEN

1. Halloween was brought to the United States by the Scots and Irish. For centuries, people of Europe celebrated two holidays at the same time—the mourning of the dead and the harvest of autumn. These sort of blended together into one celebration.

2. All Hallows Eve (Halloween) was a time for witches, ghosts, and spirits to roam about. People dressed up to scare them away, just as boys and girls now dress up just for fun and to "scare" people at Halloween. We also feast on lots of candy and other treats.

3. Orange and black are Halloween colors. Why? Because it's tradition. For centuries the orange has represented the harvest and the black has represented death.

4. It was believed long ago that if you were a witch, you might have an imp to help you, such as a bug. Perhaps that's why toy bugs and spiders and lizards are so popular at Halloween time to "scare" people. Buy an assortment of Halloween candy shapes—white ghosts, black cats—and graph them. Then enjoy eating them.

5. Witch comes from the Saxon "wica," which means "wise one." In ancient days, witches told fortunes, chanted, and mixed herbs together in big pots to be used as medicine. Use orange, black, and yellow at the easel this week for painting scary or friendly witches.

6. Bring in a large pumpkin and have children agree on the eyes, nose, mouth shape for carving. They can draw them on with a felt-tip pen. Carve the shapes with a knife (save the seeds for counting) and when dry, light the jack-o'-lantern with a flashlight or small electric candlestick. Sit around the lantern and listen to Halloween stories, or records.

The jack-o'-lantern is a symbol of Halloween that was brought to us from our European ancestors. In Ireland, children carve out potatoes and in Scotland, children carve out turnips. They light them with a candle on Halloween night so that they can see where they're going, and also scare away spooky creatures.

7. Dial-A-Witch. A witch gets many calls at Halloween to haunt houses and scare people. She's so busy that she has to have a telephone answering service. Have students record Maggie's taped message, such as, "I'm sorry, but Maggie is out haunting a house at Ghost Thrill Lane. Please leave your message at the sound of the scream."

WOBBLE AND HIS RELATIVES

1. Body movement. Children can stalk, grab, jump, pounce, and tumble like a playful kitten. At play, kittens are preparing for the real world just in case they have to catch their dinner.

2. Wobble is a tame or "domesticated" cat, which means that he can live in a house with people. Tame cats are related to the big cats such as the lions, tigers, and cheetahs. How many pictures of big cats can the children find in picture books? Would they scare Wobble?

3. Cats are rarely born singly; they are usually born in a litter (more than one) both domestically and in the wild. Where are Wobble's brothers and sisters? Were they all selected by a witch to become a witch cat? Write a letter from Wobble the Witch Cat, to Freddie the Farm Cat (his brother) and Wanda the Waitress Cat (his sister), and others that children can dream up. Children can set up correspondence boxes with letters From Wobble and letters To Wobble from these domesticated relatives and also From/To those in the wilds of Africa or at the zoo. This is a good opportunity for children to write to formulate questions, and to locate answers.

4. Torn paper cat. Using black construction paper, gently tear two rounded shapes for Wobble (one for the body and one for the head). Tear ear shapes and a tail. Glue them together or paste them down onto a gray, white, or orange

background. Using orange scraps, tear eye shapes and long whisker strips that can be curled around a pencil. Glue these onto the black cat. Now, children can tell the story of *Wobble the Witch Cat* and Maggie.

BOOK

Simon's Book
by Henrik Drescher. New York:
Lothrop, Lee & Shepard, 1983.

ABOUT THE BOOK

1. Story Starters. Each child can begin writing a story and deliberately stop at a thrilling point! Place all stories in "trick or treat" bags. Have each child select one at random to finish.

2. Have students collaborate on a monster book (authors and illustrators). One or two can write the story and one or two can illustrate it; or let the monster do it.

3. Notice the colorful endpapers at the beginning and ending of the book. Make a watercolor wash over a white 9 × 12 sheet of construction paper. When still runny, use a pen with India ink to create splashy looking endpapers for a book, as in the text.

4. Guide students to examine the borders around the pictures in this book. Have them include fancy borders to enclose their illustrations. Begin to take note of borders in a variety of picture books—some are flowers, some are designs, some are animals, some are intersecting lines, and so on. A study can be made of just borders. Students can create a variety of borders and put them around written reports.

SIMON'S MONSTER

1. Simon's monster was misunderstood. Discuss that word. He wasn't what he appeared to be. He was not scary, but friendly. Write the ending to *Simon's Book* from the monster's point of view.

2. Create a giant free-form monster shape and let the students decide how to paint it. Remember, it's gentle and will probably like pastel colors.

3. Students can make clay models of the monsters and create a friendly monster village with buildings and roads "paved with gold or silver." What does the monster flag look like?

4. Long ago in the 1800s in England, very scary books were written that were called "penny dreadfuls." They cost a penny, were written on very cheap

paper, were read, and thrown away. Simon's Monster will probably know all about "penny dreadfuls." With the help of the monster, students can write a "penny dreadful" on newsprint paper. Share these in class.

MORE MONSTERS

1. On three 9 × 12 pieces of white construction paper, draw interesting borders using felt-tip pens or crayons. Draw splotches of color at random. Paint over the sheet with a watercolor wash. Allow to dry. Then, students can print a story (using a felt-tip pen) on this most unusual background sheet.

2. Students can make monster puppets from large paper bags that fit over their heads. Have a friendly monster class meeting and each monster can introduce itself by telling its name, age, favorite food, favorite TV program, favorite magic trick, and so on.

3. On a sheet of paper, cut a little round hole that is not big enough for the monster to fit through. The story would be different, wouldn't it? Write the ending with this new twist.

4. Cut out monster shape feet from colorful construction paper, and have students use these to keep track of the monster books they read, listing author, title, and so on. These tracks can be put up all around the room, since monsters walk all over everything.

5. If Simon's monster works all night, what midnight snack would you leave for him? What kind of a thank-you note would he write back? What kind of a snack would he request for the next night?

6. Since this monster likes books, make a Monster Library card. What shape would it be? What would the name of the monster library be? What are some of the book titles that would be on the monster shelf?

BOOK:

Arthur's Loose Tooth
by Lillian Hoban. New York:
Harper & Row, 1985.

MEET ARTHUR AND VIOLET

1. This is "An I Can Read Book" that has large print and helpful pictures on each page. Read it aloud to very young children. Some six- or seven-year olds will feel comfortable reading it on their own.

2. This is a good story to record on cassette tape, so that children can listen and follow along with the text. Perhaps older children could record it in the school library for younger children to enjoy.

3. Arthur and Violet are two young chimpanzees who are having some fun with their baby sitter. Read the story aloud first so that children can enjoy it. Then talk about the action of the story as far as Arthur is concerned; what happened first, second, third?

4. Retell the story from the point of view of the baby sitter. Is she a pleasant baby sitter? What things do baby sitters need to know when they come to our home? (Bedtime and bedtime procedure, telephone number where parent or relative can be reached, food preferences, do's and don'ts, and so on.) Using stick puppets, have children role play the information that is necessary for the sitter.

In some areas of the country, there are "Baby Sitting Schools" that help older children to work with young children. They get a baby sitter's diploma too. Is there such a school in your area that is run by the Scouts or the YWCA or YMCA? Students could role play this at recess. (Example: A telephone number for them in case of a question or problem, how to pack a "goody bag" to take along filled with books, games, crafts, and so on.)

5. Have students compose a Want Ad for a baby sitter. They will need to include their own name or nickname, age, the names and ages of other children in the home, their favorite food, favorite hobby, pets, and any other information about themselves that they want the sitter to know. (Maybe this could really be used as helpful information for the next sitter.)

FEARS

1. Children can identify with Arthur's fear because it is real. Young children in grades K-2 are in the developmental stage when baby teeth are loose, teeth are missing, new teeth are coming in, and this is very important to them. Form a "Tooth Fairy Club" and make large tooth-shaped name cards for student's desks. Students can print the number on the card that represents lost teeth. Invite the school nurse or a dentist or dental hygienist to address the class about tooth care. Encourage children to ask questions.

2. Tooth Count. Have children count the number of teeth they now have on top and the number on the bottom. They can count silently from inside, using their tongues, but not fingers. A hand mirror is helpful too. Record the numbers and make comparisons. (Some students are very unhappy to be among the last to lose their teeth. Explain that the body operates in its own way and in its own good time. Besides, getting a second set of teeth a little later means "less wear and tear" on the teeth they will have for life.)

3. Violet is afraid of the dark but the "creepy crawlies" didn't try to get her when the baby sitter encouraged her to go outside to gather sticks for the s'mores treat. What helpful hints can children share about how this real fear can be overcome?

"I CAN READ"

1. Chimpanzee starts with "ch" which is a digraph—it makes up its own sound. Have students list as many words as they can that begin with the "ch"

(chimp) sound. Then, list or be on the lookout for words that end with the chimp sound. (The word "church" begins and ends with the sound.)

Other digraphs for students to be aware of as they read through storybooks are: "sh" (the quiet signal), "th" (the only time in school when it's ok to stick out your tongue) and "qu" (the "kw" sound, or quiet sound).

2. Students who are ready can practice manuscript printing using the words in the story. Find all of the names of people and copy them, then all of the names of places, and all of the names of things. These are called "nouns"—names of persons, places, things.

3. Double vowels. Go through the book and find all of the words that have double vowels (vowels side by side). (Examples: Violet, treat, Captain Fearless.) Which vowel do we often hear when two appear together? Look for double vowel words in the newspaper.

4. Silent Reading. "A student learns to read by reading," is a familiar phrase. Build a silent reading time into your day even if it is only one day per week (preferably two or three times per week). For this, establish with the children that they can take any book with them from an assortment in the book area, but they must stay with it during the whole time, which is five minutes. It is important in the beginning not to have children jumping up and changing their book every few seconds; they will have to stay with their choice for five minutes. As they begin to "read" the pictures or some words or the story, the time can be gradually lengthened. Keep changing the books. Children like to bring their own in as well.

BOOK:

The Very Worst Monster
by Pat Hutchins. New York:
Greenwillow Books, 1985.

ABOUT THE BOOK

1. After reading the book aloud, go through and have students retell the story using pictures only.

2. Describe a monster—ears, eyes, nose, teeth, hands, feet, hair, body. Tear a monster shape from a very large sheet of green paper, using many ridges and squiggly lines. Using paint or a felt-tip pen, add the features that were carefully observed when we read the book.

3. Make up some monster growls to teach Billy. Hazel can learn them too. Have them "sing" them together.

4. "Worst Monster Baby in the World" Competition Time. Make grotesque baby monster puppets on a craggy stick. Interview the parent monsters and have

them tell the terrible things their monster does around the house that they're so proud of.

5. Create a prize that would be fitting for a "Worst Monster Competition."

FUN WITH MONSTERS

1. Are little monsters always bad? We have heard people say, "My little brother (sister) is a monster!" but they don't really mean it. Students can make monster headbands, and then behave like the sweetest monster in the world.

2. Create a School for Monsters. What would Billy and Hazel have to be taught? Write everything in squiggly lines.

3. These monsters are very well dressed. Make sketches of designer monster clothing, such as designer jeans, designer sweaters, flowered dresses, hats, leg warmers, and the like. These can be collected and put in a Monster mail-order catalog. What will the cover look like? What will it be called? What are the prices?

4. Notice that the monsters wear clothing, but they are not wearing shoes. Students can work in teams of shoe salespersons. They can design a monster shoe that is so comfortable, so magical, so unusual, that all of the monsters will be growling for a pair of these shoes. They won't be able to make them fast enough, and will become as rich as a monster.

5. Have a monster dress up corner. Use old Halloween costumes, wigs, false noses, old hats, construction paper moustaches, old boots, and the like.

MORE FUN WITH MONSTERS

1. The class can make a Monster Family Album, showing not only Hazel and Billy and their parents but also pictures of two sets of grandparents, aunts and uncles, and other relatives at family monster events like Monster Christmas, Monster Picnic Day, Monster Halloween Party, and so on.

2. Students can make a newspaper ad for a baby sitter for Monster Billy and Monster Hazel. List the qualifications for a monster baby sitter.

Have students make out a baby sitting report on Billy and Hazel for the night that they were selected to baby sit with them. (Remember how they like to swing from the curtains, scare people, and so on.)

3. Monster School. Billy and Hazel like to go to Monster School to learn more about monsters. They will learn about Big Foot, reportedly living in the United States and Canada. It's hairy, smelly, and ten feet tall. What else can we find out about Big Foot?

The Loch Ness Monster or "Nessie" has been reported floating in Loch (Lake) Ness in Scotland. It's a freshwater lake, about 800 feet deep. The monster reportedly has a long neck and a small head. Hazel and Billy are interested in knowing more about this particular monster. Find information at the library.

Dragons are especially popular with Hazel. The dragon is a symbol of good luck in eastern countries (Japan, China), and a symbol of evil in western countries (Europe, the United States). The Chinese believed that ground up bones and ground up teeth of a dragon placed in hot water and boiled to make a tea, would cure anything. What other information can we find about dragons? Write it on dragon-shaped paper for Hazel.

4. Hazel wants to ride on a unicorn and bring back its horn, grind it up and make it into a monster drink for her aunt who is ill. Where can we write to a unicorn, much less ask it for a horn? Hazel gets what she wants, and we have to at least make the attempt. Start thinking and planning.

BOOK:

There's a Nightmare in My Closet
by Mercer Mayer. New York: Dial Press, 1968.

HOW TO MAKE FRIENDS WITH A NIGHTMARE

1. In this book, the boy "confronted" his nightmare and that took courage. Explain the word, "confront." Students can discuss a nightmare that they know. Draw or write about this nightmare in an effort to help confront it.

2. We have rules for many things, such as "What to Do in Case of Fire," and "What to Do If We Get Lost in the Shopping Mall," or "What to Do If We Spill Paint." Let's make a list of rules entitled "What to Do in Case of a Nightmare." This discussion may be very useful for helping a younger brother or sister, too.

3. Have every child make a nightmare puppet, and have the puppets scare the nightmare.

4. Have the children create a large nightmare from an old bedsheet. From felt or cloth material, glue on facial features. Prop the nightmare in the corner, with an "I Am Afraid of＿＿＿＿" sign (some examples are "school," "school bus," "losing my lunch or lunch money"). Make them close to the real fears that children experience. Talk them through to help the nightmare alleviate his fears. Then, have the children tell something that the nightmare told them it is afraid of, and talk it through. One day the nightmare could just disappear because it is no longer afraid; or, it could change from ghostly white to a nightmare made of bright, sunny striped, flowered or plaid material because it no longer enjoys being scared, and wants to be seen. The children have helped it to overcome those old fears. Use it for creative play period, or prop it up in a cozy reading area and let it enjoy good books along with everyone else.

5. What would a nightmare like to eat and drink? Leave some food on a plate for it so that it will eat it and feel good, and stay at school all night and not roam around. (Make sure the food is gone the next day.)

NIGHTMARES = NIGHT GOBLIN, FROM OLD ENGLISH

1. "Things that go bump in the night." There are many tales about night-mares and goblins that have been around for a long time. They are nothing new. There is an old Cornish prayer that goes like this: "From ghoulies and ghosties and long-leggety beasties and things that go bump in the night, Good Lord, deliver us."

2. On white paper cut in the shape of a ghost, write a letter to a nightmare. Find out where it lives, and what it does when it is not scaring people. Find out if there is a School for Nightmares; where it goes to receive career training. Ask for additional information too.

3. Job Qualifications. Write a Want Ad for a Nightmare. Specify the exact area to be haunted, times, skills necessary, hoots and screeches required, and salary. Post all of the Want Ads on a small bulletin board, and have class members respond to the ads. The person who wrote the Want Ad can decide who will be selected for an interview, and who will be offered the job.

4. Paint a nightmare. On 9 × 12 white paper, using white crayon only, create a nightmare. Then, use a watercolor wash over the entire page (any color) and the nightmare will appear.

5. What does a nightmare find boring? Make a large, gray construction paper ghost shape. This is the nightmare's stationery. Together with the students, compose a letter from the nightmare to the class explaining a typical, boring night. Make another large, gray construction paper ghost shape to put right next to the first one. On this one, have the students paint big, red dots. Have students write a letter on this stationery explaining what gives the nightmare goose bumps.

DAYDREAMS

1. If a nightmare involves scary thoughts that come in the night, then daydreams could be nice thoughts that come in the day. Have students make a list of pleasant words about people (friendly, helpful . . .), pets, nature, school. Create a pleasant daydream.

2. Make a set of glasses with colored cellophane lenses and oaktag frames. Have the children listen to music or a story with the headphones on, using first the yellow glasses, then blue, red, pink, purple, green, and so on. How do the different colors make us feel?

3. A bulletin board to make your dreams come true. On colorful pieces of paper cut in the shape of a star, have everyone write down a school daydream. Place the stars three-quarters of the way up from the bottom, on a bulletin board that has been covered with rainbow-colored wrapping paper. On a dark sheet of construction paper, have children trace around their hands, put initials on them, and cut them out. Place these hand cutouts close to the bottom of the bulletin board, under the stars, as though they are reaching. Think of a catchy title, and

have the children print it at the top of the board. Each day, work to make these school daydreams come true and as they do, connect a hand to the appropriate star with a piece of yarn.

BOOK:

What's Under My Bed?
by James Stevenson. New York:
Greenwillow Books, 1983.

ALL ABOUT BEDS

1. Have students write down anything they can think of about beds on a little bed-shaped sheet of paper entitled, "Things I Know About Beds." (Perhaps working with a partner would be helpful.)

2. Have students look for pictures of different types of beds in magazines, newspaper ads, catalogs. Look for pictures of the following types of beds, and cut them out: crib, cradle, brass, bunkbed, roll-out, double, queen, king, waterbed, and other. Make a booklet and paste them inside in alphabetical order. Students can pick their favorites. Then, "shop" in the catalogs, newspapers, magazines, for mattresses, sheets, pillowcases, pillows, comforters or quilts or bedspreads. Cut out the bedclothing and paste it on one page. (Make comparisons in small groups. Older children can do cost comparisons for math.)

Many of the sheets/pillowcases are interesting for boys and girls because they have their favorite characters on them. Write a story about the boy or girl who could not wait to get into bed at night because the characters from the sheets came to life.

3. Historical Facts About Beds. From colonial days we have the saying, "Sleep tight, don't let the bedbugs bite!" People say this cheerily as a goodnight greeting. What does it mean? At one time, people did not have box springs and mattresses. They slept in four-poster beds that had boards connecting them in a rectangular shape. Then they strung ropes across the boards from side to side, and tightened them. When the ropes began to stretch and sag, it was time to tighten them up again, or "sleep tight." Instead of mattresses as we know them today, people stuffed straw into big sheets of material and sewed them up. Often, the straw was filled with bugs that just might slip through and bite the sleeper. That's where the other part of the saying, "don't let the bedbugs bite" comes from.

Wayside Inns. In colonial days there were no modern motels, hotels, or campgrounds and campers that children enjoy today. In fact, ladies and children did not travel much at all because it was unsafe. The men who did travel stayed with friends or at an Inn that had beds for men only. In fact, the beds were rented out by the space—sometimes there were five men to a bed. If you went to bed early, you got a space on the end. If you were the fifth one in bed, you got a space in the middle (if you could find it).

Older students can write a story from the point of view of the bed in the wayside inn. Were the people heavy? Did they snore? Who were these people? Where were they going? Were the horses noisy outside? Were some nights busier and noisier than others?

BEDTIME

1. Why is bedtime often a bad time for youngsters? Students can pretend to be a famous "Bedtime Expert," and give advice about good bedtime habits. (Students can use puppets or the taped interview approach.)

2. Bedtime Snacks—For or Against. Conduct an opinion poll. Then, do some library research and find information on the subject. Do some foods really give us nightmares? Do some really help us to go to sleep? (Example: We know that warm milk releases tryptophane, a chemical that relaxes people.) Maybe a letter to a nutritionist would be helpful here.

3. Become an inventor. Construct a different bed of the future that will fold up during the day and be used as a functional item, other than a chair.

NOISES UNDER THE BED

1. List all of the possible things that really could be making noise under the bed (mouse, cat, register blowing air, and so on).

2. The last page in the book is done with cartoon bubbles for conversation. Rewrite the dialogue in the bubbles. Have everyone say something—even the dog.

3. Students can make a sound tape of night noises and see if classmates can identify them. Turn out the lights and play the tape again. Does this make them sound even more scary?

4. Make up riddles about the night. Use the four-line format, such as I am _____, I _____, I _____, What am I?

5. Have children vote for their favorite bedtime story in three different categories. Children can record their favorite bedtime stories and these can be used during rest time.

6. Why do we have bedrooms? Early settlers all lived in one room, where they ate, slept, and worked. Would children feel better about going to bed if we all lived in one room, or if we all slept in one room?

BOOK:

Zarelda's Ogre
by Tomi Ungerer. New York:
Harper & Row, 1967.

ABOUT THE BOOK

1. In folk tales, ogres, giants, and monsters are usually very large, bois-terous, and overpowering, but a little short of brains and can be easily persuaded when an appeal is made to their greed. Does greed enter into the story when the hungry ogre smells Zarelda's food cooking?

2. Using the description on the first page of the text, have children outline large ogres on long sheets of butcher paper. Color or paint them in according to the formula given: sharp teeth, bristling beard, big nose, and so on.

3. Have children learn the chants and recite them. There is one theory that the storytellers used to sing their tales. This was long before they were written down, and some have suggested that the chants and rhyming parts are still a part of the singing storyteller.

4. Open the book to the picture of Zarelda and her father on the farm. How many animals can be identified? Look carefully! Put them in alphabetical order.

5. What color is Zarelda's cat? Who else is famous for having a black cat? Long ago, witches were not only old hags, but young and old women, men, and even children. Often, they had a "familiar" (such as a cat) to perform tasks. They were not always mean, but some were kind and helpful. Could Zarelda possibly be a witch?

Where did Zarelda learn to cook—bake, braise, simmer, stew? What do all of those cooking words mean? Let's find out.

6. Since Zarelda has never seen or heard of an ogre, she is not afraid when one tumbles into her path. Discuss the term, "ignorance is bliss."

FOOD FIT FOR AN OGRE

1. Zarelda is quite a cook! What words could be used to describe the meal? Students can pretend to be the ogre, lick their lips at the end of the meal, and just let the words come out! Write them on a big paper bib.

2. Turn to the Menu Page for the typical midnight snack at the ogre's castle. Zarelda makes the food look very attractive. (Notice the shoes on the poultry, and the decorative fish, and the way she piles things up so that they make a design.) Everything is numbered for the reader's convenience.

Make little cards with the menu names on them, and have children make up even more names of fanciful midnight snacks.

Each student can become the ogre's official color photographer. Make a picture of a ravishing dish that is unbelievably colorful and appealing! (Even if children don't know the names, the dishes can still be colorful, piled high, and designed creatively.) Staple the "photos" together and label them for Zarelda. What will students call the book?

3. Imagine the smells at midnight. Have students take a deep breath, then another deep breath, and imagine that they are smelling the food cooking in the kitchen. Describe these smells musically with "tra-la-la" type descriptions with emphasis on different notes. (Examples: "It smelled absolutely TRA LA la-la-la LAH!", or "It smelled just like Tra LA la LA la LA," or "MMMMMMMMM-mmmmmmmm-la la la!" or YUMMMMM La Tum La Tum, Pum! Pum!")

4. Make out an invitation for Zarelda for her next ogre banquet. Perhaps it could be in the shape of a castle, or one of her food specialties.

THE BEAUTIFUL LADY OGRESSES
SHARE BEAUTY RECIPES

Since ogres know the secrets of the earth and the ways of plants, the ogresses have many beauty secrets. Print these recipes on 3×5 cards, and have students copy them and illustrate them. If students' families are campers, these will be especially helpful.

Set up Zarleda's Unisex Salon in the classroom. Props could be added for role playing. Some of the following recipes can be copied and even used:

- The inside of a lemon peel rubbed over teeth helps to whiten them.
- The inside of an orange peel rubbed over the skin relieves chapped hands.
- Cut a grapefruit in half; squeeze the juice into bath water for a refreshing soak.
- Cold tea, used as a final rinse after shampooing hair, adds a glossy look to brown hair.
- For a fresh feeling on a hot face, gently smooth a cucumber slice over the face. Rinse with cool water.
- A bit of baking soda on a moist toothbrush is a good tooth cleanser.
- Soak finger tips in a small bowl of soapy water for five minutes to clean grubby finger nails.

This could be made into a booklet. What suggestions do students have for a title? Do they have any other health or beauty suggestions?

BOOK:

Python's Party
by Brian Wildsmith. New York:
Franklin Watts, 1975.

PARTY INVITATIONS

1. Students can make a roster of names and addresses of the animals that attend Python's party. Put the names in alphabetical order and make up interesting names for the street, tree, cave, and so on.

2. Print an invitation to Python's party on the shape of an owl or other animal. Use rubber stamp/stamp pad set if available. What information will we need? (Place, time, date, type of party and name of host.)

3. Students can design a colorful, eye-catching party invitation that opens up in an unusual way (not like a book, but perhaps with three vertical folds, or diagonal folds). Print information with different colored felt-tip pens, or with letters cut from glossy magazines. The letters or words could be different colors. Make the invitation so exciting that people won't be able to wait to see what the party itself will be like.

4. If you could invite only three of the animals from the book to your party, which ones would you choose? Why them?

5. If we could choose one of these animals to take as our partner on a school field trip, which one would we choose? Why? Each student can make a black and white "snapshot" with this new partner.

PARTY TRICKS AND GAMES

1. Assign students to look though the book and take note of all of the tricks that were performed by the animals. Categorize them according to animals that used props, (hyena), and those whose tricks depended upon cooperation with other animals. How many are there in each category?

2. Each student can vote for the trick that was most enjoyable. Work in small groups with students who liked the same trick, and figure out a way to perform the trick. Give a demonstration to the other groups.

3. Have several books available on magic and magic party tricks, party games, and the like. Children can choose one to practice and master. Then, perform it at "Python's Pretend Party."

4. People associate circus clowns and animals with funny tricks. Make clown puppets or animal puppets from paper bags. Have the clown puppets interview the animal puppets just before and after their circus act. Remember

the old saying, "all the world loves a clown," so the animals will automatically be put in a very good mood by the clowns and will be very responsive.

5. Make a large cloth python from camouflage-print material, and stuff it with fiberfill. Put felt features on with glue.

Children can interview the animals inside and keep us posted as to what they're talking about.

Children can read books to the animals inside to keep them entertained.

Children can use the python as a pillow during free time for quiet reading— beware!

6. Operation Rescue! Suppose the elephant was out of town that day and did not come along in time to help the animals. Plan a rescue mission. Be careful! What supplies will we need? How can we trap a python?

PARTY TIME

1. Rewrite the story, only this time change the title to "Owl's Party," or "Zebra's Party." It would be an entirely different party. Does python show up— invited or uninvited?

2. We hold many parties throughout the year—parties as a family, and parties as a country. Use several outdated wall calendars to help list the special holiday parties that we celebrate as a nation. We can fill in our own family parties to complete the list.

3. Party Etiquette. Invite the python to a party, but first list all of the rules for party etiquette that we expect all of our guests to follow. That way the python won't be singled out, yet he'll know what behavior is expected.

4. Finally, plan a real class party with invitations, party etiquette, menu, party agenda. Enjoy the party. Later, write it up as the "social event of the year" and plan to submit it to the school newspaper for publication. If you don't have a school newspaper, make a newspaper. Use the front page of a local or national newspaper as a border, put plain paper in the middle, and have students print the information about the big event.

REPRODUCIBLE ACTIVITY SHEETS
FOR
MONSTERS, OGRES, AND
SCARY THINGS

Name ______________________ Date ______________________

MONSTER POURQUOI STORY

"Pourquoi" (poor kwa') is the French word for "why."

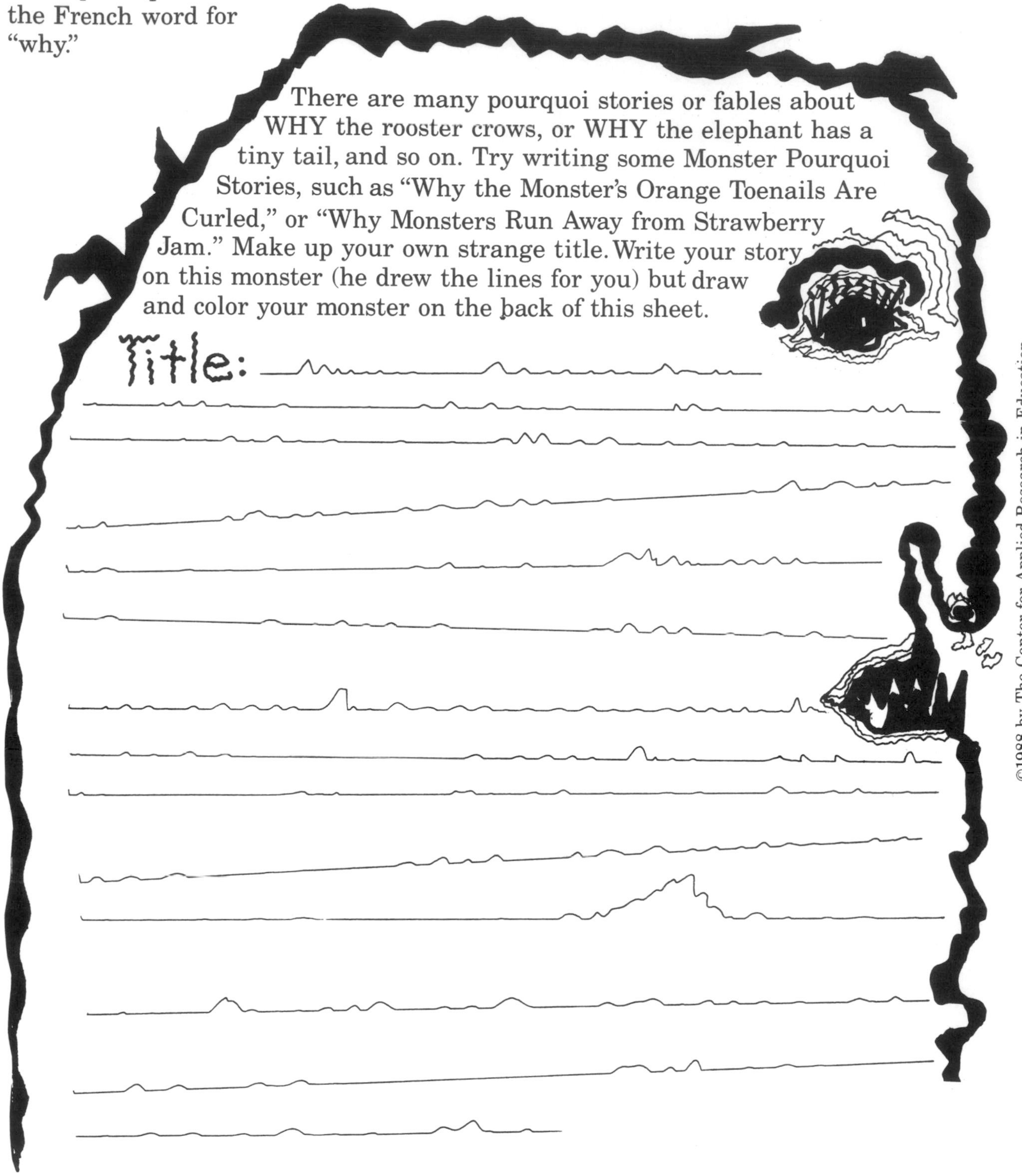

There are many pourquoi stories or fables about WHY the rooster crows, or WHY the elephant has a tiny tail, and so on. Try writing some Monster Pourquoi Stories, such as "Why the Monster's Orange Toenails Are Curled," or "Why Monsters Run Away from Strawberry Jam." Make up your own strange title. Write your story on this monster (he drew the lines for you) but draw and color your monster on the back of this sheet.

Title: ______________________

Name _____

Date _____

NO MORE RHINOCEROS? THAT'S PREPOSTEROUS!

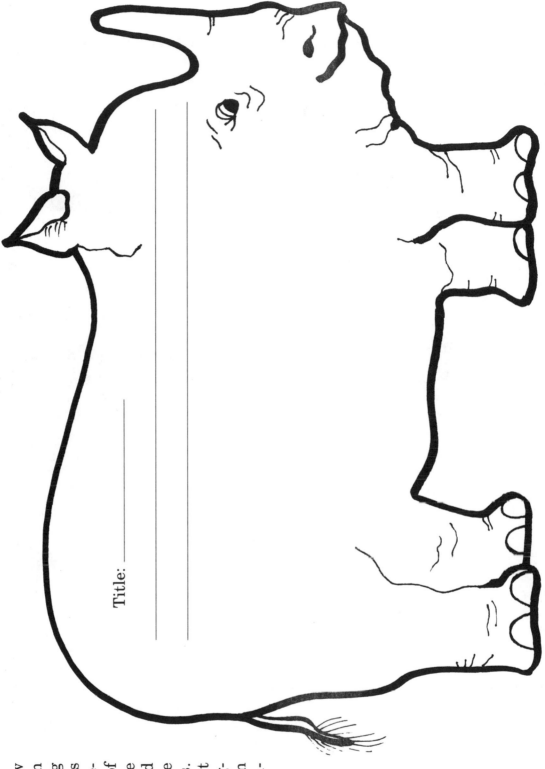

Title: _____

Did you know that the rhino is in danger of becoming extinct? For centuries some people have believed that the horn of this animal can be ground up and used as a medicine to cure all kinds of illness. Write a story about how this rhino "magically" saves his own species from becoming extinct.

HOW TO BE A GOOD HALLOWEEN WITCH

Ms. Good Witch has a new baby and also a full time career as a Halloween Witch. October is her busy season.

On the back, write five things that Baby Witch will have to learn from Mother, in order to become a good Halloween Witch!

Some words to use:

jump   black   orange   moon

broom

magic   "EEEEkkkk!!"

dark

Also, on the back, draw a picture of a baby witch when it grows up. Make it look very, very scary!

Since Ms. Witch is too busy to color this photograph, you can do it. She likes bright colors!

There is an old saying that "cats have nine lives." What does that mean?

Speaking of "nine", this Mother Cat came up with NINE SAFETY RULES FOR HALLOWEEN. Turn the page over, and see if you can list nine rules for a safe Halloween.

Discuss your NINE SAFETY RULES FOR HALLOWEEN with your friends. Compare lists. Maybe you can think of MORE than nine!

What special rules will the kitten have to learn in order to become a **SPOOKY** Halloween cat? Can you think of nine rules?

When you color the cats, make sure the kitten has nine stripes on its tail.

This very busy witch is advertising for a new cat to be her assistant. Help her to fill out the requirements. She likes colorful words.

The cat must be:

1. _____

2. _____

3. _____

The cat must have:

1. _____

2. _____

3. _____

Three things the cat must be willing to learn:

1. _____

2. _____

3. _____

Telephone Number of Busy Witch: _____

Address of Busy Witch: _____

Name _____   Date _____

After completing the following story chain, make a real story chain using hand-made paper chains and paper clips. Hang it in the classroom.

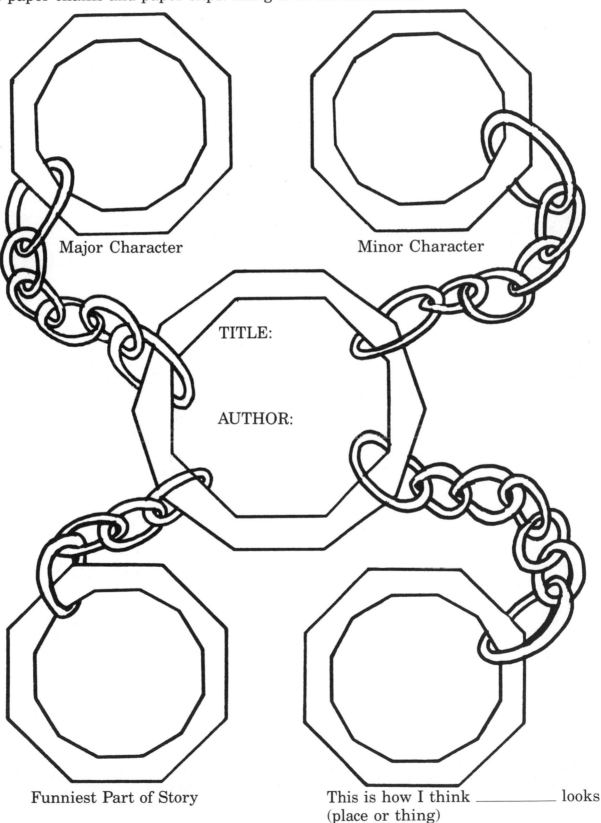

Major Character   Minor Character

TITLE:

AUTHOR:

Funniest Part of Story   This is how I think _____ looks
                                  (place or thing)

Name _____   Date _____

THEME AND PLOT

The *theme* is the message of the story. The *plot* is the plan for getting across the message.

Select a book: Title _____

Author/Illustrator _____

What is the *theme* or the "message" that the author is sending to you?

DEAR READER,
What I am trying to tell you is

What is the *plot*, or the plan of action, for sending this message to you?

1. At the beginning of the story...

2. Then, things began to happen, such as...

3. Just before the ending of the story...

4. At the end of the story...

DID YOU GET THE MESSAGE, or "theme"? SUM IT UP IN ONE SENTENCE:

_____

_____

Name _____

Date _____

THE MONSTROUS BUBBLE BATH

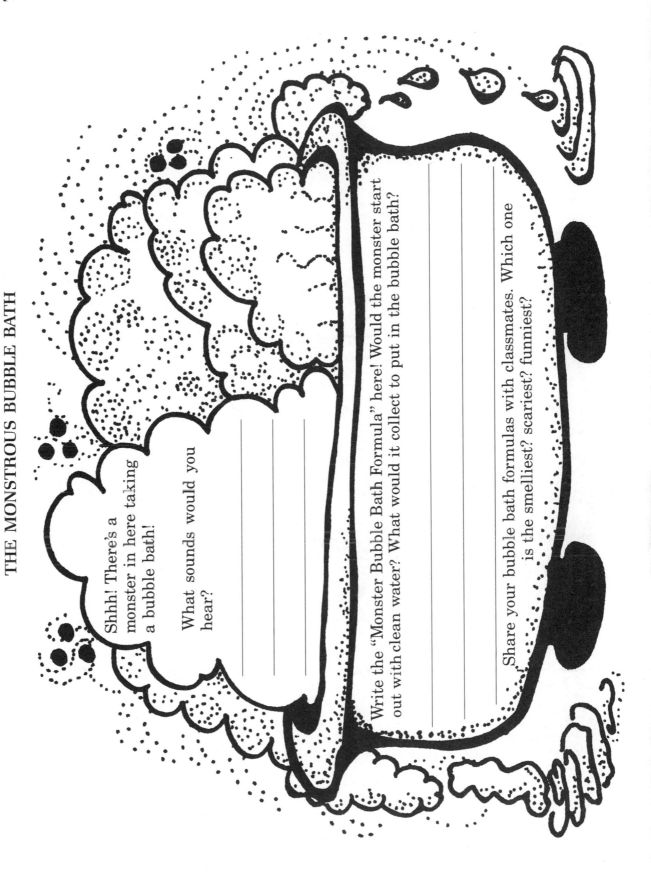

Shhh! There's a monster in here taking a bubble bath!

What sounds would you hear?

Write the "Monster Bubble Bath Formula" here! Would the monster start out with clean water? What would it collect to put in the bubble bath?

Share your bubble bath formulas with classmates. Which one is the smelliest? scariest? funniest?

Name _____   Date _____

These are the footprints of a five-legged monster! A scary exercise is written on the footprints. Do the exercise, and the scary thing will go away.

1.
Stand very still!
Raise your arms over your head.
Flap them at the monster while
    you count to ten.
1–2–3–4–5–6–7–8–9–10.
Hands at sides, feet together.
The MONSTER is looking at you!

2.
Look to the left.
Look to the right.
Twist your body to the left.
Twist your body to the right.
Do this five times while
    saying, "Gr-r-r-r!"
Look the monster in the eye.
Hands at sides, feet together.
The MONSTER is wondering what's
    going on!

3.
Put your right arm behind your back.
Lift your left foot up to touch your
    right hand.
Grab your ankle and hop seven times.
Feet together, hands at sides.
Put your left arm behind your back.
Lift your right foot up to touch your
    left hand.
Grab your ankle and hop nine times.
Feet together, hands at sides.
GOOD, The MONSTER is turning
    blue!

4.
Run in place ten times.
Clap your hands together eight times
1–2–3–4–5–6–7–8.
Open your eyes wide.
Show your teeth and growl!
GOOD! The MONSTER is turning green!

5.
Shhh! The monster is running away!
Wave bye-bye to the scary thing!
Sit down, cross your legs, fold your arms.
Put your face up to the sun.
Feel the warm sun on your face, arms, legs.
Feel the warm sun in your tummy.
Smile! The monster isn't coming back!
Take a rest—you earned it!

On the back, draw a big picture of this scary looking, five-legged monster! Shhh! It's sleeping!

Name _____   Date _____

Farmers use scarecrows to scare away the crows from their crops; but scarecrows are supposed to scare the crows and not be afraid of them. This poor little scarecrow is frightened every time the crows come flying by. Please write a story that shows the scarecrow that it has nothing to fear. Write it on the scarecrow so it won't forget!

If you need more space for your story, use the back of this sheet.

Name _____   Date _____

A SCARY HAIR STORY

Use your imagination and think up some scary words to describe a haunted house. Then, listen for the sounds that you hear coming from the house. Go inside the house and tell what you see. Make this such a scary story that your hair will stand right up straight!

Title _____
_____
_____
_____
_____
_____
_____
_____
_____
_____
_____
_____

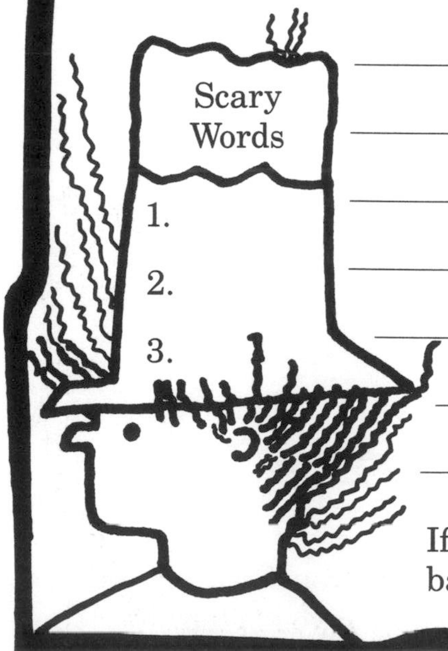

Scary Words

1.
2.
3.

_____
_____
_____
_____

If you need more space for your story, use the back of this sheet.

THE HEADLESS MONSTER MAIL ORDER CATALOG   7–12

This monster has been invited to a special party. It needs some new clothing and is looking through a MONSTER DESIGNER CATALOG. The catalog contains many items such as designer boots, jeans, sweaters, and other things that a monster would like to own. It even has designer monster heads. Help this monster to select six items from the catalog. Draw them in the spaces provided. The monster likes bright, bold colors, and flashy items.

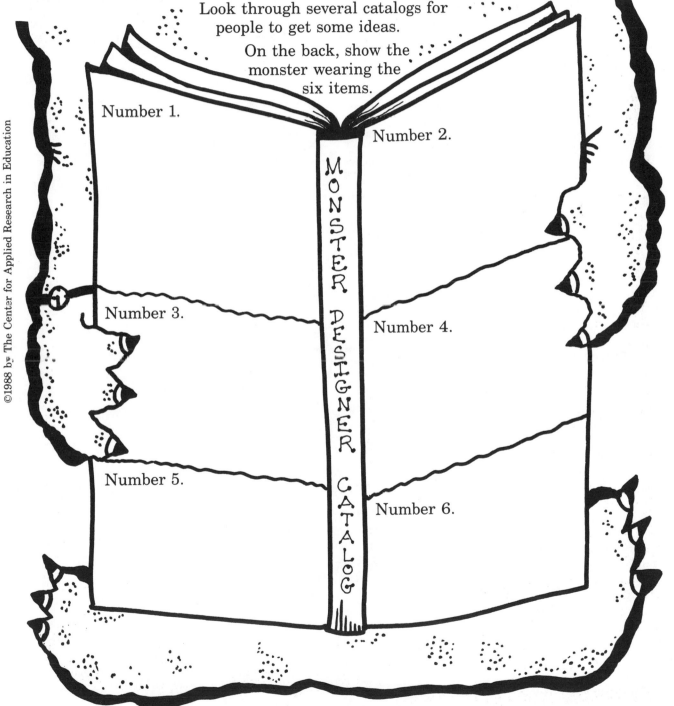

If you select the giant monster head, make it from construction paper and attach it to this monster so that we can all see what it looks like. EEEKKK!

SECTION 8

Heroes and Heroines

BOOK:

Three Cheers for Mother Jones
by Jean Bethell. Illustrated by Kathleen
Garry-McCord. New York: Holt, Rinehart and
Winston, 1980.

THE STORY FORMAT

1. First Person Narrative. This story is written in the "first person" which may be the first time some children read this format. It means that there are sentences such as "Yes Ma'am," *I said*, rather than "Yes Ma'am," *said Jamie.* Also, there are sentences such as "I liked it," instead of "Jamie liked it."

This new format can be exciting for some children. It is the way that students write naturally in their own journals or diaries. Help students to set up a journal. Staple several sheets of white paper in between a construction paper cover. Allow daily time for journal writing so that children can keep a record of thoughts, feelings, events. Encourage illustrations. Discuss whether this is to be a private or a shared journal.

2. Autobiographies. Many autobiographies are written in the first person. Older children may be interested in locating several in the library and reading one or two. Somehow, they seem more personal. Encourage children to write their own introductory autobiography.

3. Oh look—chapters! For some children, this may be a first introduction to storybooks with chapters. Chapters serve as a natural divider between events in the story line. "Chapter" is from the Latin "capitulum" which means a part or a section.

A simple technique for outlining chapters. Examine the chapter titles and dates. Have students divide a sheet of plain white paper into nine sections (one for each of the nine chapters in the book), and label the squares one to nine. In each of the nine sections, have them do the following: (a) write the main thing or event that happened in that chapter, (b) draw a picture to accompany the main event or main idea of the chapter. Now, students have an outline of the story and can report on the story by using this technique.

4. Draw a Story. Students can read another short story and outline the story in visual form with only a few written words as text clues. Start with squares for the beginning, middle, and ending of the story, and use one or two squares in between.

THE BOOK

1. Read the story aloud to the class. It may come as a complete surprise to some children that at one time children worked in the mill for twelve hours a day and were not allowed to go to school to learn. (This book has a message for children who refer to school as "boring." Contrast their boring day with the boring day in the mill.)

2. The book provides many opportunities for contrasting the past and the present for children. For example:

- daily life (hard, dangerous work in mines and mills)
- children's diseases from hard work
- child labor laws and children's rights (back of book)
- parents' feelings and parents' rights

3. Role playing. Simulate a scene where a child from the book meets with a student from the classroom.

4. Discussion: Who is the real hero or heroine of this book? What would Mother Jones say about schools today if she came back for a visit? Write a script.

5. Today's Mother Jones! Who is the Mother Jones in your neighborhood, community, city? What is this person fighting for?

HEROES AND HEROINES

1. Hero refers to a man and heroine refers to a woman. Let's take a look at the heroines that we have in the history of our country. (Suffragettes, women in education, medicine, first ladies, and the like.)

2. People make a difference. Start looking at positive and negative attitudes of people. Who are the people on TV who make a difference in our world?

3. Language development. "You can catch a lot more flies with honey than you can with vinegar" and "a smile is contagious" are expressions that convey definite messages. What are they? Can you locate more sayings by asking adults or by checking resources in the library?

4. Nonverbal communication. What hidden messages do we convey nonverbally by a frown, slumping shoulders, yanking something out of someone's hands, tears? Have students demonstrate some of these actions and have other students tell how the actions make them feel.

5. Become a Hero/Heroine! Encourage students to select the cause each one could devote some time and energy to. After discussion, have them vote for their cause. Work as one large group or in small groups to help make a dream come true. (Examples: Causes can be as simple as making cards or gifts for senior citizens in homes for Christmas; making greeting cards for children in the hospital; making a cassette recording of songs and cheerful messages for people who are confined, and sending the cassette to a local health service organization for home visits; striking up a correspondence with a pen pal.)

BOOK:

Abraham Lincoln
by Ingri D'Aulaire and Edgar Parin. Garden
City, NY: Doubleday & Co., 1957.

ABOUT THE BOOK

1. This book is a winner of the Caldecott Medal—a medal that is given yearly in the United States for outstanding illustrations in children's books. Have other Caldecott medal winners available so that children can see the gold and silver medallions on the books. Have children scout around in the school library and public library for other Caldecott Medal winners, and bring them to class. They can be read aloud and the pictures can be enjoyed.

2. After reading this book aloud, use it as a resource. Have students do some of the following activities: (a) Draw and label Abe Lincoln's house; (b) Draw and label the typical food to be found in the kitchen cupboard; (c) Make a comparison of Abe's meal and special treats with a meal of today with special treats; (d) Draw Abe's old and new bed, and describe it in written form.

3. Bring in an old shovel and have children use it to write on with charcoal or chalk, just as Abe did.

4. Have students pretend to be Abe Lincoln sitting quietly in the woods making speeches to the squirrels. Record the speech on a cassette and share it with the group.

5. List, diagram, and describe the many types of boats on the river. On a map, find the rivers on which Abe traveled.

THE BIG WORLD

1. Storytelling. People never tired of Abe's true tales about slave trading and river pirates. Write, practice, and tell an Abe tale.

2. When Abe was twenty-one years old, he set out in the world. List the places that he saw. Illustrate one that is not shown in the book. Locate them on the map.

3. Context clues. There are many sayings in this storybook, such as "If you make a bad bargain, hug it all the tighter," and "With malice toward none and with charity toward all," and "fair and square." Find more. What do they mean? Can we understand the meaning from the text clues, or do we have to do more searching to find the meaning?

Locate a resource book of old sayings. For some children this becomes a hobby or an interest. Have interested students form a Word Club, and earn extra credit for learning to spell and use a variety of the words in a sentence.

4. Fables. Abe tells the fable of "The Monkey Who Wanted a Longer Tale." What is the real message? Have students think of a message that they would like to get across (don't litter, be honest rather than a teller of fibs, be a true friend rather than an enemy...) and have them formulate it and then write it in the form of a fable with an interesting title.

5. Discuss what Abe's wife called, "wilderness manners." How can people change habits? What would students like to change? What pet peeves do students have? Is it silly to have pet peeves? Discuss.

A CLOSER LOOK AT THE STORY

1. Characters: List the major and minor characters in the book. Draw them and describe their traits. For what reason(s) is Lincoln especially remembered?

2. Setting: This is where the story takes place. How many different settings are there in this story? Draw all of Abe's homes, or all of Abe's places of work, or all of the scene shifts in the first half, or second half, of the book.

3. Discussion. Sit around in a circle and tell interesting tales about Abe: What tidbits of information make Abe Lincoln seem more "human" to us? For example, tell some of the "Honest Abe" stories, some of his pranks, and how he used his tall stovepipe hat for stuffing important papers and bills. (Would this have anything to do with the old saying, "Keep it under your hat?")

4. Make a large stovepipe hat for the classroom and put good books under there for students to read. Abe Lincoln would have thought this was a real "treasure"—to find so many good books in one place. Have students realize the importance of the quality and quantity of books available since the days of Abraham Lincoln.

BOOK:

The Story of Paul Bunyan
by Barbara Emberly. Woodcuts by Ed Emberly.
Englewood Cliffs, NJ: Prentice-Hall, 1967.

TALL TALES

1. There is an element of truth in tall tales and they are highly imaginative and playful. Using the book, do the following:

• Make a list of names and places that are real.

• Make a list of events that are rooted in fantasy (outlandish).

2. Woodcut. How appropriate that a book about Paul Bunyan and trees is illustrated with woodcuts. Find books to explain this process. Find other books that are done in this medium.

3. Creative Writing. Students can divide a journal into seven spaces—one for each day of the week—and write in the diary as though they are Paul Bunyan. Be fanciful and outlandish.

4. Create a giant Paul Bunyan for the classroom bulletin board. (Have one student lie down on a large sheet of butcher paper, and trace around the edge. Then fill in details with paint or felt-tip pen.)

Next, create a long white beard from shelf paper that can be rolled up under Paul Bunyan's chin. Have each student write a tall tale and fasten it to this rolled up beard. What fun to unroll it and read the tales!

5. Make Tall Tale Books. Get in the spirit of the fanciful tall tales and cut paper so that it is six inches wide by eighteen inches long. Students can write the tall tales on the tall paper and collect them all in a tall folder.

WAKE UP, PAUL BUNYAN!

1. Pretend that Paul Bunyan is coming back for a visit today. Have each student write out a question that he might ask. Place them all in a little box. Then, have everyone draw a question from the box. Can the student answer it, or find out the answer?

2. Invite Paul Bunyan for lunch. Using the book as a guide, what would the menu of today be?

3. Write a TV script for an interview with Paul Bunyan, using the book as a guide for the questions and answers.

4. Make a huge figure of Paul Bunyan from cardboard. Cut holes for eyes and arms and let the children "wear it" for the interviews

TODAY VERSUS YESTERDAY

1. Plan a trip for Paul Bunyan along the Mississippi River. What would he see today that wasn't there in the old days? Illustrate and explain.

2. Make a list of modern inventions. Cut up the list. Each student gets one to illustrate and discuss. (Have the children draw diagrams, write a report, or give an oral report to communicate.) Some modern day inventions for Paul Bunyan to learn about could be instant glue, computers, microwave ovens, frozen foods, and skate boards.

3. From the library, get a book about logging and lumber. List the ways that trees are useful to man in terms of the wood, paper products, seeds, fruits.

4. How can we explain "reforestation" to Paul Bunyan? Let's try!

5. Make a giant front page of a newspaper showing the return of Paul Bunyan with interviews and headlines including "What Paul Bunyan Says About_____," and "What Paul Bunyan Thinks About_____," and "Paul Bunyan Laughs As He Visits_____."

6. Draw a house plan for Paul Bunyan. Would he still live in just one room? How many rooms would he have? Where would he choose to live?

BOOK:

What's the Big Idea, Ben Franklin?
by Jean Fritz. Illustrated by Margot Tomes.
New York: Coward, McCann & Geoghegan,
1976.

LETTING THE STYLE OF THE BOOK BE THE TEACHER

1. This book, while filled with factual information, is categorized as a story-book rather than an information book or a biography of Benjamin Franklin. The vast amount of information is presented humorously, and in a way that is easy to read and enjoy.

Conduct an experiment in social studies. Read this book to half of the class while the other half is not present. Then, read a factual information book about Benjamin Franklin to the other half of the class, while the first half is not present. Then, have each half prepare a "Meet Benjamin Franklin" impromptu program. They can work in teams to present the information that they have learned from the books. The format can be question and answer, interview, news reporting, puppet presentation.

What did your class discover from this experimental technique? Be sure to discuss it with them. Usually, the class discovers that they do learn from both types of books that were presented, but the social studies information presented in the storybook format used by this author, Jean Fritz, is unique and children are usually eager to read more books by her. The famous person is presented in a friendly, next-door-neighbor manner that appeals to young people.

2. Some other books to include in your program of famous people by Jean Fritz, are: *Where Do You Think You're Going, Christopher Columbus?; Can't You Make Them Behave, King George?; And Then What Happened, Paul Revere?; Will You Sign Here, John Hancock?* Make history and social studies come alive in your classroom with this literary approach to dispensing factual information about important people in our past.

FROM THE BOOK

1. Benjamin Franklin had a pen name (Silence Dogood). Later in life his pen name was Richard Saunders. A pen name is a person's literary signature—the name used for creative writing, poetry, letters, when the real person wants to remain anonymous. Make sure that children understand the concept of remain-

ing anonymous. This does not give people the right to write graffiti or poison pen letters, but it gives them an opportunity to create a piece of writing (often from the heart) that they prefer to get feedback from as a bystander. Samuel Clemens had a pen name that is famous (Mark Twain) and he used it throughout his life.

Have students select a grand-sounding pen name. Provide a bulletin board where outpourings of creative writing can be tacked up. Collect the writings and make a class volume.

2. Benjamin Franklin was so famous that he has had streets, schools, colleges, libraries, hotels, banks, stores, and so on, named after him. Is there a Benjamin Franklin building in your town? Suppose students became famous, or at least well known. Have them draw a picture of the building they would like named after them. Tell something about the building and the famous person that it is named for (self).

3. Soap and candles were "big business" in Benjamin Franklin's day. Why? Is it true today? What has changed? How would a candle shop of today be different?

4. List Benjamin Franklin's Rules of Good Behavior and have students rate themselves just as he did.

5. Form a "Leather Apron Club" and discuss things (information) that you read in books.

PRINTER, INVENTOR, CREATIVE GENIUS

1. Inventor. The Franklin stove, or "the Pennsylvania fireplace" is only one of Benjamin Franklin's inventions. List his inventions. Work in teams to invent a different stove (or other implement, appliance).

2. Franklin organized the first circulating library in the United States. Start a classroom library and have each child write a story, or bring in one book from home to contribute or lend for classroom use only. Use a 3×5 card to list the title and author. Children can take turns being the librarian-of-the-week.

3. The first United States postage stamp (5 cents) bore the likeness of Benjamin Franklin. Design a postage stamp at today's price. Decide whether Franklin's picture or one of his inventions will be shown on the stamp. What colors will be used? Examine real stamps to note design, the amount of print, and so on.

4. Franklin's proverbs (or Franklinisms) are well known. Some include: "An ounce of prevention is worth a pound of cure"; "Snug as a bug in a rug"; "A word to the wise is sufficient"; and "Never leave to tomorrow that which you can do today." Discuss these with the children. Find more proverbs and discuss them. Have students select their favorites. After working with proverbs, have children write their own.

BOOK:

Runaway Slave, the Story of Harriet Tubman
by Ann McGovern. Pictures by R.M. Powers.
New York: Four Winds Press, 1970.

ABOUT HARRIET TUBMAN

1. Three Adjectives. What word would we select to describe Harriet Tubman as a young girl? As a young woman? As an older woman? Make three big classroom lists, using all of the contributions.

2. "Tricky" was the word for Harriet. What were some of the tricks that she played on people so that she wouldn't be discovered? Can students generate more tricks?

3. Write an interview with questions and answers. Students can be TV news reporters asking Harriet Tubman's mother and father to talk about their daughter.

4. Harriet Tubman lived to be over ninety years of age! She spent her last years in Auburn, New York. Locate it on the map. Is it near a lake or several lakes? What is the closest big city to Auburn? Where is Auburn in relation to our city?

5. Harriet Tubman was described as the Moses (great leader) of her day. Students can nominate candidates for the "Moses of Today." Have them explain why they chose those candidates.

6. Bravery. Let's take a close look at this word. Find it in the dictionary. Discuss its meaning. Learn to spell it. It involves taking chances, doing good deeds, quick thinking, careful planning but with the ability to make last minute changes. Find another book about some person who shows the qualities that make him or her a brave person.

THE UNDERGROUND RAILROAD

1. Double Meaning. The term "underground railroad" was used to describe a secret or undercover route for slaves to escape to the north and into Canada, but no railroad was involved.

Railroad terms were used for the routes, such as station, station master, conductors. What did these titles mean? Why would such titles be used? (Railroad terms would be meaningless to anyone who was listening and did not understand the special meanings.)

Double meaning words. Do any of our words have double meanings? Think about it; brainstorm. What do we come up with?

2. The term "under." Look in the dictionary to find out how many compound words you can list that begin with "under." How many do we know? Make an "Undercover Agent Book" with the words and definitions "under the cover." Learn to spell at least five; when you learn to spell u-n-d-e-r, the rest becomes easier.

3. Do we have any underground or secret agencies going on in our country today? (CIA, FBI to name but two.) How about underground activities in the world?

4. The Underground Railroad moved by night and was swift. During the day, everything was quiet and still. Describe the feelings of the people on the move at night—how would they feel? Describe the feelings of the people hiding out during the day—how would they feel?

MAP SKILLS

1. Find these states on the map—Ohio, Indiana, Pennsylvania. They were the most heavily traveled routes on the Underground Railroad.

2. Runaway slaves crossed over into Canada by way of Niagara Falls, New York, and Detroit, Michigan. Locate these two cities on the map. How far apart are they?

3. Find Lake Erie on the map. Many runaway slaves used this lake to sail into Canada. The points of departure were Erie, Pennsylvania, and Sandusky, Ohio. Locate these cities on the map. Why were these cities selected?

4. Locate Québec in Canada. Many slaves reached this area as their destination.

5. Plan an escape route for Harriet Tubman and her runaway slaves. She made about nineteen trips back to the south to help between 250 and 300 people reach safety. How many people does that average per trip?

BOOK:

Crazy Horse, Sioux Warrior
by Enid LaMonte Meadowcroft. Illustrated by
Cary. Champaign, IL: Garrard Publishing, 1965.

SIOUX INDIANS

1. In the book, this tribe is described as the most colorful and exciting of all of the North American Indian. Why? What other North American Indian tribes can we locate information about? Let's put them in alphabetical order and find out more about them, such as their clothing, food, crafts, habits.

2. The Sioux were brave and fierce and their names made their enemies shudder, according to the book. "Crazy Horse" is one interesting name. Have students make up Indian names from nature that would "make people shudder," such as "Rumbling Volcano," "Falling Rock," "Flooding Waters," and so on. What special names are referred to in the book?

3. Indians measured their age by "six winters" (age six) or "nine winters" (age nine). Have students measure their age in terms of winters and graph it on an interesting winter shape.

4. Make a diary for Curly. Write in it for one week as Hump trains him to hunt for buffalo. Use information from the book to make it more realistic.

5. "They are one sleep away" is a phrase used by the Indians to measure time. It means, "they are one day away." Using a real calendar, have students figure out when the next big seasonal holiday is, and refer to it in terms of sleep. Using the calendar, have students figure out when other holidays and birthdays occur and refer to them in terms of sleep, or phases of the moon, or in other imaginative ways.

INDIAN TRIBES OF NORTH AMERICA

1. Have children imagine a time before cultivated plants (agriculture and farming) when people had to follow the buffalo herds in order to hunt for food. Tepees had to be strong but light, and possessions were very few. Contrast this with our way of life today in terms of homes, food, possessions such as clothing, furniture, toys, and so on.

2. Buffalo were important animals. People hunted them, ate them, used their hide for clothing and tepee coverings, and used their bones for tools and needles. Read library resource books on buffalo and find out all that you possibly can about them.

3. What other types of homes did some Indians have other than tepees? Where can we locate this information? Children can construct different types of dwellings from scrap material.

4. Have each student bring in a bar of soap. Students can make a carving from a bar of soap by using a blunt instrument. (Sometimes it is easier to do a carving after making the same item in clay to get used to the three-dimensional quality of the art form.) The "ivory" carvings can be put on display, and it will make the room smell wonderful. What can we do with the soap shavings?

5. Indian children made their own toys from sticks, dried grasses, scraps of materials. Students can make an Indian toy such as a ball, doll, or boat, using items from nature.

6. Explore Indian crafts by making clay pots or bowls. Find authentic Indian designs in the resource books from the library and gently engrave them on the outside of the bowls. Gently imbed pretty pebbles, shells, or beads into the bowl also.

MORE ABOUT INDIANS

1. Storytelling. Indians placed great value on storytelling for entertainment. When tribes got together this was one highlight—to talk about hunts, storms, crafts, animals, sky, and the like. Plan a storytelling pow-wow and have each student tell a wow of a story!

2. Discuss the sign language of Indians. Make a class dictionary chart of sign language. Then, have students compose a story using sign language. Write it on paper torn from crumpled brown paper bags to simulate bark. Use sticks dipped into paint for the pictures.

3. Totem poles. Many Indian tribes carved totem poles in the shapes of animals that they worshipped or feared. Students can work in small groups and make cylinders from large pieces of sturdy paper stapled together. Then, each group can decorate and paint the animal of their choice. Eventually, pile all of the individual cylinders of totems on top of each other for a giant classroom totem pole.

Individual class members can make their own totem poles using cereal boxes.

4. Sand painting was a favorite craft of some Indian tribes. Mix sandbox sand together with dry tempera paint and shake it in a glass jar. Make a variety of colored sand. Use the bottom of a box as the "frame" to hold the painting. Gently spread sand evenly along the bottom of the box. Using a blunt instrument, trace a design in the sand. Then, slowly sprinkle on colored sand to complete the design. Make several.

5. Encourage students to make musical instruments using items from nature. Sticks, stones, rocks can be beat, tapped, and scraped to make sounds. Create simple rhythms and creative movements to accompany them.

BOOK:

Bicycle Rider
by Mary Scioscia. Illustrations by Ed Young,
New York: Harper & Row, 1983.

LOCATING INFORMATION

1. Find information about bicycles at the library. On some of the first bikes the front wheels were large and bikes were called "ordinaries." Why? While you are at it, find out what "pedal power" is.

2. Devise a Bicycle Trivia Game. Locate interesting bicycle information. Put it on a little card. On the reverse side make up a question for the information. ("This was the fastest vehicle on the road in the late 1800s." Answer: Bicycle.)

3. Bicycle Fashions. Design a bicycle outfit. Bicycles changed the style of women's clothes from hoopskirts to culottes.

4. Check the Want Ads. Find out the cost of used bikes. How do they compare with the cost of new bikes? Students can compose a Want Ad for a bike that they want. What can we do to earn money for the bike?

5. Bring in a real bike to class. Have children locate parts that move, parts that are stationary. Label the parts by looking at a bicycle manual or a book on bikes. What are some of the bike tools necessary? Bring in samples (tire pump and gauge, wrench to tighten bolts, wax for cleaning/polishing). Perhaps a bicycle repair man could be invited to class to talk about bike care.

BIKE RULES

1. Right of Way. Suppose a bike, a pedestrian, and an automobile reach a corner at the same time. Who has the right of way?

2. Cut out wheel-shaped cards. Print a bike rule and a bike tip on each card. Make a small bulletin board of these cards.

3. Make a "Bike Inspection Check List" for all parts of the bicycle. Then, compile the information so that there is a class list. Duplicate it and have the students take it home and check their own bicycle. (Perhaps this bicycle safety information could be shared in a school newsletter, or with other grade levels.)

4. For bicycle safety write to: National Safety Council, 444 N. Michigan Avenue, Chicago, Illinois 60611.

5. Plan a bike race on the playground after school. Students can plan an obstacle course (use milk containers loaded with rocks). Go one at a time, have a stop watch available and record time.

MORE ABOUT SPORTS

1. Does the title of this book let the reader know in advance what this story is all about? Discuss titles. Come up with several more ideas for a title for this story.

2. Athletes often endorse products. Look for newspaper and magazine ads for athletes and the products they endorse. Do they fall into certain categories? What would the boy in the story endorse? Ask students what they would endorse, and why?

3. Make Picture or Symbol Signs for the following: "No Bikes Allowed," "Walk Your Bicycle Here," "Only One Person on a Bicycle," "No Racing Allowed," and "Do Not Ride on the Grass."

4. Students can design a bicycle license plate for their bike. Use a symbol or logo and two colors.

5. Is there a bike path in your community? Plan one on paper that is in a nearby park, or playground and street area. Submit your plan to the principal (and then perhaps to the city council).

6. "The Runaway Bike." Make up a fanciful story, with illustrations, about a bike that does not want to race and deliberately steers off course or "runs away" right in the middle of the race. How will this end, and what is the bicycle rider thinking and saying and doing? Make this an action-packed tale!

BOOK:

Johnny Appleseed
by Carol Beach York. Illustrations by Joan
Goodman. Mahwah, NJ: Troll Associates, 1980.

JOHN CHAPMAN

1. Find the birthdate of this American folk hero. Does the birthdate coincide with the birthdate listed in other resources? Sometimes they vary. Why? How were birth records kept long ago? (This source: 1774-1845.)

2. According to this folk story, some people said that "when he was born he came right out of the ground with a sack of apple seeds over his shoulder." Discuss this amusing, descriptive phrase. How could children describe themselves in relation to their interests?

3. John sewed apple seeds into leather pouches and gave them to families who were leaving Massachusetts for Ohio. Find these two states on a map of the United States. If students had a choice, what would they give to people going west? Write or diagram.

4. It's said that Johnny Appleseed walked across the state of Pennsylvania! How far is that? Find the information in a world atlas. Would point of entry and point of departure have an effect on the distance?

5. Imagine Johnny Appleseed with a pan on his head. Have a large one available for children to try on. The pan may serve as an inspiration for creative writing about Johnny's journey and the friendly people that he met.

6. Storytelling. People gathered around in the evening to listen to Johnny talk about animals who were his friends. Have a "Johnny Appleseed Storytime" recording session. Children can record their stories on cassette tape and then listen to one after the other. Make illustrations.

APPLE TIME

1. Apples were especially popular with early American settlers because they could be stored over the winter season in pits dug in the ground. How else could

apples be fixed to last longer? (Apple cider, dried apples, applesauce, apple butter.) Today it's a good idea to store apples in the refrigerator. What things do we store in our refrigerator that could not be stored underground? Children can make them up in riddle form on tiny cards—"I'm thinking of something that is white and would go sour"—and write the answer on the back.

2. Make up a dictionary of apples using terms such as: grafting, insecticide, rootstock, dormant, photosynthesis, and the like. How many more terms can we think of? Bring in a book on apples from the library.

3. Visit an apple orchard, if possible, and learn apple facts from the tour guide. On returning to school make plans to paint a class mural (or picture) of the trip, as you munch your apples.

4. Apple trees are often sprayed with pesticides by helicopter. Some apple tree pests are moths and aphids. Diseases such as "apple scab" and "powdery mildew" have to be checked. What other diseases is this fruit to be protected from? Check with your local Farm Bureau for information about crop protection.

5. Put five apples in a row. Examine them very carefully. List all of the ways that they are alike. List all of the ways that they are different.

MORE ABOUT APPLES

1. Use paper apples for counting. Cut out 100 apples from red construction paper and have the children put them in order to gain practice in rote counting.

2. Make apple-shaped subtraction facts, with the answers on the reverse side. They can be called the "June drop" facts. June is when many apples fall from the trees because the tree is only able to support just so many.

3. There are over 7,000 varieties of apples with some interesting names, such as "Granny Smith," "Jonathan," "Winesap," "Delicious," "Rome Beauty," and so on. How many are grown in our area? How many more names can we find? Examine an apple closely and make up a colorful name for this very special apple. Tell what's different about it—is it seedless? What color is it inside and outside? Is it smooth or bumpy? Is it a healthy food? How can it be eaten?

4. Apple Recipes. Have children be on the lookout for apple recipes in magazines and newspapers. Cut out the recipes. Compare them. Make a booklet of them. Copy one to take home for a holiday treat.

5. List words that describe eating apples—crunchy, juicy, chewy, noisy.

6. Language Development. Suppose Johnny Appleseed decided to start distributing other fruit seeds, such as orange, grapefruit, plum, peach, grape, and so on. Then what would he be called? What could we call him if we couldn't use the word "seed" in the title? (Johnny Orange Planter, Johnny Orange Grower, Johnny-seven (a packet of seven seeds in a pouch)....)

7. Apple Homonyms, or "Applenyms." Make matching apples and print homonyms on them. Scatter them on the ground (floor) and have the children match them. Homonym starters: sew/sow (Johnny sewed seeds into a pouch for people to sow when they arrived.).

REPRODUCIBLE ACTIVITY PAGES
FOR
HEROES AND HEROINES

Name _____   Date _____

Tall tales have some truth to them, but they are exaggerated and make us laugh and not quite believe them.

Write your own tall tale on this tall character. Keep pasting more paper strips in the middle for a really tall tale! Then cut out your tall tale, paste it together, and tack it onto a bulletin board.

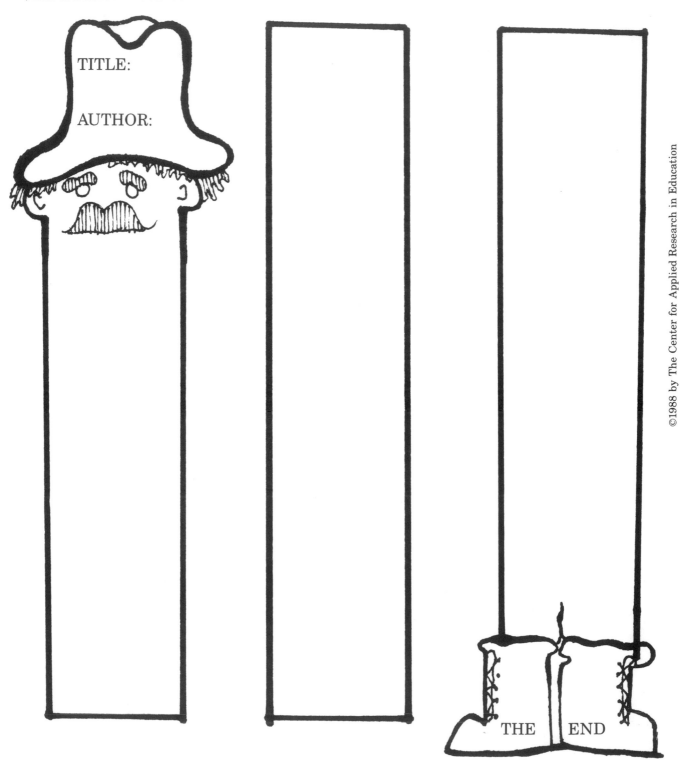

TITLE:

AUTHOR:

THE   END

Name _____

THE BETSY ROSS FLAG COMPANY

In order to work for The Betsy Ross Flag Company, you must be able to answer the following questions:

- How many stripes are there on the flag? What color are they? Are they all the same length?

- How many stars are there on the flag? What does each star represent?

- What does each color of the United States flag represent?

  Red is for _____

  White is for _____

  Blue is for _____

- Who designed the American flag? What do other United States flags look like?

- What do flags of foreign countries look like? What symbols do they have on them?

THE BETSY ROSS FLAG COMPANY ASSIGNMENT:

When you have answered the questions above, you can work for the company. The company is in the process of designing a new flag.

This is your assignment the first day on the job.

- Draw two new United States flag designs.

- What is the story behind your new flag designs?

Share your flag designs with classmates. Actually make one of your "favorites" from construction paper.

Design 1

Design 2

Name —————————————————————   Date ————————————————————

Children's Book Week is celebrated in November. Design a stamp for this very special week. You may want to use your favorite book character, or a scene or symbol from your favorite story.

Examine many first class postage stamps for ideas. Make several different sketches before you create your special stamp.

SUGGESTION: Send a copy of the stamp design to The Postmaster General, Washington D.C. 20260, along with a letter suggesting that a postage stamp contest be held every year for Children's Book Week in November. The winning stamp(s) can be selected from designs submitted by school children just like you!

Name _____   Date _____

STORY CHARACTERS

8–4

In good children's literature, the character undergoes some type of change, and is a better person at the end of the story.

Select a story and write: TITLE _____

AUTHOR _____

Draw and describe the following in the three spaces provided: (1)What the character was like in the beginning of the story. (2) What happened that caused the character to change. (3) What the character is like at the ending of the story.

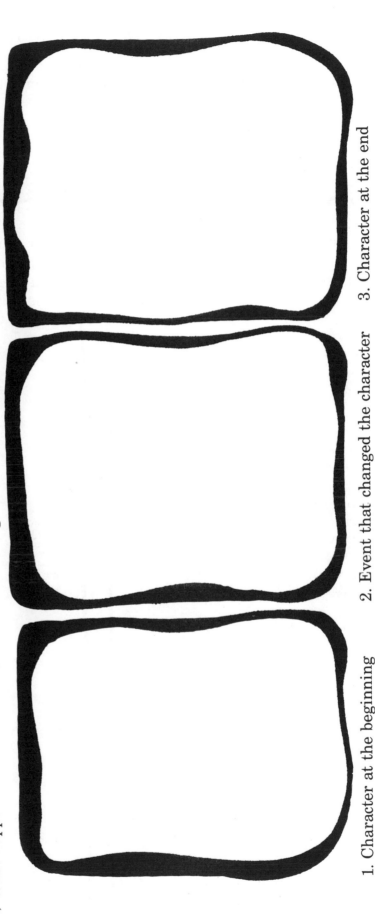

1. Character at the beginning   2. Event that changed the character   3. Character at the end

Write a story of your own. Create a situation that causes the character to experience growth and change, and to become a better person at the end of your story.

Name _____   Date _____

THE JOURNAL OF MY HERO/HEROINE

I have read ____ books about people who have made the world a better place. The

real life character that I most admire is:_____

I met the character in this book: TITLE:_____

AUTHOR:_____

Journal Notes
If the person you admire kept a journal or a diary as a young person, it's possible that this could be found there. What is the person thinking, feeling, doing?

Entry 1

Entry 2

Entry 3

Journal Notes
Enter some notes in the journal of this person at the height of his or her career. Remember what the person is thinking, feeling, doing.

Entry 1

Entry 2

Entry 3

Name _____   Date _____

I am not too much different from the people I admire. I, too, have hopes and dreams. Some day I would like to accomplish something worthwhile. My thoughts and feelings are recorded here. (Share them with others.)

JOURNAL NOTES OF

_____

(your name)

AS A YOUNG PERSON

Entry 1

Entry 2

Entry 3

JOURNAL NOTES OF _____

AS A SUCCESSFUL ADULT. (Write it as you hope and dream it to be.)

Entry 1

Entry 2

Entry 3

©1988 by The Center for Applied Research in Education

Name _____   Date _____

YOUR STORYBOOK TICKET

TO _____
ADMIT ONE   (title)

BY _____
                             (author)

Suppose you could go to live in a storybook. Think about all of the books that you have read or the stories that you have listened to. Select one that you would like to live in for awhile. Fill out your ticket above.

The plane leaves in twenty minutes! Fill out this questionnaire while you are waiting. Enjoy your visit!

1. Why did you select this book?

_____

_____

2. Whom do you plan to visit there?

_____

_____

3. What do you especially want to see? List three places or things.

_____

_____

_____

4. How will the storybook characters greet you when they first see you?

_____

_____

5. What will you do while you are there?

_____

_____

Have a nice trip! On the back, draw yourself into a picture with the storybook characters.

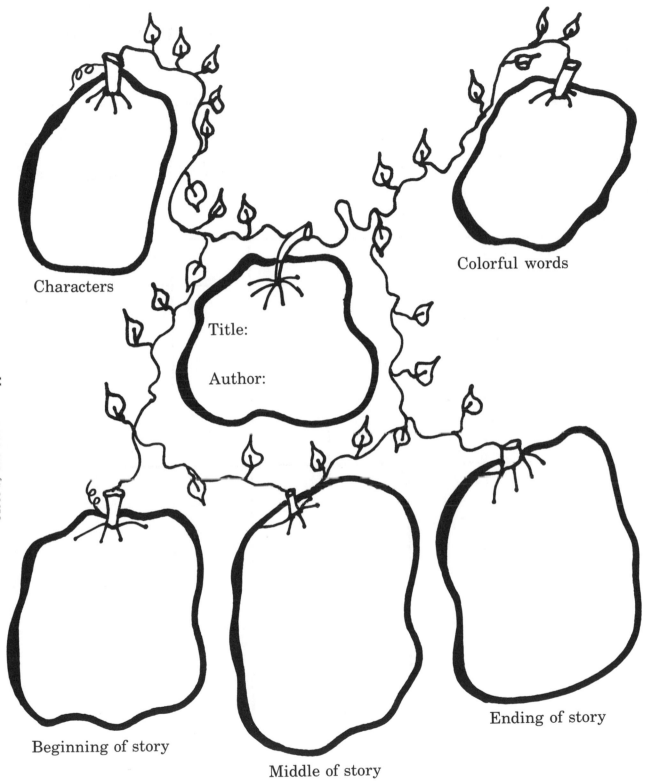

Characters

Colorful words

Title:

Author:

Beginning of story

Middle of story

Ending of story

Name _____

Date _____

A READING JOURNAL

Date	Book	My Rating	Rating Explanation	New Words	Category: (Fantasy, Mystery)

Name _____   Date _____

SPIN A STORY

Cut out the spinner and attach it to the middle of the wheel with a paper fastener. Then spin until the spinner lands in Section A—that is your major character. Spin until the spinner lands in Section B—that is your setting, or where your story will take place. Spin again, until you land in Sections C and D.

Make up a story with the help you got from the story spinner. Keep spinning again and again for more good stories. Later, use a paper plate and a spinner and create your own story wheel.

SPIN ME ONCE, SPIN ME TWICE, THREE IS BETTER, FOUR IS NICE!
NOW SPIN YOUR STORY

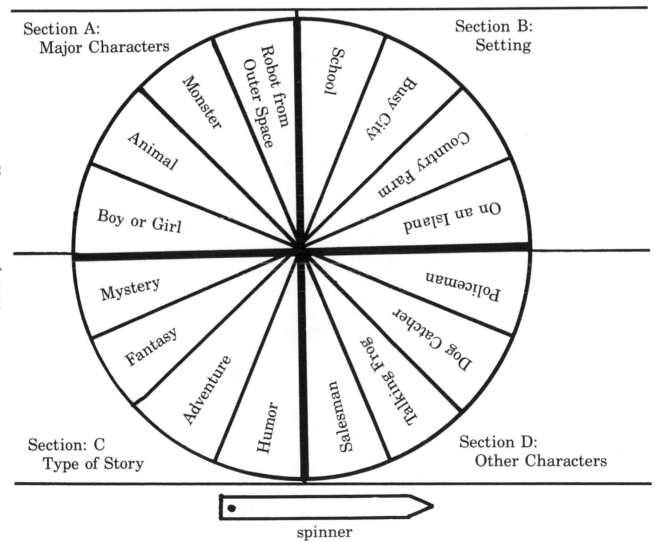

A "spinner" of tales, or a "spinner" of yarns, means that a person is a good storyteller. Be prepared to write or tell your story.

SECTION 9

Problem Solving

BOOK:

Perfect Pigs, An Introduction to Manners
by Marc Brown and Stephen Krensky. Boston:
Little, Brown & Co., An Atlantic Monthly Press
Book, 1983.

PAGE BY PAGE

1. The book is done in cartoon style and will inspire children to draw cartoons. Cartoons are an excellent vehicle for having children write dialogue between characters, and to have them realize what the character is thinking inwardly and saying outwardly.

2. Have the children illustrate manners similar to those in the book, using different animals.

3. After going through the entire book, concentrate on "a good manner each day."

4. In the book, which manners are practiced indoors and which are practiced outdoors? Which are applicable in both an indoor and an outdoor setting?

5. Have each child select his or her favorite book section and add one more manner to the section.

6. Discuss manners. Are all of the manners in the book of equal importance?

PRACTICING GOOD MANNERS

1. Set up a felt board so that children can reenact the book manners using felt pig figures.

2. Have the students make a giant construction paper "Good Manner Piggy" for the classroom. Consult the pig for advice about solving problems; make this into a writing exercise or use cassette tape.

3. Role playing. Set up a corner of the room where children can act out the right way and the wrong way to behave in a given situation.

4. Catch children in the act of using good manners. Reward children with verbal praise so that the good manners become "contagious." A construction paper Good Manner Piggy Award that the child could pin on would also be good reinforcement.

5. Have the children look through the book again. What manners listed under each category can we use while at school? Let's list them.

MORE PRACTICE WITH GOOD MANNERS

1. Make a "Good Manner Book" to take home and share.

2. Have a "Good Manner Shag Rug" where children can go to think about their behavior when it is negative. Perhaps they can decide when they are ready to return to the group.

3. School manners. What other categories can be added to the book? Brainstorm for some ideas. Some suggestions are: Good Manners on the Bus, Good Manners During the Assembly Program, Good Manners During Fire Drill. Have the children work in groups to illustrate them, similar to the format used in the book.

4. Practice good manners. Take time to practice lining up quietly and orderly; practice walking quietly in the hall; practice going to the lunchroom and going through the line. Children need to continually practice these behaviors in a positive atmosphere and to be praised for desired behavior, rather than just being told about it or scolded. Everyone feels better, too, if the class is not continually lining up "on the run." Good manners are both "caught" and "taught."

BOOK:

Ramona Quimby, Age 8
by Beverly Cleary. Illustrations by Alan
Tiegreen. New York: Dell Publishing, 1981.

READING FOR PLEASURE

1. If children have not met the many interesting characters in Beverly Cleary's books, get them from the library and have a special week where they can read about *Henry Huggins, Henry and Ribsy, Beezus and Ramona, Henry and the Paper Route, Ramona the Pest,* and so forth. Create a library of these books, make little library cards, and have children sign them out for one week. Share the stories and the books.

2. The books listed in number 1 are great read-aloud books and everyone will enjoy a good laugh at the same time. Group two or three young students with readers from the fifth or sixth grade, who can read them aloud to the youngsters.

3. Enlist the aid of older readers (grades 5, 6, 7) to record the stories on cassette tape for a listening library for younger children.

4. Ramona liked "Sustained Silent Reading" (D.E.A.R. — Drop Everything and Read). Try this in your classroom. (Work up to it gradually—five minutes for the younger readers, ten minutes for the older readers, until you can sustain it

for about twenty minutes.) Children learn to read by gaining practice with reading.

SCHOOL

1. On the way to school, Ramona was "happy because her family was happy" and "happy because they could depend on her." Have students discuss this in relation to their own feelings on the way to school.

2. "My Very First Day At School Ever." Who can remember? What memory is outstanding? Let's draw, write, or tell about it.

3. "My Very First Day At School This Year." What memory is outstanding? Let's draw, write, or tell about it.

4. Self-concept. "What Do Others Think of Me?" Ramona overheard a teacher's comment and got upset. What other people think about us is very important. Work on self-concept and the idea that each child is special and has something special to offer to the group. Encourage children to begin to describe classmates in positive terms; for example, "Susie has pretty eyes," "Gary has a nice smile," "Steven has such a good singing voice," "Evelyn is always willing to help others," "Claire is willing to share her toys."

5. After-School Snack. Ramona is hoping for something other than apple juice and graham crackers. Make an after-school nutritious snack book for Ramona.

6. Ramona is caught eating something and liking it. She finds out that it is tongue, then she won't eat it. Have children talk about this. Why won't they try something new just because it looks or smells different?

For snack time, tell children that you are having something new. Call it something unusual and then have it be something very, very ordinary and delicious. Examples: Green Flop (sherbet), Orange Stuffing (sherbet), Milk Mud (chocolate drink), Parrot Eyes (striped peppermint round candies).

"Turn the table" and have students think up unusual names for gum drops, crackers, celery, carrot sticks, olives, and the like.

MORE FUN WITH RAMONA

1. What's in a name? "Picky Picky" tells us something about the Quimby's cat. Discuss names of pets and what they tell us about them. If children could rename their pets, what names would they choose?

2. Show animal pictures from magazines, and have the children name them.

3. Ramona is reading a "medium boring" book. Can students name one that they have read?

4. Supernuisance. Have students list and discuss "pet peeves."

5. Have an "I Can't Believe I Ate the Whole Thing!" Lunch Day! What menu would make each child say that?

6. Fake Sobs for Mean Parents. Have students demonstrate theirs.

7. "Grown-up tea and toast" is what Ramona had when she got sick. Have students tell about their favorite "I'm feeling a little better food."

BOOK:

Everett Anderson's Friend
by Lucille Clifton. Illustrations by Ann
Grifalconi. New York: Holt, Rinehart &
Winston, 1976.

LATCHKEY CHILDREN

1. Everett Anderson is a latchkey child, in an apartment building where there are other latchkey children. Discuss what is meant by "latchkey children." Form a discussion group for the latchkey children in your class. Make giant, colorful key-shaped name tags to be put around the neck with bulky yarn. Have children print name, address, and phone number on it.

This group can discuss topics such as, "What I Can Make for Myself to Eat." Have the children practice opening and closing jars of peanut butter. Each child, using a plastic knife, can spread peanut butter on crackers. Serve this snack to the entire class.

Role play: "How I Can Help Out At Home." Children can pick up items from the floor, hang up jackets, put toys in one special spot, and so on. Have them help make up the list.

A special-interest note about latchkey children in your weekly, biweekly, or monthly newsletter that is sent home to parents, would be helpful. Other children can invite them home occasionally or arrangements can be made to do things after school one or two days per month. Some schools have after-school programs specifically designed for latchkey children. Perhaps parent volunteers may be interested in this.

2. Have all children practice printing their name, address, and phone number, including area code. Keep this information on a 3 × 5 card in a lunch box or jacket pocket. Each morning when attendance is taken, call out the children's names and have them respond with their phone numbers.

3. Using a toy telephone, have children practice dialing or using push buttons to "call" numbers where help could be provided if they need it: Operator, Fire Department, Police Department, neighbor.

4. On a real telephone (disconnected) have children practice dialing the fire department or police department and calmly giving name, address, and stating the problem.

5. List some DO's and DON'Ts for children on the way home from school. Elicit responses from children.

MAKING NEW FRIENDS

1. Everett Anderson thought that he would not like the new people in 13A, but to his surprise, he did. Discuss this with children. Why do we make up our minds, sometimes, before we know all the facts? Is this wise?

2. Students can draw a picture of a very good friend, and in one sentence tell or write what they like about that person.

3. Have children make greeting cards from construction paper, with a pleasant message or a get-well message. Put them in a "shoe box store." When classmates are ill, there are ready-made cards that can be mailed to let them know the class is thinking about them.

4. There is an old saying, "You can't judge a book by its cover." Discuss this with the children. It really means that you can't tell what a person is like just by looking at him—which is partly what Everett did.

Select large and small books at different reading levels from the library, and deliberately change the covers on them. Have children select the book by the cover, and then open it up. They are very surprised! This is especially effective when you can put a drab cover on a beautifully illustrated picture book, and a splashy cover on a textbook with tiny print and no pictures that is at an advanced reading level. Have children show the cover and the inside. The point here, again, is that we can't judge the inside by the outside. (The book is only the vehicle for making the point—the books are all fine in their own right.)

MORE OF EVERETT ANDERSON

1. The Everett Anderson books are written in rhyme, so it is best to go through the book once with the children to enjoy the rhythm and the rhyme, and then to discuss the book later. Tell the children that we are going to listen first and that we'll talk and ask questions later, and stick to this plan.

2. In *Everett Anderson's Goodbye,* the story is about a death of a member of the family. The reader is made aware of the misery that Everett is feeling, and of an understanding mother who just waits and lets him work out his grief. The message is that we should take one thing at a time, and go slowly.

3. In *Everett Anderson's Year,* go through the months of the year and see what Everett is thinking about with each new month. Then, have students go through the months of the year and write or draw what they are thinking. Are they similar?

4. Other books in this series are *Some of the Days of Everett Anderson* and *Everett Anderson's Christmas Coming.* They are all books that get us talking about "feelings" rather quickly.

5. In *My Friend, Jacob,* the author deals with the special friendship that grows between a young boy and an older boy who is somewhat delayed in his development. They each have something to offer one another; they each help one another. It is a very special kind of friendship from which they both benefit, and children will benefit from being exposed to this point of view.

BOOK:

Alexander and the Terrible, Horrible, No Good, Very Bad Day
by Judith Viorst. Illustrations by Ray Cruz. Hartford, CT: Atheneum, An Aladdin Book, 1972.

ABOUT THE BOOK

1. Retell the story of *Alexander and the Terrible, Horrible, No Good, Very Bad Day.*

2. Have students write or tell about their very own terrible, horrible, no good, very bad day.

3. Have students write a class story together about Alexander in which he has another terrible, horrible, no good, very bad day. (Children enjoy incorporating their own experiences into the story.)

4. Have students write an individual or a class story together about Alexander and the Super, Marvelous, Trouble-Free, Very Good Day!

5. Students can write a story taking a middle of the road approach where Alexander has some good experiences and some not so good experiences, yet survives with a smile.

6. Mottoes. Talk about what a "motto" is (a word or expression to use as a guide). Think of some mottoes, or expressions, that we use in our language. Look in the library for inspirational books that suggest words to live by. What would a good motto be for Alexander? "There's always Tomorrow" could be a starter. What else?

SOLVING PROBLEMS

1. Problem solvers are people who look for solutions. If one thing doesn't work, they find out why; then they try another approach. Promote problem solving in the classroom by giving problem situations. Let children work on their solutions in small groups.

2. Form a "Problem Solver" Club. Problem solving isn't always easy, but students can consider options or choices. Problem solvers do not feel helpless because they know there is a way out. Decorate a shoe box with the Problem Solver logo or emblem that the club chooses, and encourage students to write out problems and drop them into the box. The Problem Solvers can meet and discuss problems and solutions.

3. Read newspaper cartoons critically. How do characters solve problems in cartoons? Can we learn from them? Do they reflect real life or are they all fiction or fantasy?

4. Positive/Negative. Use cartoon characters to state a problem. Then have blank bubble shapes drawn over the characters. In one shape, have the students write thoughts that show that the person is thinking negatively—that there are no solutions. In the other shape, have the students write thoughts that show that the person is thinking positively—that there are some solutions to this problem. Children can work these out in small groups and share the process of problem solving.

MORE PROBLEM SOLVING

1. Talking to Myself. Have students keep a journal. What are they saying to themselves? ("Yes, I can do it" or "I'll never make it!" or "It's not the end of the world," or "Maybe next time.") Have them monitor their own thinking, because what we say to ourselves affects the way we feel and affects the way we solve problems. Have students check at the end of the week for positive/negative entries in their journals.

2. "It's OK to Make an Honest Mistake!" We learn from making mistakes. Have students form an "Alexander Support Group" and write or tell about a mistake they made. How will they handle the situation the next time?

3. Problem Solving on Tape. Have students tape record their problem, and identify themselves by a number. Have students listen to the "problem" tape and answer on a "suggested solution" tape.

4. Have stuffed animals in the room for children to snuggle, cuddle, and talk to on a terrible, horrible, no good, very bad day. (Cut, stuff, and sew from material if large animals are not available.)

5. Hang a kite from the ceiling in the corner of the room. Let children "fly a kite" to get their minds off their problems, when they have a terrible, horrible, no good, very bad day.

BOOK:

The Tenth Good Thing About Barney
By Judith Viorst. Illustrations by Erik
Blegvad. Hartford, CT: Atheneum, An Aladdin
Book, 1971.

LOSSES

1. This book offers a very positive treatment of the death of a boy's pet cat named Barney. In order to relieve the child's sense of loss, his mother asks him to think of "ten good things" about Barney. Thinking of "ten good things" about a variety of difficult situations can be helpful for children.

2. The book reinforces the idea that it is OK to cry, to feel sad, and to feel a sense of loss when a pet or a loved one dies. Children may be helped by discussing this.

3. Another message in the book is that "it might not feel so bad tomorrow," which gives the child hope that in time this awful feeling will be lessened. Some children may require more discussion time than others.

4. Be certain to make the book available for children to go to and to go through on their own. Take particular notice if a child goes to the book repeatedly; some help may be needed with a problem, and you may have to discuss it with the child, or to seek counseling for the child.

INFORMATION ABOUT FEARS AND LOSS

1. Children who experience loss are concerned with who will take care of them. Caretakers need to be capable, warm, and have the best interests of the child at heart. Food becomes important and a child may feel best eating the foods that he/she eats when ill.

2. Both Science and Health courses offer opportunities to introduce the subject of death into the curriculum. The attitude of the teacher, nurse, counselor, or principal is of utmost importance when dealing with this tender subject. Proceed with caution and according to school policy. Ask children from whom they would want to hear "bad pet news." This also gives a clue as to whom they would want to be with in case of other bad news.

3. Acknowledge that death is sad because it is a final earthly goodbye. Talk about how we can help someone who is grieving (introduce the words "grief" and "grieving") over a loss; for example, remember the good things, be patient with the person, be gentle and generous with hugs, try to include the person in activities.

4. Physical contact is important to someone who has experienced a loss. When discussing this book, have the children sit close together so that they are touching. You might have them hold hands.

5. Let it out! It is important not to postpone grief, or to deny grief. Children need to be reassured that it is OK to cry. Parents need to know that children should be included in the process of working out family grief. They sense when an adult is not being honest with them.

LOSS THROUGH DEATH, SEPARATION, DIVORCE

1. If a classmate becomes ill and must leave school temporarily, discuss it with the children. What can they do to help? They can send cards, make something to send, keep in touch.

2. When a classmate returns after an illness, prepare the children if there is a change in appearance. Again, gentleness and tact are required of everyone.

3. Teach young children to cook in school. Make snacks, using simple recipes. This enables the child to achieve a measure of independence and not to feel so helpless.

4. Children experiencing loss need to wear extra clothing for warmth. Warm clothing reduces loss of heat—a condition that results from having received a shock.

5. Some children may be able to discuss customs surrounding death; especially if the school policy calls for treating this subject in the curriculum. For example, in Mexico the Zapotec Indians still celebrate the Days of the Dead. The first and second days of November are set aside to remember the dead. Four items are set out for the dead: incense is burned so the spirit can find its way; flowers are put out to please them; water is left out for drinking; and bread is left for eating.

6. In Latin America, families with children who died set out toys, cakes, and candies at the doorstep for the child angels. They do this one night each year on All Hallows Eve (Halloween). They set off firecrackers to guide the child angel home. What ritual took place when burying the pet cat, Barney?

7. In China, white is the color of death. In our culture, people who are in mourning wear black. To express emotions, have children draw or paint to music.

8. Other books that address the subject of death and that are appropriate for young children are:

- *Grandma Didn't Wave Back* by Rose Blue. New York: Franklin Watts, 1972.

- *Everett Anderson's Goodbye* by Lucille Clifton, et al. New York: Holt, Rinehart & Winston, 1983.

- *My Grandpa Died Today* by Joan Fassler. New York: Behavioral Publications, 1971.

- *New Mother for Martha* by Phyllis Green. New York: Human Science Press, 1978.

- *The Bear Who Saw the Spring* by Karla Kuskin. New York: Harper & Row, 1961.

- *Annie and the Old One* by Miska Miles. Boston: Little, Brown & Co., Atlantic Monthly Press, 1971.

BOOK:

It Could Always Be Worse
by Margot Zemach. New York: Scholastic
Book Services, 1976.

PAGE BY PAGE

1. Contrast the family picture on the first page with the last family picture in the book. List the contrasting words that help describe the family.

2. What noises would we hear in this house? (Crying, quarreling, clucking, honking, crowing, and so forth.) Reread the story aloud, and have children create sound effects for the background. Tape record the story with sound effects made by the children, so they can listen and enjoy it again.

3. The Rabbi is a religious person to go to for help. Who are the people that we go to for help besides a rabbi? List them. Who do children personally go to for help? Ask them.

4. Examine the pictures carefully for all of the action taking place.

5. Examine the pictures for the different expressions on people's faces. What are they communicating by these expressions? Try some nonverbal communication messages with face and body—happy, sad, grumpy, scared, wonderful, surprised, and so forth.

VARIATION ON A THEME

1. Explain that "variation on a theme" means that a story with a certain message could be told in a variety of ways. (There are over 100 versions of *Cinderella*.) Compare this book with another by James Stevenson: *Could Be Worse!* New York: Greenwillow Books, 1977. How is it the same? How is it different?

2. Have children list complaints and then discuss them. Are some more important than others? Are some picky? Do some show lack of patience?

3. Pet Peeves. Have children list their "pet peeve"; this can be a picky complaint, not a critical problem. Students can make bumper stickers to advertise their pet peeve.

4. Round Robin Story. Have a round robin "It Could Always Be Worse" story with small groups of five to eight students. Have them present it to the class in the form of a dramatic play.

PROBLEMS AND SOLUTIONS

1. The Rabbi was a problem solver. Have students think of other ways that this very same problem could be treated.

2. Have children list school problems (lunchroom, recess, bus, auditorium) and work out some possible solutions.

3. Correspondence Club. Establish a "pen pal" club. This can be done with another class in the same school district, or with another class in a different city or state. Students enjoy writing letters if they know they will receive an answer. Send them all together in a big envelope.

4. Count Your Blessings. Have students get into the habit of looking for all of the good things in their lives, and all of the good opportunities that are available to them. Do this regularly; for young children you can use a hand puppet that helps with counting and with suggestions (nice school, good friends, good things to eat, nice treat, sunny day, good health, all wearing clean clothes, all wearing shoes, all have a paper and pencil to work with, and so forth).

BOOK:

Say It!
by Charlotte Zolotow. Pictures by James
Stevenson. New York: Greenwillow Books,
1980.

DESCRIPTION OF A WALK IN THE WOODS

1. Have the students listen carefully to recorded instrumental music on headphone sets. Students can pretend to be walking in the woods as they listen. Have them draw and label three things that they hear that could possibly be something in the woods. (For example, a loud trumpet could be an animal call; bass notes could be a large animal walking, and so forth.)

2. Print descriptions from the book directly onto cards. Mix them up. Students can paint the one that they get. Make it any season. (For example, "It's a wild, wondrous dazzling day!" "It's a golden, shining, splendiferous day!" "A brook bubbled over mossy green rocks." "Clouds were gray purple." "The pond shivered into a million zigzagging streaks of color.")

3. Make a picture showing an animal on the gound or up in a tree (hidden by brush or grass or swirling leaves) but watching the girl and her mother.

4. Go for a real autumn walk around the school playground or in the school neighborhood and stop periodically to smell, to look, to listen, and at the end to think of a word or phrase that describes the experience. Record the individual comments on an experience chart. Have children think of a beginning sentence, and print each comment with a name after it.

Later, make the experience story on a reproducible ditto and send it home for children to read.

SAY IT IN HOW MANY WAYS?

1. In the story, when Mother said, " That's what I've been saying all the time," she meant she was saying "I love you." List all of the ways that Mother said it.

2. Have a "Say It" Pal. Every student can print his or her name on a small paper. Put them together and have a drawing. Have the student keep the person's name a secret. The student then does something special for that person that day. (For example, the student could ask to sharpen their pencil, let them get ahead in line, and so forth.) At the end of the day, see if the students can guess who their "say it" pal is.

If students want to know who their "say it" pal is for the day, have them all take a name. Then, individually, call upon them to spell the name of their pal, while everyone listens very carefully to hear if it's their name that is being spelled out loud.

3. Declare every Wednesday as "Say It Day!" At the end of the day, have the children tell one nice thing that they did for someone and one nice thing that someone did for them. (Children need to distinguish between giving and receiving.)

4. For a math lesson, bake cookies together that make you "say it."

SAY IT SOME MORE

1. Make a "Say It" Badge. Children can trace and cut out a leaf shape and print the two words, "Say It" on the badge. Pin or tape it on. People will ask, "What does it say?" or "What does that mean?" Answer: "I love you." Watch them smile.

2. Children can draw and tell about "A Favorite Say It Day in the Life of _____." It can be real or fantasy.

3. Students can look in magazines for glossy colored pictures of favorite foods that make you "say it." Paste them on a chart. Use these for beginning and ending sounds, or long and short vowel sounds.

4. Children can wear their favorite "say it" color to school on a designated day. Make a "say it" color graph of these favorite colors. Use real swatches of material.

Have students record their favorite "say it" snack. Give the list to the room mother for the next party; perhaps something can be selected from this.

REPRODUCIBLE ACTIVITY SHEETS
FOR
PROBLEM SOLVING

TRIAL BALLOONS

There are many ways to solve a problem. How did a character solve a problem in a book you read?

What other ways could the character have used to solve the problem? Think of five of them. Write them inside the "trial balloons." Turn over the page and write a new ending to the story using one of your ideas!

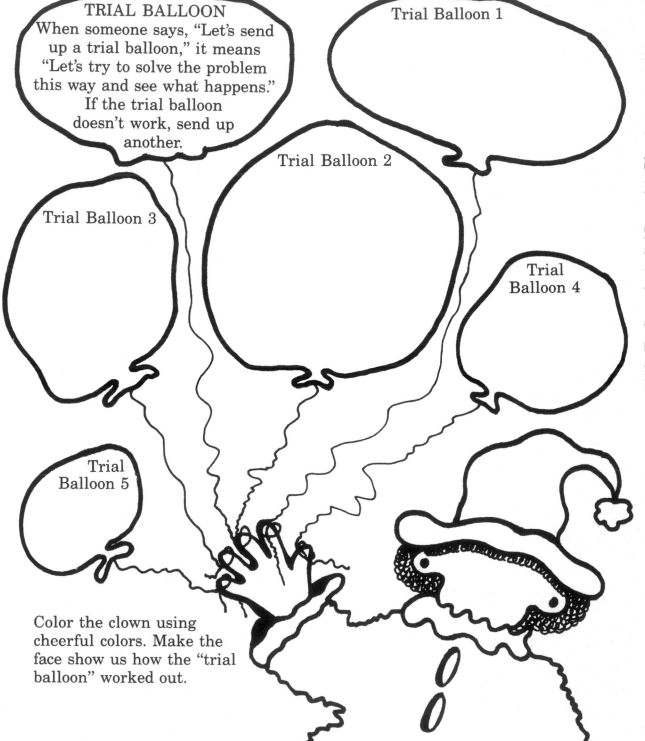

TRIAL BALLOON
When someone says, "Let's send up a trial balloon," it means "Let's try to solve the problem this way and see what happens." If the trial balloon doesn't work, send up another.

Trial Balloon 1

Trial Balloon 2

Trial Balloon 3

Trial Balloon 4

Trial Balloon 5

Color the clown using cheerful colors. Make the face show us how the "trial balloon" worked out.

Name _____   Date _____

ENJOY THE FLAVOR OF PROBLEM SOLVING   9-2

Step 1: Write the problem.

In many stories that we read, the characters have problems to solve. Select a story that you know, and use these four steps to show how the character was helped. You can become a creative problem solver on your own! Use these four steps to help you work through a problem.

Step 2: List some possible ways to solve the problem.

Step 3: Select one way to try to solve the problem.

Step 4: Check back. Did it work?

What color will you make each section?

You can also have a classroom problem-solving session where everyone works on the same problem.

Name _____   Date _____

THE TEDDY BEAR DRUM MAJOR PROBLEM SOLVING FORMULA 9–3

This Drum Major won first prize for problem solving. He is willing to share his formula with you. Although he does a lot of fancy footwork and is a "high stepper" he suggests using these four steps for problem solving.

Make sure that you have all of the facts!

1. WHAT IS THE PROBLEM?
(Write it down.)

2. WHAT ARE SOME POSSIBLE WAYS TO SOLVE IT?
(The sky's the limit.)

3. SELECT ONE SOLUTION AND TRY IT.
(Write down what you will do.)

4. DID IT WORK? If not, go back to 2 through 4 again.

Name _____   Date _____

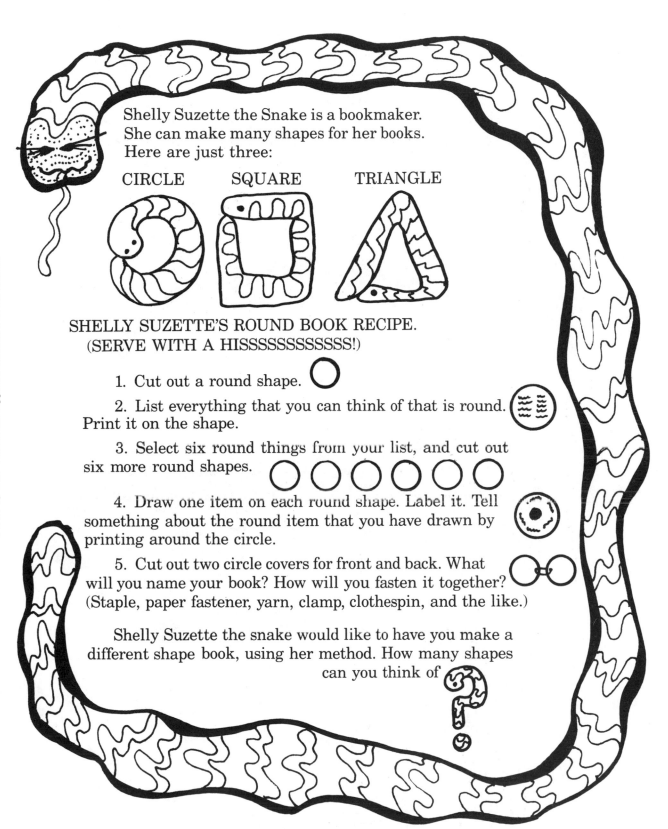

Shelly Suzette the Snake is a bookmaker.
She can make many shapes for her books.
Here are just three:

CIRCLE   SQUARE   TRIANGLE

SHELLY SUZETTE'S ROUND BOOK RECIPE.
(SERVE WITH A HISSSSSSSSSSSS!)

1. Cut out a round shape.

2. List everything that you can think of that is round.
Print it on the shape.

3. Select six round things from your list, and cut out
six more round shapes.

4. Draw one item on each round shape. Label it. Tell
something about the round item that you have drawn by
printing around the circle.

5. Cut out two circle covers for front and back. What
will you name your book? How will you fasten it together?
(Staple, paper fastener, yarn, clamp, clothespin, and the like.)

Shelly Suzette the snake would like to have you make a
different shape book, using her method. How many shapes
can you think of

A CIRCLE SHAPE BOOK

1. Cut this large hamburger out around the circle. Use it for a cover. Trace six more circles.

2. Cut out the six small circles on the next page. Paste each one in the middle of a big circle.

3. Write colorful adjectives to describe each item. Write them around the edge of the circle.

4. On the cover, print a special name for the hamburger, and the author's name. Staple it on top or on the side. Color the cover to make it look appetizing!

Sample Page →

Crispy, crunchy, fresh green lettuce!

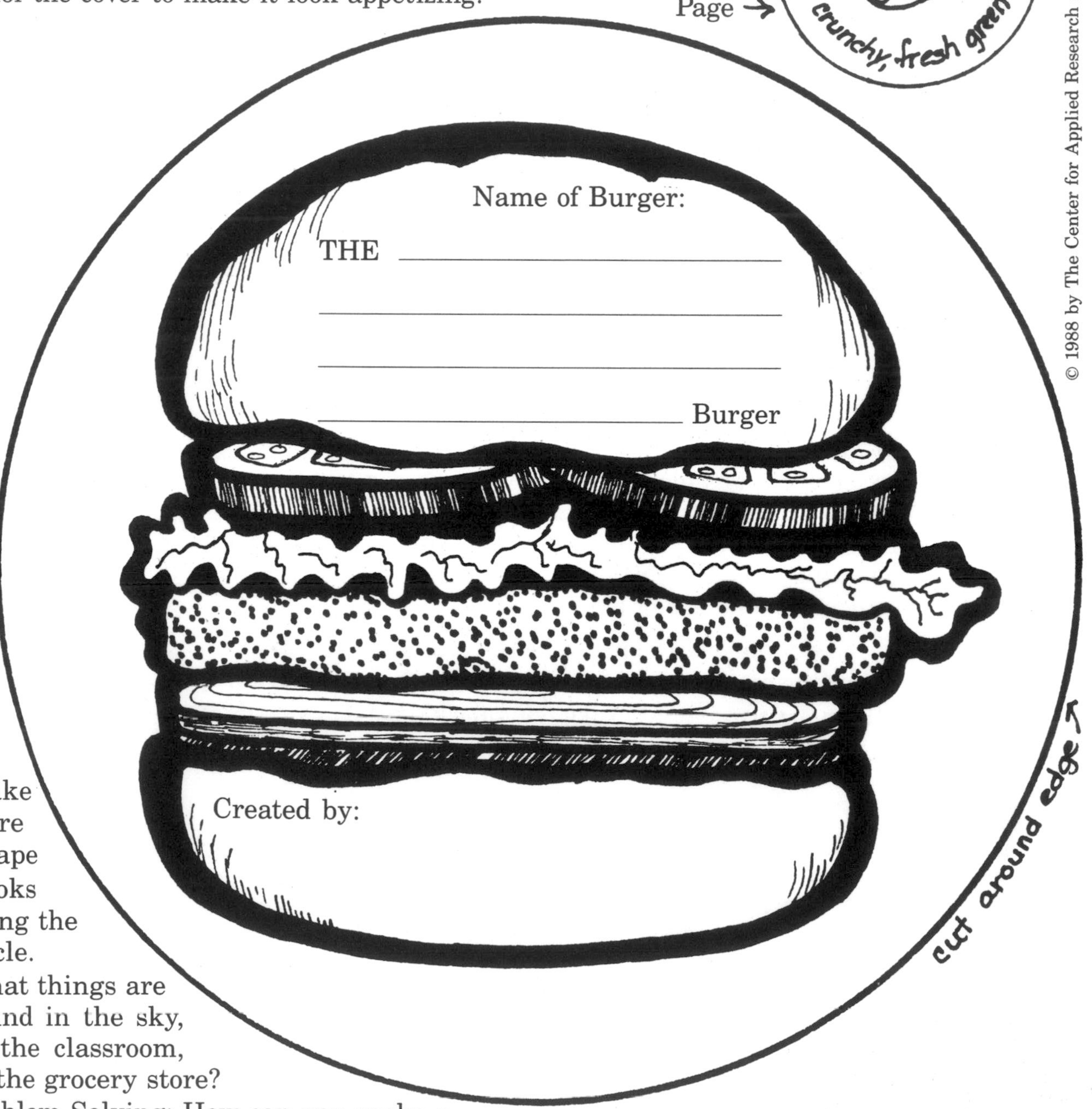

Name of Burger:

THE _____

_____

_____

_____ Burger

Created by:

Make more Shape Books using the circle. What things are round in the sky, in the classroom, in the grocery store?

Problem Solving: How can you make a 3-D Circle Book; a puffy book using material; a real circle book that you could eat?

cut around edge ↗

Name _____   Date _____

A CIRCLE SHAPE BOOK

Cut and paste each one onto a larger circle. Write descriptive words for each item around the large circle. Three are done to get you started. Color or paint them so that they look delicious!

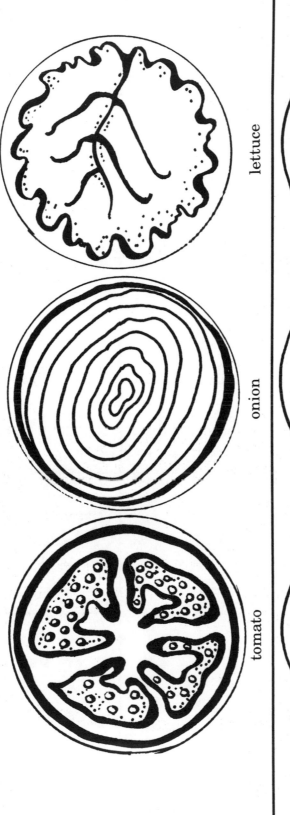

tomato

onion

lettuce

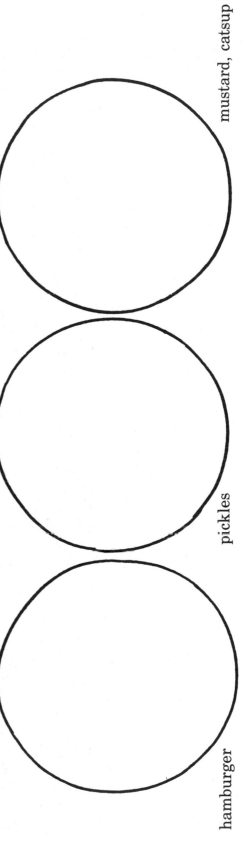

mustard, catsup

pickles

hamburger

STORY STARTER CARDS FOR PROBLEM SOLVING

Cut these into four "story starter" cards. Select one that you would like to finish first. Draw an illustration to go along with the problem and with the solution. Compare your story with those of your classmates.

Title:

Once there was a little, brown, furry mouse who walked in his sleep. His next door neighbor, Mr. Clancy Cat, was always prowling around at night to catch him.

One night the sleep-walking mouse left his house and his safe garden. He turned the corner and stepped in front of two glowing, yellow lights. Only, they were not lights... they were the gleaming eyes of Mr. Clancy Cat!

Title:

On the top of a big green hill, in a big yellow house, there lived a family with two sisters. One sister was always happy  and one was always sad. The sad one had lost her bright, red umbrella and the rainy season was coming! She was afraid of rain and deep puddles because she had not yet learned to swim!

Title:

Mark asked Frankie if he would like to play baseball at recess. Frankie was very pleased and said, "Sure would! You can count on me!" Later, Billy came up to Frankie and said, "Five more minutes until recess. Remember, it's your turn to bring the basketball today," and off he went. Frankie gulped. He had made two different promises—one to Mark and one to Billy. Now what?

Title:

Tommy was a new student at school, and he felt so alone! Everyone had good friends and laughed and played together. Soon it would be time for lunch, and he didn't even feel hungry. That was unusual for Tommy who loved to "eat everything in sight," according to his Mom.

Name ——————

Date ——————

MORE STORY STARTER CARDS

Cut these into four "story starter" cards. Select one that you would like to finish first. Draw an illustration to go along with the problem and with the solution. Share your story with those of your classmates.

Title:

The teacher asked Mark and Mike if they would help pass out the birthday treats. Mark had lemon lollipops so everyone was happy. Mike had cupcakes with orange frosting and everything was going along fine until he came to the last group. There were only two cupcakes left, and there were six students waiting for their treats. "Oh, no!" thought Mike, "now what?"

Title:

Mrs. Jones left the room for a minute and Joey and Jill were mixing paint. Brad came along and purposely knocked into Joey just as he was pouring purple paint into a small juice can. "Oops!" laughed Brad as the paint spilled all over the table and onto the floor. Brad quickly took his seat and got busy. When Mrs. Jones returned to a "purple disaster" she asked, "What happened?"

Title:

Arthur walked up to the teacher's desk and said that he had something to tell her. "Jimmy keeps pinching me every time we line up, and I don't like it!" The teacher said, "Why don't you tell Jimmy that you don't like him to pinch you?" Arthur's eyes filled up with tears as he explained that he had tried, and that if Jimmy knew that he was telling the teacher he would be pinched even more. "Dry your eyes," said the teacher. Then she added, "We'll think of something."

Title:

Mr. Anthony called the class together for a group meeting. "This is serious," he said. "Today is the third day in a row that someone has reported that their lunch money is missing. Any suggestions for how we, as a group, are going to deal with this problem?"

SECTION 10

Poetry

BOOK:

Rabbits, Rabbits
by Aileen Fisher. Illustrations by Gail Niemann.
New York: Harper & Row, 1983.

CREATIVE ARTS

1. Children can illustrate the different seasons of the year by using sponge painting, or a combination of construction paper and paint. They can make two rabbit cutouts, one brown and one white, and paste them in the appropriate season of the year.

2. Fuzzy rabbits. Gently tearing the paper gives it a fuzzy, uneven edge. Children can make a body shape, long ears, head, feet, and tail by gently tearing the paper. Then paste it together for the fuzzy rabbit. Eyes, nose, and whiskers can be gently torn and added with a different colored paper. (For this art technique demonstrate the difference between a quick rip of the paper (uncontrolled) and a gentle tear (you control the shape).

3. Creative Movement. Read the rabbit poems aloud while children act them out.

4. Have children demonstrate some of the sayings, such as a "nose full of twitches."

LANGUAGE

1. Record the poems on cassette tape so that children can listen to the rhythm and the rhyme as they silently read the book.

2. Children may listen to the recorded poems on a headphone set and move and clap to the rhythm.

3. Read "Thinking" and discuss the idea of "words in your head." Sit around in a poetry circle and have children take turns telling a "word from their head." Other children can then think of a word that rhymes with it.

MORE ABOUT RABBITS

1. Have available the book *Listen, Rabbit* by A. Fisher. It is a story told in rhyme, about a boy who desperately wants to make friends with a cottontail.

2. Proportions. A rabbit's back feet are four times the size of the front feet. This makes it possible to hop. Show these proportions using the ruler.

3. The submarine rabbit. Just as a submarine surfaces with the periscope first, the rabbit emerges from its burrow with ears first. A rabbit can move each ear independently; can people? Rabbits can wiggle their ears; can people? The

ear, like an antenna, can be moved to catch noises but the rabbit does not need to move its whole head. Have children put their hands up to their heads like antennae and move their right hands to the right, then their left hands to the left, and so forth.

4. The Fur Coat. The rabbit actually has two fur coats—the outer guard hairs which repel rain and wind, and a downy inner coat which keeps the heat close to the body. Do we have inner and outer linings in our coats, and if so, why?

5. Rabbit Whiskers. The rabbit uses its long whiskers to feel the walls of the burrow. To demonstrate how a rabbit feels its way through a burrow, have students form two lines. Then, blindfold one classmate and let her find the way between the two lines by using outstretched arms (whiskers) to guide her.

6. Invite a pet rabbit (in its cage) to visit the classroom for a day. Children can examine the rabbit closely, and draw it.

BOOK:

Speak Up
by David McCord. Illustrations by Marc
Simont. Boston: Little, Brown & Co., 1979.

CREATIVE ARTS

1. Read "Butterfly" aloud to the children. Read it again. Then, have them make their own versions of the butterfly that the author is so delightfully describing. Hang them all up, around a copy of the poem that has been printed on large chart paper (you, an aide, or older children can print the poem).

2. Not all of the poems are illustrated. What a perfect opportunity for children to draw an illustration just from the words in the poetry. Accept all illustrations, since they are the child's personal expression.

3. The sun is described in "Skyviews" as an "unbuttoned button in the sky's blue shirt, with not one hole to hold it." Have students print the words and illustrate the sun in an unbuttoned sky.

LANGUAGE

1. This book is rich in language development for children. Consider the poem, "How to Learn to Say a Long, Hard Word." This is a fascinating poem to work through with children.

2. "Riddle-Me Rhyme" is excellent for chanting and choral reading by the group. Be sure to have the students try, "Riddle-me, Riddle-me, Ree," and "Riddle-me, Riddle-me, Ro."

3. "Those Double Z's" will delight the students. This could lead to a great deal of interest in words with double letters.

4. "Farther and Further" may be the way to finally settle this question and learn the difference in a fanciful way.

5. "Limericks" could lead to an entire reading of more and more, and eventually to writing some.

CREATIVE MOVEMENT

1. "Roller Coaster" is an excellent poem for role playing by five or six children at a time. Others will catch the movement and join in later.

2. "The Windshield Wipers' Song" is a natural vehicle for creative movement and role playing.

3. Puppets are a great help for children who have some difficulty with body movement. Children who are self-conscious about movement can go behind a screen (or hanging bedsheet) with a bright light, and make a silhouette that can be seen on the other side. Masks help too.

4. Have other David McCord poetry books available for children, such as: *Far and Few*, *Every Time I Climb a Tree*, and *One at a Time*.

BOOK:

Hailstones and Halibut Bones
by Mary O'Neill. Illustrations by Leonard
Weisgard. Garden City, NY: Doubleday, 1961.

ADVENTURES IN COLOR

1. The colors are explored rhythmically and sensitively. Divide children into small groups and have them practice the various poems for choral reading. Read aloud in groups and record on tape for replay at a later time.

2. Set up a Color Table, and change the color weekly. For the "Red Table" have different objects, materials, and foods available. Children can bring in items from home. Have them use the five senses and have Something Red to See, Something Red to Hear, Something Red to Smell, Something Red to Touch, Something Red to Eat. Use this as a challenge for all of the colors.

MORE ADVENTURES

1. Painting with only one color. For the different poems, mix the color in a variety of tones and have children paint with three or four shades of the same

color. They can illustrate something from the poem. (For example, orange. On a light orange background, have students paint with bright red orange, yellow orange, and light orange (add orange to white.) Do this for all of the colors; it makes a striking painting. Frame them in yet another tone of the same color. Copy the orange poem with an orange felt-tip pen, and make a display outside your classroom door to share with everyone.

2. Cooking in Color. Make fruit-flavored gelatin for a color salute, and for an experience with food that changes from a liquid to a solid. Also, use food coloring and add it to vanilla frosting to make a rainbow of frosting colors for cookies.

EVEN MORE ADVENTURES

1. Put a prism on a sunny window ledge; what happens when the sunbeams shine onto the prism? What happens when we move it?

2. Investigate a Rainbow. Check for this information in a science book in the library. What makes a rainbow?

3. Have a crazy color day, when nothing matches—one red sock, one blue sock, and the like. Enjoy all of the color combinations. How many colors are represented? Which one is there the most of? the least of? What is the very biggest patch of color? the smallest?

4. It's time to get out the scrap box. Sometimes the scrap box is filled to overflowing and needs to be sorted. Sort the scraps according to colors. Make a picture using all of the tones of just one color.

5. Be sure to have two more poetry books by this author available. One investigates the type of breezes and winds that blow in *Winds*. Illustrations by James Barkley, NY: Doubleday & Co., Inc., 1970. Another gem is *Fingers Are Always Bringing Me News*. Drawings: Don Bolognese. NY: Doubleday & Co., Inc., 1969.

BOOK:

What I Did Last Summer
by Jack Prelutsky. Illustrations by Yossi
Abolafia. New York: Greenwillow Books, 1984.

PAGE BY PAGE

1. Children will be able to relate to the sequence of these poems, from the first one entitled "The Last Day of School" where the young boy is "tickled to bits" to be free, to the last poem which depicts the end of the summer vacation and

is entitled, "Boring!" For this reason, the book is timely either at the beginning or the ending of the school year.

2. A poem entitled, "The Fourth of July" has some excellent descriptive words for fireworks, such as: "cascaded," "great torrents," "ignited the sky." The illustration helps to describe the words. Painting red, white, and blue fireworks with a fluid medium (such as thinned tempera paint that a student "pushes" along glossy white paper by blowing through a straw) will help to capture the explosions! Work more with the language of this poem for some "fireworks firewords."

3. After reading "The Museum," children will understand and sympathize with the idea of wanting to touch things in the museum. Where else do children want to touch things, and are not allowed to do so? Why not? Lead children to the conclusion that if thousands of people came through and touched things (gritty hands, tugging hands, ice cream cone hands, and so forth) soon the furnishings would not be worth the visit.

4. Make sure to have other copies of poetry books by Jack Prelutsky available for children, such as: *Zoo Doings, The Snopp on the Sidewalk,* and *Rolling Harvey Down the Hill.* Also, he has a collection of Read-aloud Books such as *It's Christmas, It's Halloween, It's Thanksgiving,* and *It's Valentine's Day* that make children giggle.

SUMMER

1. Write a poem about a summer heat wave, using a form such as cinquain, haiku, or concrete poetry (see Activity Pages).

2. Write a question/answer chant about summer for choral reading (it doesn't have to rhyme).

3. Make a Sun Poetry Book. Make large red, orange, yellow, and gray circles that represent the sun. Send "messages from the sun" with red representing sunburn (the hottest day) to gray representing a cloud cover (the coolest day).

WHAT GOES ON IN SUMMER?

1. Have a "Summer Beach Box" with swim goggles, fins, suntan lotion, sun glasses, straw hat, and the like. Let children apply the lotion and put on the hat and goggles for "inspiration" while they write summer poems.

2. Have a "Summer Sports Box" with baseball, bat, glove, tennis racquet, soccer ball, and the like. Children can donate the items for one week of "summer sports poetry."

Get copies of weather maps that show, in color, the weather patterns that change each day and each month. (*USA Today* is an excellent newspaper source for a giant weather map.)

Students can write and learn rhythm chants for the various states (two-liners). Some examples:

"Hi, Alabama! How are you?"
  "Very hot, and thirsty too!"
"Hi there, Georgia! How are you?"
  "Ripe with peaches, and we're warm too!"
"Hi Colorado! How are you?"
  "80 degrees, with skies of blue."
"Hi Arizona! How are you?

  "_____"

3. One more resource that is a "must" for young children is *The Random House Book of Poetry For Children*. These 572 poems for today's child were selected by Jack Prelutsky and illustrated by Arnold Lobel.

BOOK:

The Poetry Troupe, An Anthology of Poems to Read Aloud,
compiled by Isabel Wilner.
Decorations by Isabel Wilner.
New York: Charles Scribner's Sons, 1977

TIPS AND RECOMMENDATIONS

1. A "troupe" is a group that reads poetry aloud for its own enjoyment and that of others. This author recommends small groups for reading poetry aloud — five or six students. Some poems require two readers, some require four.

2. Make presentations to other classes no longer than ten or fifteen minutes. For younger children, three or four short pieces would be a pleasant listening experience.

3. Ask for volunteers to read poetry aloud with you. Select readers from all reading ability levels. Enlist the aid of the librarian.

4. Leave them wanting more when performing for an audience.

5. Let children help select poems to read aloud.

RHYTHM AND RHYME

1. Have students move to the rhythm, when appropriate. For example, when working with the first poem in this collection, entitled, "Did You Feed My Cow?" children can nod while saying, or after saying, "Yes, Ma'am!"

2. Folk Rhymes. There are many four-liners in this category. Children can easily memorize them and feel successful. Be prepared for lots of smiles and laughter and a good time.

3. This book is divided into sections such as Chants, Repetitions, Narrations, Observations, Characterizations, and the like. There is such a variety under each heading that there is something to appeal to everyone! Enjoy!

POETS

1. Build a poetry stage from a large box. Set it on a desk top and the children can stand behind it when reading poetry aloud. Children can make and use puppets for poetry reading, using this stage.

2. Have children's groups practice their reading and then record the poetry on cassette tape. Encourage critiques and retaping.

3. Make video tapes of the children performing in their poetry troupe.

4. For a touch of the dramatic, use tambourines and rhythm sticks, or a drum, to announce the selections to be read aloud by the poetry troupe. Children can have a beginning and an ending speech for the audience. The children could write it together, taking their cues from the poetry in the book. For example, "Are you here to read poetry?" "We are!" "Will we enjoy it?" "You will!"

5. Poets have good memories! By memorizing poetry, the memory span is increased.

REPRODUCIBLE ACTIVITY PAGES
FOR
POETRY BOOKS

Name _____

Date _____

RHYTHM AND RHYME TO READ ALOUD

When writing poetry to read aloud, try the "QUESTION AND ANSWER METHOD."
Decide *whom* or *what* you are going to ask questions.

<u>SAMPLE</u>: Asking Questions of Those Who Lay Eggs

"How many eggs have you, Mrs. Hen?" "Let me see, I think there's ten."
"How many eggs have you, Mrs. Duck?" "Four big ones, Am I in luck!"
"How many eggs have you, Mrs. Frog?" "Nine tucked underneath a log."
"How many eggs have you, Mrs. Chick?" "Three scrambled, two fried,
one poached — Take your pick."

Now, you can try a question and answer chant. Who is doing the talking — animals, furniture, toys, friends, strangers, a bat and a ball, a tennis shoe and a stone? You are the author, so you can decide. Write two different chants below.

1.

2.

USING DESCRIPTIVE WORDS

Think of a sentence as a rubber band. Try stretching the sentence, or expanding it, as a way to get ready to write poetry. The first one is done for you. Do the other three. On the back, try using other colors. Put a purple star next to your favorite one.

Purple

As purple as a _grape_ .

As purple as a _ripe_ _grape_ .

As purple as a _juicy_ , _ripe_ _grape_ .

As purple as a _grape_ .

As purple as a _shiny_ , _juicy_ _grape_ .

As purple as a _ripe_ , _grape_ .

Orange

As orange as a _____ .

As orange as a _____ .

As orange as a _____ , _____ .

As orange as a _____ , _____ .

Green

As green as a _____ .

Yellow

As yellow as a _____ .

Name _____ Date _____

THE MONSTER PUPPET BRINGS OUT THE POET IN YOU

Color, cut, fold, and paste this one-eyed monster of a story teller. It will help you tell stories and poems. Staple or paste a strip along the back of the folded circle, and insert your hand in the strip to move the monster mouth. Put a bright red tongue in the middle. See the sample.

Sample

fold

POETRY THAT SINGS

Use any form of poetry that you like to write two poems about birds. Write them on the birds.
Remember to use
    colorful words.

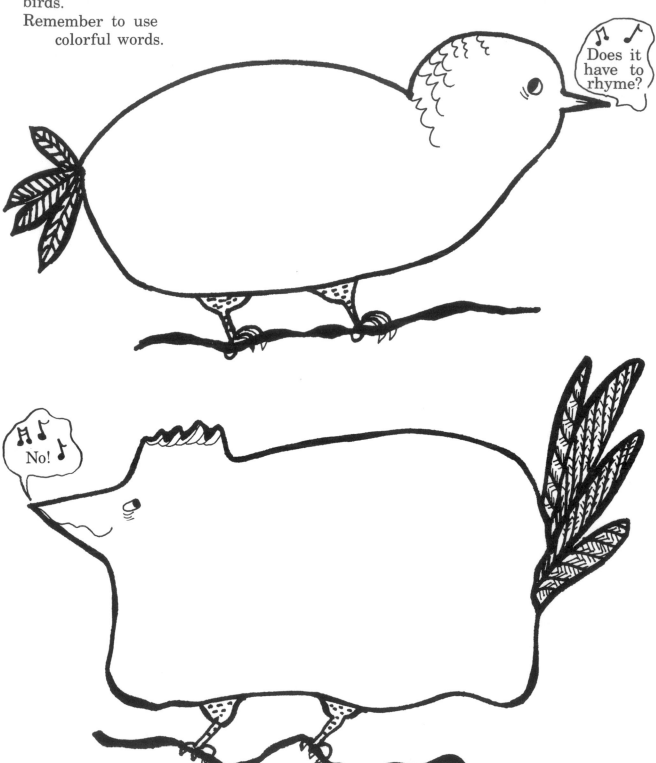

Name _____   Date _____

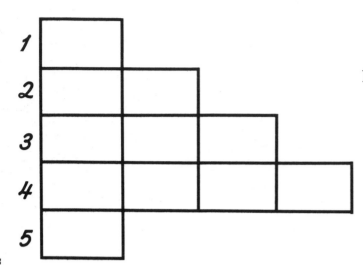

Cinquain is a French stanza of five lines.

    Line 1 —Subject word

    Line 2 —Two words that describe Line 1

    Line 3 —Three "feeling words" that end in ING

    Line 4 —A complete sentence.

    Line 5 —One word that sums it up!

Here are some samples of cinquain poetry done by students:

MOM	SPRING
Mom	Spring
Pretty, tall	Warm, green
Loving, hugging, kissing	Raining, glistening, changing
I like my mom.	I'm glad it's spring.
Great!	Fabulous!

Try some cinquain poetry. You will begin to get a feel for words that are related. You will also have something to show for your effort. You are working with both <u>process</u> and <u>product</u>.

1 _____   1 _____

2 _____ _____   2 _____ _____

3 _____ _____ _____   3 _____ _____ _____

4 ____ ____ ____ ____ ____   4 ____ ____ ____ ____ ____

5 _____   5 _____

Illustrate your work using construction paper cutouts or paint. Make a display.

©1988 by The Center for Applied Research in Education

POETIC LICENSE*

Write a poem about any subject, or story that you have read, using the poetic form you like the best.

This Official Poetic License is hereby granted to _____
(your name)

Write poem below:

_____
_____
_____
_____
_____
_____
_____
_____

From the Great State of _____

on this day of _____ in the year _____.

OFFICIAL
"IT DOESN'T HAVE TO
RHYME"
S E A L

*To deviate from conventional form or fact for the desired effect.